THE CHIEF SECRETARY

The Right Honourable Augustine Birrell

THE
CHIEF SECRETARY

Augustine Birrell in Ireland

by

Leon Ó Broin

"*And as for history, be damned to it. What's
history done for me? To this melancholy plight
am I reduced.*"   BIRRELL IN OCTOBER 1919

1969

Chatto & Windus

LONDON

PUBLISHED BY
CHATTO & WINDUS LTD.
40 WILLIAM IV ST.
LONDON, W.C.2

*

CLARKE, IRWIN & CO. LTD.
TORONTO

SBN. 7011 1447 9

PRINTED IN GREAT BRITAIN
BY R. AND R. CLARK LTD.
EDINBURGH

To Cáit and Nóirin

ACKNOWLEDGMENTS

BEFORE I leave the reader to what I trust will be interesting reading I must say a sincere 'thank you' to a number of people who helped me in putting this book together. It will be apparent from the text that I have drawn deeply on original sources and for permission to do this I am indebted to Her Majesty Queen Elizabeth, Mrs. E. J. Nathan, Mr. Mark Bonham Carter, Mr. C. P. Magill, the Hon. Anne MacDonnell, Mr. R. J. Stopford, Mr. Adrian Robinson, the Earl of Haddo and to the authorities of the Public Record Office, London, the British Museum, the National Library of Ireland, the Irish State Paper Office, the Department of Western Manuscripts in the Bodleian Library, to the libraries of Oireachtas Eireann, the Dublin Corporation, the Royal Dublin Society, and the Universities of Dublin, London, Liverpool and Newcastle upon Tyne. I would also like to thank Hutchinson and Co. Ltd. and Alfred A. Knopf Inc., New York, for permission to reprint extracts from Lady Cynthia Asquith's *Diaries 1915-1918*.

For information, guidance and practical assistance I am grateful to David Garnett, Raymond Mortimer, G. C. Duggan, Joseph Brennan, D. S. Porter, Fergal McGrath, Christopher Fyfe, Bulmer Hobson, Charles Cundall, Roger Highfield, Cathal O'Shannon, Breandan Mac Giolla Choille, Denis Gwynn, William O'Sullivan and Ailf Mac Lochlainn, and to my wife Cáit, my daughter Noirin, Eileen Crowley, Anna MacAuliffe, Joan Lally and Doreen Callan.

My friend Owen Dudley Edwards gave generously of his time to examine and transcribe the relevant papers at Haddo House, Aberdeen, helped by Mrs. Margot Longley; to them both, as well as to the Earl and Countess of Haddo who facilitated their work, I am much obliged.

Finally, I have to acknowledge a great debt to two of Birrell's kinsmen: Mr. J. C. Medley and Sir Charles Tennyson. Mr. Medley, who is a great-nephew of Birrell's and his executor, unearthed and placed at my disposal the documents now deposited in the Bodleian, and otherwise helped and encouraged me. Sir Charles Tennyson who, in his delightful *Stars and Markets*, has given the best account that exists of Birrell's domestic life, gladly supplied me, in conversation and correspondence, with the further information I sought and, moreover, read my manuscript and made valuable suggestions for improving it.

Dublin, June 1969   LEON Ó BROIN

CONTENTS

ILLUSTRATIONS

The frontispiece is reproduced from *Things Past Redress*, by Augustine Birrell, by kind permission of Messrs Faber and Faber

CHAPTER I

A Reluctant Chief Secretary

1907–1911

M R. BIRRELL'S tall, burly, bespectacled figure was easily recognized as he came aboard the mailboat at Holyhead. It was an unusually villainous day in January 1907, and the Cabinet Minister, making his first official visit to Ireland, was feeling anything but happy. He was a bad sailor at all times and, though he would not admit it to anybody, the prospect of spending the next three hours on a rolling, lurching ship had him unnerved. He had made this ugly crossing a couple of times before and knew what to expect. So, without being obviously impolite, he cut short the Captain's greetings and went down below. He walked unsteadily, for that morning in his hurry to catch the train at Euston he had stumbled and strained a cartilage. It was a nuisance, happening at this time, for on the morrow in Dublin Castle he would have to carry the Sword of State before the Lord Lieutenant, and he could imagine how he would look as he limped through St. Patrick's Hall and what people would say, seeing him for the first time.

When he reached his cabin he dismissed the steward and, quickly swallowing a couple of tablets, lay down just as he was in his great coat, closed his eyes and hoped for sleep that he feared would not come. His mind was active with foreboding and resentment. Would he be sick? Very likely. Why had *he* been appointed Chief Secretary for Ireland, with responsibility for trying to solve the insoluble Irish Question, when it was being said in the Opposition press that he was the most subtle Parliamentarian in the Liberal Party? Surely he was entitled to something better than this. He knew that this was a post no minister fancied, and that all of them did their utmost to avoid. When the Prime Minister, Campbell-Bannerman, told him of his intentions, he had an answer ready for him. 'Wouldn't So-and-so be far better than I?' he said, naming a colleague. 'Good heavens,' the Prime Minister replied – somewhat unfeelingly, one would think – 'but he's a good friend of mine', as much as to say that nobody in his senses would send a friend to that benighted country. What could he do then, not being well-off enough to refuse, but accept the unwelcome charge? He was determined, however, at the first opportunity to tell the Prime Minister that he could have his province back whenever he wanted it.[1] The post nevertheless had compensations; the salary was an improvement on what he had before – it would need to be – and there was an official residence in the pleasant Phoenix Park, not far, he gloomily remembered, from the spot where, only twenty-five years earlier, a Liberal predecessor of his had been murdered on what was also planned as a peace-making mission.

He must have slept, for he was suddenly aware that the pitching and tossing had ceased, and that the steward, standing at the door, was telling him that they were 'in'. Birrell rolled off the bunk and limped up on deck. He felt bruised, drugged and dishevelled, and the debonair Captain's effort to cheer him up as he left the boat did not relieve his misery. 'Chief Secretaries as a rule don't last long', he remarked, and from the way he looked at Birrell as he said this, it was obvious that he felt the latest arrival would be no exception to the rule. Another few sea-crossings would cool his ardour.

The carriage that awaited Birrell at the pier head took him into Dublin and out to the Chief Secretary's Lodge. There he had a bath, slept for a couple of hours, then dressed and went to the Castle where Aberdeen, the diminutive Viceroy, was giving a dinner for him. It was an occasion he found amusing. Around him sat men who corresponded to the characters of Thackeray's *Sketch Book*: Sir Fiat Haustus, Sir Blacker Dosy, Mr. Sergeant Bluebag and Mr. Counsellor O'Fee.[2] The conversation roamed haphazardly over an infinity of subjects, but before the port was brought in everyone was talking about something that had just happened. There had been a riot in the Abbey Theatre over a new play and the police had been called in to quell it. How typically and delightfully Irish, Birrell thought. He had come to Ireland wondering how to deal with the popular pastime of cattle-driving, and here, on his first night, he was presented with a problem of theatre censorship. As he limped up to his bedroom that night, he recalled again and again the exotic name of the piece that had hurt the susceptibilities of the audience. It sounded like something that might be said of a politician. *The Playboy of the Western World.*

2

Birrell was fifty-seven when he was appointed Chief Secretary. He sat in a government that was unusually talented. Five of its members, including Birrell himself, were men of outstanding intellectual quality, while among the others were men more celebrated in later times, like Lloyd George and Winston Churchill. Margot Asquith linked him with Chesterton, Belloc, Max Beerbohm and Bernard Shaw as men whose conversations were perpetual feasts of delight; his cultivated and independent personality was illumined by flashes of humorous declamation. John Morley at a meal was so captivated by his talk that he forgot the pretty young woman at the other side of him.[3] He had no superior as an after-dinner speaker. In parliament he was equally impressive. His manner was unaffected and he was able to make the wittiest of observations without the suspicion of a smile. When the Speaker called him to order on one occasion for some glaring irrelevance, he blandly said: 'I'm sorry, sir, that you didn't call me to order before. I've now said all the disorderly things that I wanted to say.'[4]

He was born in 1850 in a suburb of Liverpool of Scottish and Northumbrian parents. His father, Charles Mitchell Birrell, a chronic invalid, was a Baptist Minister, but Birrell himself was probably never baptized and later he strayed from non-conformity while remaining, as he put it, theologically-minded but unorthodox. He confessed to being shocked by the irreligious atmosphere of the House of Commons when debating religion, and to having a soft corner in his heart for religious minorities such as the Roman Catholics and Jews. In discussing what happened at the

Reformation he gave vent to the view often quoted since by Catholics that 'it is the Mass that matters: it is the Mass that makes the difference, so hard to define, so subtle is it, yet so perceptible, between a Catholic country and a Protestant one, between Dublin and Edinburgh'.[5] And he prefaced this statement by saying that nobody nowadays save a handful of vulgar fanatics speaks irreverently of the Mass and it was doubtful whether any poor sinful child of Adam, not being a paid agent of the Protestant Alliance, could witness, however ignorantly, the Mass without emotion. He had a cynical view of life; he did not believe in the human race; greed and gain and high prices alone made idlers work. As between Catholics and Protestants, however, of whom he was to see a lot in Ireland, he had a preference for the former. 'The Church of Rome', he said in 1913 when the Ulster crisis was at its height, 'seems determined to frustrate my pious efforts, and I think she is right to do so–although she but postpones the Day of Reckoning. However, I would sooner be split by the Babylonian Whore than by Sir Edward Carson.'[6] Years later he quoted Hartley Coleridge's statement that Ireland would be a delightful country if it was not for the Catholics and the Protestants. 'I have never', he said, 'been able to make up my mind which of the two has been Ireland's worst enemy. I dislike the Protestants more than I do the Catholics, but the latter may be the more insanitary to the life of a nation.'[7]

Birrell was never anything in politics but a Liberal and joined that party while earning a modest livelihood at the Bar which he later supplemented with a couple of directorships and the salary that went with the Chair of Comparative Law at University College, London. He was first elected to parliament in 1889, as the member for West Fife. H. H. Asquith represented East Fife, so that, as Birrell sarcastically commented: 'What a grateful thought, that there is not an acre of this vast and varied landscape which is not represented at Westminster by a London barrister!'[8] For eleven years Birrell and Asquith shared the representation of the shire, never without contested elections in which Birrell always had a much larger majority against his Tory opponent than

4

Asquith had against his. Birrell used to quote against himself a remark made by one of his staunchest supporters: 'I canna reckon how it is, Mr. Birrell, that ye always hold your seat so easily, while *a really clever man*, like Mr. Asquith, only gets in with the greatest difficulty.' However, in 1900 Birrell was defeated in West Fife, while Asquith held his seat until the 1918 General Election.[9] Birrell shared in the Liberal's great victory of 1906. He indulged the people of North Bristol with a glimpse of the Promised Land and was elected as their parliamentary representative until his retirement.[10] West Fife had been as ideal as any constituency could be, he told Campbell-Bannerman, but he loyally accepted the change of constituency and was glad that the shunting had been done with elegance and propriety. A change of air was wholesome.[11]

His first ministerial appointment, in 1906, was as President of the Board of Education, in a government which was so individualistic that Birrell could find in it neither a clique of intimate friends round the Premier, Campbell-Bannerman, nor a clique of enemies concerting against him.[12] 'I remember well taking possession of that office,' he told the House of Commons. 'My courteous predecessor . . . introduced me to the Permanent Secretary. I shook hands with half a dozen gentlemen, heads of different sub-departments, and then, with rather more sorrow than I thought I should have displayed in the circumstances, my predecessor took up his hat, coat and umbrella, and went out to enjoy a crust of liberty. . . . I felt at once naturally and properly in the hands of the very experienced chief. I was indebted to him and shall always remain indebted to him, for the loyalty of his service, and, for the most part, for the accuracy of his information. He gave me a bird's eye view of the nature of my duties. He generally instructed me, very gradually, into the mysteries of the machine, and for many a long day I was pretty helpless in the matter. . . .'[13]

He held this post for only a year during which an Education Bill of his had to be abandoned because, in his own words, it had come back from the Lords 'a miserable, mangled, tortured, twisted *tertium quid*'. It had been fiercely assailed on religious grounds in the Commons, but he had managed to send it to the Lords with a substantial majority.[14] In November, 1906, he told his chief that 'the situation is getting warm, and as they say when ladies are in the straw, it will be worse before it is better'.[15] A month later he recognized there were good reasons for leaving the Board of Education. 'The only thing they could do after the rejection of the Bill', he said modestly, 'was to get rid of the Minister ... so I was dispatched to Ireland', in January, 1907, to replace James Bryce who was going as Ambassador to the United States. He told his friend Asquith that he hardly dared to forecast the future. He had responded to 'the moral imperative', and only vaguely hoped that the Authority from which it is derived dated from Heaven rather than from another place'.[16] A wise Tory had once advised him never to ask for anything, never to refuse anything, and never to resign anything, and hitherto he had followed it to the letter. He was prepared to go to Ireland if this was what Campbell–Bannerman wanted.[17] It was; Campbell–Bannerman told the King that Birrell had most of the requisite qualities for the Irish Secretaryship, literary sense and knowledge, sympathy, good-nature, humour, and breadth of view. 'He had a most thorny task in his present Office and as you know all sorts of people raged around him, but he came out on friendly terms with them all. After the storm of last session, also, a change is not undesirable in the Education Office.'[18a]

John Redmond, the Irish leader, was a party to the change. He had found Bryce's administration lamentable in the extreme. It was said that Bryce was perenially athirst for information and as eager about a new fact as about a new mountain to climb.[18] He could see interesting sides of questions but lacked the capacity to resolve them.[19] Whatever the reason the Irish members did not want him and were very happy to learn that the succession was to go to a man with qualities that had survived the ugly debate on the Education Bill. Indeed, Birrell's stock at this time was extraordinarily high. He was regarded as a very likely successor to Campbell–Bannerman, and the *Irish Times* marked his new appointment by warning the Irish Unionists to be on their guard against the most subtle and experienced Parliamentarian in the ranks of the Liberal Party, and the best man in the Cabinet.[20]

3

When appointed to Ireland, Birrell was prepared to confess that he knew little about that country save as a tourist, but he had read a great deal of Irish history, and he had a certain amount of background information that he had derived from Irish political speeches and from the novels of Edgeworth, Carleton and Trollope. And long before he ever became a minister he had, from the backbenches of the House of Commons, watched the denizens of 'the Irish Quarter', solid and compact under Charles Stewart Parnell, and torn by internal dissensions after the affair with Kitty O'Shea, and Parnell's tragic death. To him Parnell was 'the most curious and interesting, because almost inexplicable, member of Parliament' with whom he had ever exchanged words. He was never in the least degree lovable, but he spread a fascination around him to which men easily succumbed. He had met him once at a small dinner-party where the other principal guest was Gladstone. Gladstone was 'all aglow' and anxious to illuminate Parnell's mind on the subject of Ireland and Irish history, but Parnell who was 'as icy as an old whig', refused to be illuminated or even to show interest. The Liberal Party lieutenants had mismanaged the row over the Parnell divorce, and this Birrell deplored. Had Gladstone been left alone, he believed he never would have written the letter that split the Irish Party, but he thought that the Irish themselves were quite capable of producing a split on their own.[21]

However, the split had occurred and it had taken nine long years to heal it. But then it was like the old days again. The cry of 'The Land for the People' arose and was backed by cattle drives and resistance to evictions which involved the Irish Parliamentary Party's popular organization, the United Irish League, in daily difficulties with the police. Sitting members of the party went to prison and large areas of the country were 'proclaimed'. This turbulence was reflected in the House of Commons where the conflict with the government became increasingly bitter. It eased off when the Liberals took office, but disappointed hopes impelled three members of the parliamentary party to resign. One of these threw in his lot with Sinn Fein and forced a by-election in Leitrim. He was badly beaten, however, and his defeat left Redmond, the leader of the reunited Irish Party, with the firm conviction that he could defeat Sinn Fein any time by a direct appeal to the Irish people. Sinn Fein was a separatist organization with links with the Irish Republican Brotherhood, and its policy was one of passive resistance to the British Government. It advocated the abandonment of attendance at Westminster and the convening in Ireland of a national council to deal with Irish affairs. After the defeat in Leitrim, Sinn Fein resumed its insignificant place in the Irish political scene. The future obviously lay with the Irish Parliamentary Party and with Home Rule for Ireland inside the United Kingdom, which they expected the Liberal government to give them.

Birrell was personally as much committed to Home Rule as any Irishman. Shortly after entering politics he had written an essay in which he asserted that the roots of Irish nationality had been driven deeper in by conquest and ill-usage. Her laws were taken from her, and her religion brutally proscribed. In the great matter of higher education she had not been allowed her natural and proper development. Her nationality had thus been checked and mutilated, but that it still existed in spirit and in fact could hardly be questioned.[22] By 1910, when he was considering the possibility of incorporating Irish Home Rule in a wider scheme of imperial federation, he declared that to drag Ireland in the wake of England was a downright stupid policy.[22a]

Conservatives, he argued, regarded the Act of Union as a fact of nature though it had really been engendered in corruption in the year 1801. Nobody denied how the Union had been carried; it had been in the school books for generations. It was manifest, therefore, that Britain's relations with Ireland would have to be modified. It was a poor state of affairs when the most that could be said for the inefficient, extravagant, unpopular English administration of Ireland was that it was better than if you were to en-

8

trust the task of spending their own money to the Irish people themselves. The Irish should be let govern themselves; experience had shown that the English could never do it. Englishmen had many gifts but this was not one of them. And, in a review in 1903 of Morley's *Gladstone*, he declared that it was as certain as anything could be in a world like this that a large measure of Home Rule would follow.[23] He had entertained thoughts like these for years, and had first hinted at them when he spoke on the second reading of Gladstone's second Home Rule Bill, following the election of 1892. That measure had been jettisoned by the House of Lords, an act so frequently repeated that it was becoming obvious that sooner or later the power of that House to function as a purely Tory organism would have to be taken from them.

When, on the 13th February 1907, Birrell made his first speech as Chief Secretary in the House of Commons–the occasion was the debate on the King's Speech–a backbencher who was later to be a Prime Minister saw him as 'a sort of fairy in spectacles'[24] but obviously a fairy of unusual physical proportions. He rose after Walter Long, a former Tory Chief Secretary, who had contrasted the prosperity and peacefulness of Ulster with the disimproving situation in Nationalist Ireland. 'I cannot help thinking', Birrell began, 'that to appeal to the Protestant garrison in Ireland and to its prosperity as an explanation for the discontent and misfortune in other parts of the country is a very singular reading of history. Supposing it had been the other way; supposing our Monarch, our Constitution, and our Church service had been those of the Church of Rome–one sometimes thinks they easily might be–and it had been the Protestants of Ulster who were subjected to penal laws and to the harsh treatment that the Roman Catholics of Ireland have received, I wonder whether then their prosperity would have been all that it now is, whether content and satisfaction with the existing régime would then exist. It is all very well to support a Government when the Government is on your side. That does not require much philosophy; it does not require anything except the indulgence of your own love of aggrandisement.'

B   9

Some reform was absolutely necessary. Like the Prime Minister, he was perfectly satisfied that ultimately the only solution that would give satisfaction to the great majority of the Irish people would be what was generally called a Home Rule Parliament. He had had no time yet to make himself acquainted with the many vexed problems that arose in Ireland, but he was bringing to the consideration of them a fresh, and as far as possible, an independent mind and a most sympathetic heart. He had assumed office at a time which synchronized with the existence in Ireland of a great number of currents of emotion and feeling. There was a new spirit abroad, and he appealed to Ulstermen to cease troubling the dry bones of an outdated bigotry.[25]

He told the House that many of the letters he was receiving contained a somewhat grim reference to the fact that the Office of Chief Secretary for Ireland had been the grave of many statesmen's reputations. Sitting opposite him that day was another of his Tory predecessors, George Wyndham. 'His name', said Birrell, 'is associated with a very great measure of land purchase in Ireland and if he is one of the statesmen whose reputation is buried in Ireland, I, at all events, congratulate him on having a noble place of sepulture. Some day after I have had my trial of office, I may be found creeping up within its shadow asking permission to shelter my weary bones beneath the same tomb.'

4

Birrell had no illusions about what lay in store for him. The Government had given a pledge 'to govern Ireland according to Irish ideas', and there were about forty boards to be administered –enough to make a coffin for Ireland, somebody with a grim sense of humour remarked. The Presidency of the Board of Education had involved heavy responsibilities but 'multiply that by ten at least', he said, 'and you get some notion of my condition at the present moment. I find these great departments of State . . . admirably manned . . . I do not doubt that they have gained . . . great knowledge of Ireland. They are the machine, and they must of necessity either work me or I must work them.'[26]

When he spoke these words he probably had Sir Antony MacDonnell, his Under Secretary, mainly in mind. With him he was to have many a tussle, for MacDonnell was no 'yes-man' but a strong, forceful independent-minded Civil Servant of unusual distinction. Though an Irishman and a Catholic he had held high office in the Indian Service and was commonly known as 'the Bengal Tiger'. Birrell had another name for him–'my rice and curry gentleman'.[27] To come to Ireland he had given up a seat on the Council of India as well as the reversion of the Governorship of Bombay. He had done this, William O'Brien said, 'in order to fight the leaders of anti-Irishism in their dingy dens in Dublin Castle',[28] which was a colourful description of MacDonnell's concern for the welfare of his native country. He had returned on the invitation of George Wyndham, who had given him a firm assurance that he would be allowed 'to compass the objects that he held to be of primary importance'. These included the maintenance of order, the co-ordination of the various Irish Boards, and a settlement of the university problem in a manner acceptable to the majority of the Irish people.

MacDonnell's Irish career began happily with the enactment of the Land Bill of 1903, an important measure that owed its origin to an agreement between a group of Irish landlords and representatives of the tenants. This encouraged him to believe that his proposals for the co-ordination of the Irish Boards under a central authority which came to be known as 'devolution' would likewise be well-received, and that, in time, Parliament, seeing that this modest scheme worked well, would give Ireland full control of her own affairs. This was not what happened. When word of what the devolution scheme meant reached the ears of the Unionists they set up a furious agitation. According to Sir Edward Carson, what was proposed was worse than Gladstone's Home Rule, or even Repeal of the Union. It was fatuous, ridiculous, unworkable and impracticable. MacDonnell was represented as a criminally unscrupulous conspirator whose aim was to destroy the Empire, and, under instruction from the Catholic bishops, to force Protestants and Protestantism out of Ireland. The Government got frightened, so that Wyndham publicly repudiated MacDonnell, and Balfour later abandoned Wyndham who had to resign. MacDonnell would have gone also had he not received powerful support in Parliament and outside it.

A consistent admirer of his was Alice Stopford Green, the widow of the author of the *Short History of the English People*. She was a person with capacity beyond the ordinary and an immense store of energy. She edited her husband's writings, and wrote some historical works of her own. She was active and outspoken in many causes, particularly those affecting the welfare of Ireland and emergent Africa, working through a host of friends whom she took pains to cultivate and inspire, and for whom she was prepared to spend herself and her modest fortune when, as sometimes happened, the need arose. Among the leading Liberal figures of the period she knew Campbell-Bannerman, Asquith, Birrell, Bryce, Morley and Haldane, and her Irish acquaintances included men as diverse in their attitudes and ideas as John Redmond, John Dillon, Sir Roger Casement, P. H. Pearse and John MacNeill. Birrell had known her when she was preparing her husband's letters for publication, and had spoken enthusiastically of their likely effect. 'They cannot fail to stir some sluggish pulses', he told her, 'and to inspire some young hearts to deeds of pith and moment . . .'[29] Later they were to tire of each other, she of what she considered his ill-timed jests and he of her dangerous associations.

It was quite characteristic of Mrs. Green to open a correspondence with Campbell-Bannerman, then leading the Liberal Opposition, about the Tory attacks on MacDonnell. Campbell-Bannerman found the situation strange, he told her; there were so many intrigues and cross-purposes that it was not easy to find one's way, and they were dealing with a Prime Minister [Arthur Balfour] who did not mind what quibbles he escaped by, provided he escaped for the moment. The Liberals and the Nationalists were trying to discover the precise relations between MacDonnell and the government and the reason for Wyndham's resignation. Meanwhile, he hoped that MacDonnell would hold on.[30]

MacDonnell did so. He served Wyndham's successor, Walter Long, for what was left of the Tory term, and the Liberals from 1906 till 1908 under Bryce and Birrell. When he went, it was because of the attitude of the Irish Party. Their first reactions to his scheme of devolution had been confused. John Redmond welcomed it as a declaration from the Conservative camp in favour of Home Rule, and 'quite a wonderful thing'. T. P. O'Connor said that Devolution was the Latin for Home Rule, while William O'Brien was particularly enthusiastic. He did not care a brass farthing whether what was proposed was called a statutory body or a legislature; whether it was devolution or revolution. He preferred to call it evolution; it was a stepping stone to all they desired. Michael Davitt, and Tom Sexton who controlled the party paper, the *Freeman's Journal*, took the opposite line. They saw in the scheme a plan to break the national unity, and to betray the national trust. Some of their dislike of the scheme brushed off on to MacDonnell. He was 'a domineering Indian satrap', in Dillon's opinion; Tim Healy described his models as Hindu, and a backbencher went so far as to say that MacDonnell 'half policeman, half Civil Servant, was the worst enemy that ever came to Ireland'.[31]

Birrell, when he came to Dublin, found the devolution proposals on his desk and, the Cabinet agreeing, he consulted Redmond and Dillon and amended the scheme in a number of respects so as to make it more generally acceptable to them. MacDonnell thought that in doing this Birrell had gone too far and had put the whole idea in jeopardy. However, Birrell went ahead and embodied the amended proposals in what he called the Irish Council Bill and this he introduced in the House of Commons on the 7th May 1907. He appeared to Mrs Green, who was in the gallery, 'cold, apparently tired and clearly had not a good hold of his subject'.[32] The night before, he was given a banquet by the Irish members as a token of their regard for him, and at this function Birrell explained the terms of the measure. It was not yet in a form that Redmond and Dillon approved of completely, but they saw that, if accepted as a first instalment of Home Rule, it would be easier for the Liberals later on to face up to the establishment of a genuine Irish parliament.

Many Irish people, amongst them P. H. Pearse and Terence MacSwiney, both of whom figured prominently later in the revolutionary movement, were of the opinion that, since the Irish Council Bill gave Ireland control over education, it ought not to be actively opposed. Pearse was the editor of the Gaelic League paper at this time, and concerned for the survival of the Irish language. A similar line was taken by the influential editor of *The Leader*, D. P. Moran. The Irish Council Bill was a miserable substitute for Home Rule, he said, but it put to the Irish a problem in tactics. If they thought they would get more by flinging it back, by all means fling it; if not, cool prudence would suggest that they should endeavour to make the best of it. His own view was that they should take it and use it for all it was worth and look for more.[33]

This seemed to be Redmond and Dillon's position essentially. But the final word did not rest with them but with a National Convention of the United Irish League, which was called to consider the proposals. However, all that seemed to be necessary was that the true character of the Bill should be explained to the delegates so as to remove doubts that had been raised in reference to the management of the denominational schools. Redmond would have to do this himself, for Dillon was prevented from attending the Convention by a grievous domestic bereavement. This was not what happened. On the eve of the Convention word went out from a caucus meeting that the Bill was to be thrown out. This meeting had been organized by the Molly Maguires, a nickname given to a wing of the Ancient Order of Hibernians which had established itself extensively among the Catholic labouring classes of the Ulster towns and villages, and their representatives actively lobbied the Convention against the Bill. So also did the formidable Young Ireland Branch of the United Irish League, but for a different reason. They had adopted the slogan 'Concentrate on Home Rule. Never mind essentials.' Impressed by the volume of discontent and anxious to maintain the unity of his party, Red-mond performed a *volte-face*, and spoke against the Bill which was then unceremoniously rejected. There was bewilderment all round. In this situation the Government could not go ahead with the Bill, and Redmond told the House of Commons that he agreed with the Prime Minister that apparently there was a mis-understanding at the Convention with reference to some of its more vital portions.

Birrell was greatly upset by this unexpected turnabout, which reflected on himself personally. For the second time within a couple of years his retention of office was in doubt. His reactions are revealed in a letter he wrote to Campbell-Bannerman from Dieppe, where he had taken himself:

24. 3. 1907

In the mournful circumstances I have thought it best to stay where I am than to obtrude my melancholy visage upon the sight of our faithful but embarrassed Commons. However, I must brace myself up to the inevitable and propose to come on Sunday. . . .

From all that I hear the failure of the Bill to secure the support of the Convention is attributable mainly to two causes:

(1) the opposition of the Bishops and priests to the Education De-partment, jealousy of the teachers etc. etc.,

(2) the disaffection of a number of the Irish M.P.s who resent (and I think justly) having been kept in complete ignorance of the contents of the Bill by Redmond and Dillon.

Our poor dear Sir Antony still thinks that if the Bill had been much less it would have got through!

Our mistake was ever to have touched Devolution at all. Home Rule we could not give and we should have contented ourselves with Land Reforms and the University Question, and in both we should have taken altogether our own line and left Sir Antony in the lurch. As it is!

I feel I am somewhat of a Jonah, certainly not a Mascoth and can only say that I am perfectly ready to sacrifice (?) myself at a moment's notice and that if you think I ought to go I will do so without any sense whatever of injustice.

As to Redmond and Dillon we have no case against them; they misjudged the situation, that is all.

Had we given them what they wanted I doubt very much what the results would have been.[34]

He told Redmond that the Irish could not be expected to risk a break-up of their Party and movement for such a Bill. As for Redmond–he had many critics. Poor fellow, what a silly monkey he looks now that the giant robe has slipped off his shoulders, was one writer's comment.[35] Others accused him of a double treachery to the Liberals and the Irish people, or deplored his irresolution. Mrs. Green was one of the latter. She had attended the Convention in Dublin and had been shocked at the one-sidedness of the debate. She was also shocked by MacDonnell's depression when she saw him. He had been humiliated by Birrell and the other ministers of the Government, who treated him as a nuisance, which he admitted he was, and now the Nationalists in a body had spurned the Bill. The lodge had become 'a sad house' and remained so, until wearied of Birrell's opposition and 'fluent talk', he resigned in the spring of 1908. Birrell told MacDonnell that another Council Bill was a sheer impossibility unless it went much further than the last one; it would have to be Home Rule of some sort. MacDonnell believed that England would not give Home Rule, and that proceeding by any other method than Devolution meant postponing to the Greek Kalends administrative reforms as well as Home Rule. He also disagreed with Birrell on the University Question, preferring a scheme of Bryce's, in which he had himself had a hand, to one that Birrell was concocting.[36] 'One more Irishman leaves the field', he told Mrs. Green, 'broken in hopes and in health because his brother Irishmen frustrated him and denied him their support.' He was going to the House of Lords as Baron MacDonnell of Swinford; but what could he be there, he said, but *vox clamantis in deserto*?[37] He had told Birrell that in the event of the Bill being defeated, Dublin Castle would cease to have any attraction for him.

He was succeeded by the sixty-four-year-old Sir James Brown Dougherty, who had been Assistant Under Secretary since John Morley brought him into the Castle in 1895 as a measure of compensation for his defeat in an election in Derry City. Before that he had been a Presbyterian minister and Professor of Logic at Magee College. He was a safe, sensible, level-headed man, and the fact that he was a confirmed Liberal and Home Ruler was deemed important in a service in which so many of the higher posts were filled by Tory-minded officials. These men were considerably alarmed when the bearded Dougherty made his appearance among them, but he made no major changes in precedent or procedure, and was gradually accepted by the younger members of the staff as 'a nice, quiet, inoffensive gentleman'.

After the Irish rejection of the Irish Council Bill, Birrell gave the Prime Minister an appraisal of the political situation. 'Redmond's position is a ticklish one', he said. 'I think he has saved himself for the present, but only by the skin of his teeth. He has very little personal control. The next session he will be watched with scrutinizing eyes by the whole country. He can't rest on his oars for a single moment. He must be up and doing, from the very first. The impression is general in Ireland that the Irish parliamentary party have allowed Home Rule to be snowed under and that it can't emerge for at least a decade. Were this impression to become a belief, Redmond and his whole party would be knocked into space, and their maintenance fund would disappear, and the Sinn Feiners, who are the Fenians and Ribbonmen and separatists in new clothes and with some new ideas, would reign in their stead. Redmond who has still got hold of the machine at Westminster must, therefore, make great play, somehow or other, next session. If he can't give us support he must fight us tooth and nail, and at least half his supporters would be just as well pleased if he decided to fight us.

'Unless, therefore, our programme contains something too good to be lost, we must bid farewell to Irish support. Personally I don't care very much about anybody's support, but I do emphatically feel that the Irish are in bare justice entitled to two things at once. One is the University, the other is Land Reform. . . .' With a university scheme and help from the Treasury he thought the support not only of the Nationalists but of Balfour and Carson could be expected. 'This would go a long way to secure peace and be a great *coup* for us and a blessing for Ireland.' Even if the Lords threw out the Land Bill this should not frighten them. It would commend itself to all their friends in the Commons. Redmond was asking that the Government should by resolution in the next session commit itself, in general terms, to the principle of Home Rule for Ireland. Without this he did not see how he could give any further support. 'He is very much in earnest about this', Birrell said, 'and from his exclusive point of view, one can understand it. But it seems to me impossible, although personally I am always ready to vote for Home Rule whenever asked to do so . . .'[38]

The Government's pledge 'to govern Ireland according to Irish ideas' had been given in the King's Speech which opened the Session of 1907 and the phrase had been devised by Redmond. What Irish ideas were was set out in the programme of the United Irish League, and they covered the two subjects Birrell had suggested to the Prime Minister for urgent attention as well as practically everything else from self-government to the development of Irish industries and the preservation of the Irish language. On the negative side there was also the question of discontinuing the Crimes Act on which the Conservatives when in office consistently relied. Redmond, for his part, had undertaken to do what he could to keep the country quiet so that the Government could proceed to develop their friendly policy in a peaceful atmosphere. But it took time on both sides to implement these promises and Birrell was made to look particularly foolish when, on the basis of some casual statistic, he declared that Ireland had never been so peaceful for 600 years only to be confronted with a great revival of cattle-driving, led by some of the Irish members of parliament. To meet this eruption MacDonnell had pressed him to change his policy and give the full rigour of the law to the law-breakers. But Birrell would not listen to him. He doubted whether in the conditions that existed a Liberal Administration should make itself responsible for order in Ireland. It would be monstrous if he had to go to war with his Irish friends and clap half of them in jail to protect his enemies, and such sordid enemies.[39] He was prepared, therefore, to ignore the inflammatory harangues of the Irish members and to deal only with overt acts of illegality. Redmond's speeches were feeble, he said, but his heart was not set on violent measures, and Birrell believed that this was the view of most of the Irish Party. It would be a pity to drive them into the field, and he did not see himself as the man to do this if he could help it. The Government would have to go slow, leaving the violent speechmakers, Ginnell and Sheehy and the rest, alone. If, however, those gentlemen took a hand at cattle-driving themselves, it would be a different matter. The important thing was to get ahead with a drastic Land Bill if it could be fitted into the legislative programme.[40]

Birrell explained to the Prime Minister that the difficulties in preventing the cattle-drives were enormous. 'All that has to be done', he said, 'is to open a gate, let loose a dog or two, and the bullocks are on the road and will wander for miles. A child can do it.... We have of course succeeded in arresting a certain number, but owing to the supineness and cowardice of the graziers, often butchers in the neighbouring town, and to the complacency of the herds, the task we are imposing on the police is a very hard and thankless one.'

'But when we do make arrests, what happens? Sometimes under a statute of Edward III of blessed memory, we haul them before a Resident Magistrate and require them to give sureties for good behaviour or go to prison for a month, for failing to give sureties. Sometimes they give the sureties and walk away and sometimes they go to prison. If they are taken to the Petty Sessions, the odds are ... that by the votes of three or four *ex officio* magistrates the fellows are discharged though clearly guilty. Here, one at once asks, where are the other magistrates? Why don't they attend and support the R.M.? The answer is cowardice of the most contemptible kind, and party spleen, which derives a malicious pleasure in seeing a Liberal Government in a hole. They want to force us to use the Crimes Act...

'Then there is that pestilent ass, Ginnell, a solitary unpopular fellow, a very bad speaker, of no personal influence, hated by his own party, but a clever writer, and as the *Irish Times* is careful to report him verbatim, he gets the limelight turned full on him. In Westmeath, he has undoubtedly instigated cattle-driving. What he wants is to be prosecuted and to defend himself at a State Trial. He also longs to be sent to prison. To prison he would have gone long ago, but for the fear that if he is sent to prison more powerful persons (Hayden e.g.) would be impelled to take his place. This is a very real fear and hitherto it has prevailed. Ginnell does not personally conduct drives, as one M.P. (Farrell), who is being prosecuted, ... has done in Longford.

'No doubt the immunity granted to Ginnell has a bad side and it has encouraged the agitation to a certain extent. Still, if I can avoid making him a hero I am anxious to do so...

'Things may get worse this winter, or they may not. That depends upon another aspect of affairs – what are we going to offer Ireland this next session? You will shudder at the question but I should be an unfaithful steward if I did not ask it and press it upon you with all the force at my command.'[41]

In time a Land Bill was fitted in. It may not have been as drastic as Birrell contemplated, but it propped up the finances of Wyndham's 1903 Act which had gone seriously awry, so that the purchase of estates for resale could be completed, and wide areas opened up for the relief of congestion. This was done in 1909 and Sir Henry Robinson, the permanent head of the Local Government Board, declared, in a prophecy that was not to be fulfilled, that Birrell's name as a result of this legislation was graven on the West of Ireland as eternally as the watercourses on the mountains. No Unionist government would have dared to bring in a measure of that kind, he said, while for a Liberal Minister to have carried compulsory purchase of wide areas for the relief of congestion through the House of Lords was a feat of statesmanship which could only be realized by those who understood the forces and the strength of feeling and influence working against him.[42]

6

Birrell's Land Bill of 1909 was a considerable achievement, but his first real triumph, and the one by which he is today best remembered, was the Irish Universities Bill which he introduced at the end of March 1908 and which became law four months later. This was his solution for the second of the urgent problems to which he had drawn the Prime Minister's attention and which, in November 1907, he had announced in Dublin that he would solve during the next session of Parliament, or resign. In fulfilling this promise he broke a deadlock that had been reached with his predecessor; not only that, but he succeeded where greater men than Bryce had universally failed. The university question was one of enormous importance to Ireland and, as Birrell told the Catholic Archbishop of Dublin, nobody in England cared a straw about it except the fanatic crowd who, stirred by the neo-Catholicism of the Church of England, saw Popery writ large over the whole subject.[43]

Bryce had sponsored a scheme which in essence was one formulated by Lord Dunraven in January 1904. It proposed a reorganisation of the existing University of Dublin so as to include within it, as well as Trinity College, the Queen's Colleges of Belfast and Cork, the Jesuit-directed Dublin University College, with Maynooth, Galway and Magee Colleges as 'affiliated institutions'. The scheme was badly received. Queen's College Belfast were the first to declare against it. They did not want to have any connection with Dublin, for they feared that Trinity College, with its long-established traditions and great wealth, would always be the predominant partner. The Ulster Unionist Council were also critical and made it clear that they would only accept the scheme if it were stripped of those features that gave it virtue in the eyes of the Catholic bishops, such as the recognition of Maynooth as an affiliated College. As for Trinity College, it was equally reluctant to accept the proposed partnership with other institutions, and in support of its attitude a 'defence committee' was set up which campaigned widely in Britain with the slogan 'Hands off Trinity'. In the upshot the scheme was abandoned, or as Arthur Balfour put it, Bryce nailed his flag to another man's mast and sailed for America. The other man was, of course, 'the bubbling fountain of wit and humour', Birrell.[44] Bryce had declared that his was the only scheme that was politically possible at the time and that he could hold out no hope of any other from the Liberal Government. But Birrell explored the alternative possibilities for himself. The result was a conviction that if the problem could not be solved by holding northern and southern interests together, they should be separated – it sounds like the forerunner of Partition. He framed his own proposals accordingly. Thus Trinity College and Queen's College, Belfast, were assured of an independent existence while it was deemed politically safe simultaneously to establish a National University, with constituent colleges at Dublin, Cork and Galway and with affiliation for Maynooth. There was a stipulation, however, that no religious test would be permitted in any of the university institutions, although this was neutralized by a provision that the Senates and Governing Bodies should be acceptable to members of the predominant denominations in each. This secured that, in all essentials, the National University would be under Catholic control.

Birrell prepared his way with great astuteness. He sought out Traill, the Provost of Trinity, and through him made friends of the Fellows of the College and their Parliamentary representatives, one of whom was the formidable Sir Edward Carson. He went to Armagh several times and got on like a house on fire with Cardinal Logue, whom Birrell's Irish nationalist friends had warned him against. They saw in the Cardinal 'a cunning little Irish peasant', a description to which Birrell would only give a qualified assent. 'Cunning he may have been,' he said, 'all peasants are supposed to be cunning and, if they are not, what would become of them?'[45] Years later, he reported that 'His Eminence, the

Cardinal, is a wily old fox, but at bottom, tho' it is a deep well, he is a good Christian man, which one hardly expects a Cardinal to be'.[46] Before he approached the Treasury about the financial implications of his proposal, and this he did with a heavy heart dreading a rebuff, he sought an assurance from the Cardinal and from the Archbishops of Dublin and Tuam that he was proceeding on the right lines, and that if his draft scheme were properly endowed it would be accepted in Ireland as a reasonable foundation for the establishment of university education on a national footing.[47] The Catholic Archbishop of Dublin, Dr. William Walsh, did not like Birrell's scheme at first and Birrell did not blame him. 'To live in a Catholic city, as the Catholic Archbishop does, with this Protestant Elizabethan institution forever staring you in the face was no doubt galling to a proud prelate.'[48] Yet no serious opposition came from that quarter. Birrell admired the library in the Palace at Drumcondra, and found the Archbishop himself a man of wide reading, pleasant manners, and most informing conversation, a man who could have told *The Times* all about the forger Pigott on whom they based their campaign against Parnell, had he been asked. Birrell also found the Jesuit President of University College, Dr. Delaney, particularly co-operative.

He approached all these people with a confidence begotten of the fact that his Cabinet colleague, Haldane, had told him how back in 1898, although then in opposition, he had obtained from Balfour the necessary credentials to explore the possibility of an agreed settlement of the Irish University Question. University organization was a subject Haldane had studied closely, and he had earlier succeeded in carrying out a much needed reform in the University of London. His Irish enquiries led him to the point when he was able to win Balfour's support for a draft bill that he believed both Conservatives and Liberals could accept. A reactionary element in the Conservative Cabinet decided otherwise. By keeping close to Haldane's draft, Birrell had a fair assurance that his proposals would have an easy parliamentary passage. He therefore insisted that the name of Haldane should be associated with his own among the introducers of the measure. It had in fact an easy passage, but Birrell told the Catholic Archbishop, Walsh, that he had never heard greater nonsense talked in all his life. 'My illustrious predecessor, the Bishop of Hippo', he said, 'was a saint and a doctor, but the honours of martyrdom have, I think, been reserved for his unworthy namesake.'[49] No time was lost to give effect to the Bill, but the election of Archbishop Walsh as Chancellor of the new National University suggested that its denominational character was likely to be more marked than had been expected, and by the end of 1908 an agitation, promoted by the Gaelic League, and endorsed by the Nationalist leaders, was in progress for the adoption of the Irish language as a compulsory subject for matriculation.

Bryce had to be placated, of course. He naturally disliked seeing his own plan dropped, and felt hurt when Balfour made fun at his expense on the emergence of the new proposals. He asked Birrell to explain to the public that in acting as he (Bryce) had done he had been really only the Cabinet's instrument. Birrell saw a difficulty about doing this, because it appeared that no one in the Cabinet had read Bryce's submissions. He told Bryce, however, that he was quite prepared, when introducing the Bill, to make it clear that Bryce had been authorized by the Cabinet to make the announcement he had made, and that the change of plan was due first to himself, and then to the Cabinet. They had all changed their minds. It was a subject full of uncertainty. With the exception of Sir Antony MacDonnell, with whom Birrell said it was his hard fate never to agree, though greatly liking the man, and one or two others, he could find nobody who backed Bryce's proposals though no doubt many of them were willing to accept them *faute de mieux*. 'The Catholic Archbishops of Dublin and Tuam and the Cardinal, tho' mighty shy at first of my definitions', he said, 'soon made it plain that they preferred two universities. This, perhaps, is not surprising, but Dillon, who is very anti-clerical, is equally clear on his preference. I leave T.C.D. out, of course, tho' personally convinced that to fight Trinity is impossible. . . .'[50]

While the Universities Bill was before Parliament, Campbell-Bannerman resigned and died shortly afterwards. His successor was not Birrell, as had once been considered likely, but Henry Herbert Asquith. The reshuffle gave Birrell another opportunity to appeal to be relieved of the burthen of Ireland. He was again unsuccessful. Asquith tried to induce Winston Churchill[51] to take the post but Churchill had other ideas, and Asquith was forced to prevaricate, telling Birrell that 'there is literally no one else could do your job – I won't say as *you* do it, but who could do it at all'. So Birrell agreed to stay on in Ireland where, he said 'at all events you are never dull'.[52] He had an exciting night when he made his first appearance in University College, Dublin, and spoke to the Literary and Historical Society on the subject of university reform. A normally placid student named Arthur Clery, one of a growing body of young men who had been bitten by the bug of the Irish revival, went quite mad. Assuming too readily that the soft words he had listened to from the Chief Secretary were as unreal as they frequently were on such occasions he tore into Birrell, 'spat on his promises, derided his non-conformist conscience and guyed all his Liberal gods. He made the platform look like some arena where a bewildered bull lay staring, uncomprehendingly, under the rain of many darts.'[53] But Birrell was no stranger to University debating societies, and this particular occasion, disturbing though it was, obtained no place in his memoirs.

More continuously and unpleasantly exciting was the affair of the Crown Jewels which disappeared from the Office of the Ulster King of Arms in Dublin Castle six months after Birrell assumed office and shortly before a royal visit to the City. The Jewels, which were worth something less than £20,000, were not really Crown Jewels at all, in the sense that they were sometimes worn by the King. They were in fact the insignia of the Order of St. Patrick of which the Chief Secretary was a member *ex officio*. The circumstances of the disappearance were deeply mysterious, but despite close and prolonged investigation, in which Scotland Yard was joined, it was never established who stole the Jewels or what subsequently happened to them. They are still missing, after sixty years.

A number of people were suspected but nothing could be pinned on them. One of these was Lord Haddo, the Lord Lieutenant's son, but this particular allegation was described by Birrell as a most cowardly falsehood. The air was thick with stories of nightly orgies in the Castle at one of which the intoxicated Ulster King of Arms, Sir Arthur Vicars–it was said that a couple of sherries could knock him over–was relieved by a practical joker of the key of the strong room which was later returned to him. If it could be done once, it could be done again. Sir Antony MacDonnell, the Under Secretary, circulated a report, in which apparently Birrell believed, that there was a connection between Vicars and a group of homosexuals in London, and it was established that he was financially badly off and had been helped out of his difficulties by a person he had helped into an official job.

At an early stage King Edward, anxious to avoid a scandal, wanted Vicars dismissed, without the public enquiry that was being demanded. He did not have his way immediately and that vexed him enormously apart from the failure to find the jewels. However, Vicars was ultimately sacked, following a private Court of Enquiry, with which he, on the advice of his lawyers, would have nothing to do. In 1920 he was taken from his bed one morning and murdered outside his house. A label with the words 'Spy. Informers beware. I.R.A. never forgets' was hung around his neck, but the I.R.A. repudiated the grisly deed.

The Crown Jewels affair was widely seen as a demonstration of extreme incapacity on the part of the Irish Government. Birrell barely knew of the existence of the Jewels, yet he had to take a share of the blame with the Lord Lieutenant and the Under Secretary.[54] The robbery had taken place within a few yards of the Chief Secretary's Office, the Headquarters of the D.M.P., the Dublin Detective Branch, the Headquarters of the Royal Irish Constabulary and the Head Offices of the Dublin military garrison. As *The Times* pointed out, there was no spot in Dublin or possibly in the whole of the United Kingdom, which was at all hours of the twenty-four more constantly and systematically occupied by soldiers and policemen.

The only relic of the regalia of the Order of St. Patrick that survived was the Chief Secretary's small star. This was handed over by Birrell to his successor and he explained that it had survived because his housemaid had kept it with his evening clothes![54a]

8

The need to do something for primary education and for the notoriously badly paid primary teachers who were an important political group in the community presented itself to Birrell at an early stage. Within a couple of months of assuming office he came, with his wife and his son, Francis, to the annual teachers' congress which was held in the Dublin Mansion House and received a wild reception, the whole assembly rising and cheering as they entered the Round Room.[55] It was the first time in the history of the organisation, the teachers' president said, that a Minister of the Crown had condescended to discuss with them in public the reform of primary education, and this observation spurred the meeting to rise again and cheer for several minutes when Birrell was called upon to speak. It was a red letter day.

Birrell assured his audience that it gave him the profoundest satisfaction that the very first time he had opened his mouth in public in Ireland should be to espouse a cause that lay at the very root of what was called the Irish Question. *The Irish Times* had called him a cheerful humbug. He did not at all recognise the truth of that description (laughter). He had reason to rejoice greatly and the first cause was that the Irish people, before it was too late, had become alive to the importance of preserving their ancient and proud language and with it the memorials of a past greatness and the prospects of a happy future (cheers).

He counselled his audience to share his cheerfulness. 'Don't be too fond of exhibiting your sores', he said. 'There are days, like the present, when it is a happiness to be alive, when even the cripple may crawl into the sun and rejoice that he is alive; they were certainly not days when Irishmen should lose faith in the future. I quite agree there is another side to the picture. An ever-dwindling population, the frightful spread of tubercular disease, and a totally inadequate provision for the national education of the country (more cheers). The scale of your salaries is most meagre and insufficient, and your chances of promotion are not only poor but most disheartening. . . .' And when he had given examples, he added with a flourish: 'Gentlemen, these are not exhilarating figures.'

From that on every sentence was punctuated with louder and louder applause. 'You are the victims', he told the teachers, 'of a highly centralized system, a Board over whom you have naturally no control, whom you cannot reach, and who do not appear to be tremendously desirous to ascertain your opinion. . . . You are entitled to say—"Whoever is my paymaster, let him pay me my due". This highly centralized system was imposed upon you by outsiders just as too many things have been imposed upon Ireland.

'How and in what way and by whom', he asked, 'is the primary education of this country to be controlled? By what means are we to obtain that further sum of public money for the purpose of supplementing the salaries of teachers and to create scholarships, prizes and bursaries so that the more quick-witted of the Irish children may reap the same advantage of secondary and higher education as would have fallen to their lot had they been born, not in Ireland but in England or Scotland. It is idle', he declared, 'to talk to me of a United Kingdom except on terms of education equality.'

The excitement of the teachers, who at this stage had reason to expect an immediate substantial rise in pay, was abated when Birrell proceeded to outline the difficulties he had to face. There was the Treasury, first and foremost, and he asked the delegates to bear in mind that there were other parts of the United Kingdom knocking at the Treasury door—'I won't say as loudly as I do, because I think that the Chancellor of the Exchequer would admit that of all his sturdy beggars I am the sturdiest (laughter). Still he has many beggars knocking at his door. As I come in, I find another fellow slipping out and I sometimes hope without anything in his pockets (laughter) so that there may be more left for me.'

And millions were needed in Ireland. There were harbours to be dredged, commerce that was threatened with extinction, railways to be made, schemes of arterial drainage awaiting attention. He often wished it were possible to pool all the money to which Ireland was entitled and having got it safe in their hands, to distribute it according to the real needs of the country as a whole. The cost of education should be the first charge.

This was postponing action. The words with which he ended his speech promised not an immediate increment but that he would do all that lay in him to procure what he was satisfied justice demanded. 'I hope', he said, 'if I remain in office a sufficient length of time and if things go on as I trust they will do, before long to come before you, not only with sympathetic words but with full hands.' He sat down to further applause and a vote of thanks having been passed the chairman called for three cheers for Mr. and Mrs. Birrell. He hoped that when they did come again they would indeed come with full hands for the Irish teachers.

In response to the vote of thanks Birrell made a second speech. He had pretty long ears, he said, and he had heard certain remarks which no doubt were not meant to be heard by him. When one of the platform speakers was saying that he had often heard promises from Chief Secretaries before and had been disappointed, a gloomy voice at the back of the hall had said, 'So we shall be again'. He (Birrell) knew it was much easier to make promises than to keep them. He was now busily occupied in trying to keep the promises made by his predecessor (laughter) but he had not made any promise to the teachers except to do his very best.

With that the Birrells left the Mansion House on an outside car and were given an enthusiastic send-off. Next day the *Freeman's Journal* complimented the Chief Secretary upon his first venture on an Irish platform. Unlike his predecessors he had neither been guarded by police batons nor protected by ticket collectors.

In time he obtained from the reluctant Treasury an additional £114,000 for the teachers which became known as 'the Birrell Grant', as well as a contribution towards the heating and lighting of schools. He left office, however, still deploring the unsuitability of the Irish educational system. This was administered by Boards nominated by the Government with balanced representation on them for Catholics and Protestants. The Board of National or Primary Education had a Resident Commissioner, one Mr. Starkie, a brilliant but ill-tempered classical scholar whom Birrell disliked. This he was alleged to have shown on an occasion when he received a deputation from the Irish National Teachers' Organization led by an aggressive individual named Mansfield who attacked the Resident Commissioner. Later a story was current that Birrell said to Mansfield: 'Starkie is a bully but you too are a bully. The only difference between you is that he is a chastised bully while you are an unchastised one.'[56] These were words Birrell might indeed have used, but the pedantically truthful[56a] Under Secretary put Starkie's mind at ease about them when he raised the matter.[57] He had been present at the interview and had no note whatever of Mr. Birrell having used any such expression about Dr. Starkie.[57a]

Birrell must have acquired a reputation for outspokenness among the teachers. On another occasion when a member of a deputation wound up an eloquent appeal by saying that he had only £100 a year and had fourteen children to support, Birrell with horror in his voice exclaimed: 'Fourteen children! Good heavens, man, that's a disease.'[57b]

9

While traditionally and theoretically the Chief Secretary to the Viceroy, Birrell, by virtue of being a member of the Cabinet, was effectively the supreme British personage in Ireland. He was a simple sort of person—he liked, for instance, to have his meals in a pub or a small restaurant— and he had no use for the unreal sort of life that surrounded the Lord Lieutenant, the parades, levees and junketing that separated an aristocracy of sorts from the ordinary people. He regarded Dublin Castle, where these functions were held and where his own office was situated as 'switched off' from the current of Irish life.[58] It was still, as Thackeray had said, 'the greatest sham of all the shams in Ireland'.[59] He shared this contempt for the hangers-on of the Viceregal Court, the 'Old Gang', with Irish Nationalists of all brands, and he deliberately kept away from the Kildare Street club which was the recognized headquarters of Irish Unionism. His happiest Irish days were those spent away from 'the respectable monotony' of life in the Lodge. 'Never was any Chief Secretary so peripatetic as I was', he said, wondering what the real Ireland, the new Ireland, the enfranchised Ireland, was thinking about and whitherwards it was tending'[60]. He liked the West best of all, and he saw a great deal of it in the company of the permanent heads of the Local Government Board and the Congested Districts Board of which he was President *ex officio*. Indeed, his idea of paradise – for the Irish presumably, because his own roots were deep in English soil – was a parish in Connacht supplied with a pious and sensible priest, a devoted and skilled Dudley nurse, and a sober dispensary doctor, although he knew from experience that this was a combination it was not always easy to find. He said this in his posthumous biography,[61] but, years before, he had told Mrs. Green that he should be quite willing to spend the residue of his days in a *Congested District*, tho' not in a *Congested Cottage*. The people were delightful and it did not lie in the mouth of a politician to say they were liars.[62] But there were sights in the West that depressed him. In the same letter he said: 'I was at Galway the other night. Oh Lord! The melancholy of it was overwhelming. Belmullet was a Pleasure House beside it. Galway and the Workhouse at Clifden will never quit my memory.'

On his travels in the country he liked best the company of Sir Henry Robinson, the Vice-President of the Local Government Board, although he was reputedly a Unionist and unpopular with the Irish Nationalists who alleged that he was 'slim' and a 'time server'. A tall thin man with large ears and a long foxy nose,

Robinson had a talent for mimicry and a story for every occasion. One of these concerned a bluff, gruff, cautious Boots in a Donegal hotel who always gave a curt non-committtal reply to a question. A Chief Secretary– it might have been Birrell– his wife and a lady friend spent a night in the hotel, and when starting off next morning the tourists crowded into the hall to get a glimpse of the great man; and one of them, more inquisitive than the others, asked the Boots which of the two ladies was his wife. 'Well, thon's a question', he replied, 'a'm not rightly able to answer you, but all ah can tell you is that last night the Chief Secretary slept with the one with the red hat.'[63]

Robinson insisted to English political visitors that as a public servant he had no positive principles or prejudices, that his main worry was to keep his successive Chief Secretaries out of trouble, but it is evident that he had his eye on the Under Secretaryship which he had little chance of achieving so long as the Liberals remained in power. Beatrice Webb said that Robinson had the characteristics of all very clever officials of seeming to be indiscreet and being at the same time a model of discretion, and she had no difficulty in assessing his attitude to the line of chiefs for whom he worked. He had liked Balfour and Long, he detested Wyndham and Hicks-Beach and found Bryce a bore.[64] But for Birrell– Liberal though he was–he had a particular regard. He found him adroit and quick to come to conclusions. He was rather easygoing, it was true, but he never kept papers. In fact 'he was an ideal chief', and if legislative work was the criterion of a Chief Secretary's success his services would rank higher than those of any Chief Secretary except perhaps Gerald Balfour. No fewer than fifty-six Acts of Parliament were carried through the House by him.[65]

Being a literary man, and liking company, he sought information as to what the new Ireland was thinking about, in Irish literary and artistic circles. The latest list of Irish publications and the programmes of the Abbey Theatre became of far more significance to him than the monthly police reports that were laid on his table. 'The plays', he said, 'of John Synge and Lady

Gregory, the poems of Mr. Yeats, A E, and Dora Sigerson, the pictures of Orpen, Lavery and Henry, the provocative genius of Mr. Bernard Shaw, the bewitching pen of Mr. George Moore, the penetrating mind of Father Tyrell (the list could easily be prolonged) were by themselves indications of a veritable re-naissance–a leap to the front rank of thought and feeling alto-gether novel.'[66]

He became a regular habitué of the Abbey Theatre, arriving as the doors opened and sitting among the sparse audience in the stalls until the manager heard he was there and came down to keep him company. A one-acter he must have seen there many times was Lady Gregory's *Workhouse Ward*. He obviously liked it anyway because he read it in an 'admirable brogue' on one oc-casion at a dinner-party with Viola, the daughter of the actor-manager Beerbohm-Tree.[66a] He expected much from the Abbey. It made merciless fun, he said, of mad political enterprises, and lashed with savage satire some historical aspects of the Irish Revolutionary. He was often amazed at the literary detachment and courage of the playwright, the relentless audacity of the actors and actresses, and the patience and comprehension of the audience.[67]

10

Other ministers were busy with legislation, too, and some of this made a great impact on Ireland. There was the Old Age Pensions Act, for instance, which was a sensational boon in a country where the standard of living was low and the population of old people high, owing to the constant emigration of the young. An old age pension of five shillings a week–a lot of money in those days–was like manna from heaven for the poor and destitute and especially for those living in areas where in the past there had been recurring famine. Before this to be seventy years of age was some-thing either to be ashamed of, if you could still work, or some-thing in the nature of an affliction, if you were being supported by your family. There were obstacles to be overcome before you

got your pension of course–a pensions officer, a pensions committee, and, if an appeal had to be taken, the Local Government
Board of which the Chief Secretary was President. There was a
means test which could usually be passed by applicants, but the resources of civilization were often taxed to the limit and beyond it
to establish the requisite age. There were many stories in circulation. One of them about the man who had perhaps reached the
fifty mark who was asked how he managed to be in receipt of an
old age pension. He replied: 'Since I knew the day that the
pensions officer was coming round to look at me, I had a real old
alibi down from the mountains waiting for him in the bed.'

The fundamental trouble was that there was no registration of
births in Ireland before 1864, while baptismal records were frequently inadequate. To prove that one was seventy in 1909 meant
going back to 1839, the year in which an event famous in Irish
folklore occurred, the night of the Big Wind. The fame of that
night may indeed be due in part to its association with efforts to
receive the old age pension. An illustration in one of Sir Henry
Robinson's books is of a woman who claimed she could remember 'atin' a potato out of her fisht the night of the Big Wind'. 'It
was a wonderful wind,' Birrell said later. 'Dickens alone could
have done it justice. It ought to have blown itself out in 1839, but
there it still was, sweeping pensions officers and local government
officials off their feet in 1908. It shrieked and whirled around every
cabin which sheltered anyone bending under the weight of years.
Though a terrible memory, it was still a priceless asset.'[68] But the
'Big Wind' played such havoc with the Treasury chest that
alleged septuagenarians had to discover other evidence. 'I always
thought I was sixty,' one of these explained to Birrell, 'but my
friends came to me and told me they were certain sure I was
seventy, and as there was three or four of them against me, and
evidence was too strong for me, I put in for the pension and got it
for a year; but now they have it taken off me, and I hope your
Honour will see me righted, for I have a long, weak and struggling
family!'[69]

Codding the Government was a game the common people,

'the cunning peasants', were uncommonly good at playing. The best exponent of it, perhaps, was the Galwayman, Padraic O Conaire, afterwards a writer of great distinction in the Irish language, who played it to enter the British Civil Service. He was living in London at the time and one of the examination subjects was Irish, with questions set in Irish to be answered in Irish. To conduct the test for them the Civil Service Commission asked Trinity College, Dublin, to suggest some capable person. O Conaire had entered under his name in English, Patrick Conroy. When Trinity consulted Douglas Hyde, the President of the Gaelic League, Hyde replied, strongly recommending O Conaire, but without knowing that he had entered for the examination. Hyde's recommendation was accepted and so O Conaire set the questions in Irish, Conroy answered them in Irish, O Conaire checked the answers and Conroy duly passed the examination. It is the only instance known to us of a man setting questions for his own examination and passing himself.[70]

The Old Age Pensions and other social legislation of that time – the first steps towards the welfare state – are associated with the name of Lloyd George, the Chancellor of the Exchequer in Asquith's government. They were measures that cost a great deal of money, as much money, as Lord Lansdowne said, as would pay for a great war. Lansdowne was expressing a viewpoint, which we have often heard since, that these social innovations weakened the moral fibre of the nation, and diminished the self-respect of the people. The extra money that was required to pay the Exchequer contribution and to re-equip the Navy which had become urgent as a result of the growing menace of Germany could only be found by increasing taxation and it was the proposals in this regard together with a Bill for the disestablishment of the Church of Wales, with which Lloyd George was also especially identified, that brought to a head the question of terminating the House of Lords veto. That House, in Birrell's words, had become a sort of pocket borough for the Tory Party. It had ceased to play the part of an intelligent Second Chamber and only exercised its critical and disagreeable functions when a Liberal Government was in power.[71] This had become for Asquith the dominating issue in politics, because in the long run, as he said, it was the issue that overshadowed and absorbed everything else. Its importance for Ireland was, of course, beyond question.

The curtain raiser for this tremendous parliamentary drama was the so-called People's Budget that Lloyd George introduced at the end of April 1909. It was a most controversial budget, although a pale, insignificant thing compared with what we are accustomed to nowadays. There were additional duties on spirits and tobacco, a heavy tax on licensed premises and a tax on motor-cars and petrol. These might have been accepted without undue criticism. The real trouble arose, however, in connection with an extension of direct taxation. Income tax, at the highest level was raised to 1s 8d in the £–that too was tolerable–but super-tax or surtax as it is now called was introduced for the first time and was levied at the rate of 6d in the £ on the amount by which incomes of £5,000 or more exceeded £3,000, and also introduced for the first time were land taxes. These, after some years' experience of disappointing yields, were abandoned, but in 1909 they set off a veritable storm of opposition. There was to be a tax of 20 per cent on the unearned increment in land values, payable either when the land was sold or when it passed on death. There was to be a capital tax of one halfpenny in the £ on the value of undeveloped lands and minerals, and a 10 per cent reversion duty on any benefit which came through a lessor at the end of a lease.

The resistance to these taxes was not confined to the Tories. There were plenty of critics of them among well-to-do Liberals. Lord Rothschild, who was a Liberal, sent Asquith a letter of protest which was signed by the principals of most of the leading financial houses. A former Liberal Prime Minister, denounced the budget as inquisitorial, tyrannical and socialistic. This was Lord Rosebery of whom Birrell said that his hatred of Ireland was that of a jilted woman[72] for the Irish had helped to bring down his government in 1895. And King Edward, who was coming near the end of his days, deplored the attempt of ministers, particularly Lloyd George and Winston Churchill, to inflame the passions of the working and lower orders against people who happened to be the owners of property.

The debate in the House of Commons on this unprecedented Budget stretched out through the summer and autumn of 1908 and ended only in early November. By that time attention had moved from its merits or demerits to the question whether the House of Lords would dare to touch it. They had often rejected Money Bills, but more than 250 years had passed since they had rejected an entire budget. The right of veto, therefore, in this respect seemed to be as dead as the right of the Sovereign to veto legislation. What would the Lords do? Asquith warned them that if they rejected the budget it would open the way to revolution. It would bring the peers and people into a head-on collision. And the King counselled Lansdowne, who led the Unionists in the House of Lords, and Balfour, who led them in the Commons, to be careful. Both warning and counsel were disregarded. On the last day of November the Lords threw out the Finance Bill which embodied the Budget motions and three days later the King dissolved Parliament. This was inevitable, because with the legislature deciding to withhold the necessary finance, the Government could not carry on. A general election was, therefore, fixed to take place in the second fortnight of January 1910, and the Liberals were concerned to find out how the Irish would now behave.

The Budget was unpopular in Ireland. An increase in the duty on spirits was a blow at the Irish whiskey industry and at the politically important owners of public houses, who, in the words of an unintentional humorist, were 'living from hand to mouth'. The Budget was also unpopular because of the revaluation of land that the new taxes was likely to bring about, while at the back of people's minds was the fact that a Commission had reported, not long before, that the country was already taxed beyond its capacity. Redmond, while not withholding his support, had remonstrated with the Government without achieving anything, and was criticized, not for the first time, for being too subservient to the Liberals.

However there was a bigger issue at stake than the Budget, and

Redmond could hardly be blamed for keeping his eye fixed on it. This was the use the Liberals could make of the situation that would follow on the removal of the House of Lords veto. Knowing, therefore, that for tactical reasons they might be reluctant to mix up the subject of Home Rule with the House of Lords issue, Redmond, even before the dissolution of Parliament, made it abundantly clear that the Liberals would have to pay a price for Irish support. The price was an official declaration on the Home Rule question. If he did not get this, Redmond said, not only would it be impossible to support Liberal candidates in the English constituencies, but he would call upon their friends to vote against them everywhere. This, he admitted, would be, in one sense, a ludicrous, and, in another sense, a very tragic position for, of all the countries concerned, Ireland was most interested in limiting the power of the House of Lords, and it was unthinkable that the Liberal leaders would deliberately force the Irish into a position of seeming to support the Lords in the forthcoming election.

Redmond had his way. When Asquith duly declared his election policy, he repeated a statement he had made on becoming Prime Minister, namely that Ireland was the one undeniable failure of British statesmanship, and that the solution of the problem could only be found by a policy which, while explicitly safeguarding the supremacy and indefectible authority of the Imperial Parliament, would set up in Ireland a system of full self-government in regard to purely Irish affairs. There was no question of separation nor of rival or competing supremacies, but, subject to those conditions, the new Liberal Government would be free to act on that policy.

The result of the election was 275 Liberals, 273 Unionists, 82 Nationalists, and 40 Labour members. The Liberals lost 104 seats; the substantial majority they had secured over all other parties in 1906 was changed into a minority of 120. They could still count, of course, on the Irish and Labour votes as regards the issues of the Budget and Home Rule; so they stayed in office. But Redmond and the Irish Party held the balance of power. Grievously disappointed, the Liberals began to wonder whether–roughly sharing, as they did, the British vote with the Conservatives– they were entitled to go ahead with their policy *vis-à-vis* the House of Lords. They looked round for a compromise and as they did Redmond was forced to remind them of the character of the Irish support. Their slogan was: No Veto, No Budget. Birrell reported on the situation on the 1st of February 1910. He had just returned, he told Asquith, all storm-tossed and snow-driven from John Bull's Other Island, whose political state and condition was highly complex and entertaining, but none the less full of historical significance and immediate political importance. Every- thing was in order provided the Government went ahead with, first, the Budget and, then, the House of Lords, placing the two issues in immediate sequence. Without these the Irish would go into opposition, and if Redmond did not lead them there, he would be knocked off his quaking throne.[73]

So Redmond once more had his way; demonstrating as *The Times* said that he was the real master of the situation. Having in previous weeks frequently used his famous phrase 'Wait and See' while the Government was trying to make up its mind what to do, Asquith told an excited House of Commons early in April 1910, that he intended to bring in a series of resolutions to curtail the power of the Upper House. The Finance Bill enshrining the Budget was then reintroduced and by the end of the month it had passed through all its stages, in *both* Houses. The Conservative Lords recognized that the General Election had settled *that* issue, whatever about the wider question of the veto. Parliament then adjourned, and during the adjournment the King died, leaving his inexperienced successor, George V, to face a most serious con- stitutional crisis, one that would involve himself personally if, as was more than likely, he was asked to create sufficient peers to change the character of the House of Lords. The Cabinet, how- ever, were not over-anxious to coerce the King, or to face another hazardous general election. So they resolved to try to settle the problem by means of a conference with the Opposition leaders. These responded eagerly enough, because they too were in a fix.

The talks, however, which began in mid-June and went on inter-mittently till the 10th of November, ended without agreement being reached. Asquith and Balfour might have come to terms, but Lord Lansdowne was adamant. He was an Irish landlord who had not forgotten the Land League, and was determined to do nothing to facilitate the passage of Home Rule. With his disruptive presence at the talks there was no need for the Irish nationalists to worry about the rumours that were in circulation to the effect that the Government were attempting to bolt, as Dillon put it, or worse still that the two Front Benches, if they settled the consti-tutional question by agreement, would probably drop Home Rule altogether.

The breakdown of the talks with the Opposition left the Cabinet with no alternative but to recommend that Parliament should again be dissolved and to secure from the King an under-taking that, if the Liberals won the election, he would create the hundreds of new peers that would be necessary to end the Tory stranglehold on the House of Lords. The King acquiesced in both courses but, in order to safeguard his position, it was agreed that the pledge about the creation of peers would be kept secret until the people's verdict became known.

The election, held in the depths of winter, and the second within a year, changed the overall picture not at all. The Liberals lost three seats and the Conservatives one, while the Irish Nationalists and Labour picked up a couple each. So far as the constitutional proposals were concerned, the Liberals, with the co-operation of the Nationalists and the rising Labour Party, had a reassuring majority of 120 which enabled Asquith immediately to introduce what was called the Parliament Bill on the assembly of the new House of Commons. This deprived the Upper House of all power over 'money bills' and restricted it to a suspensive veto on other legislation of two successive sessions. By the end of May over 900 proposed amendments had been disposed of and the Bill was ready to go to the Lords.

By that time also the Irish Party was making up its mind as to what it should do at the Coronation of the new King, whether

The Earl and Countess of Aberdeen at St Patrick's Cathedral
during George V's visit, July 1911

they should absent themselves from the official functions as they had traditionally done or attend these functions in order to demonstrate that the Home Rule, that was now showing on the horizon, involved no sort of hostility to the King or the Empire. Their decision was to maintain the old position and to explain why. The first words of their explanation made it clear that when the day came for the King to enter the Irish capital to reopen the ancient Parliament of Ireland, he would obtain from the Irish people a reception as enthusiastic as ever welcomed a British monarch in any of his dominions. This was an opportunity the King never had, but when he visited Dublin after his coronation the tremendous welcome he received nourished a theory or an illusion he held that there existed between the Irish people and the Crown a bond of understanding that was quite independent of politics and parties.

But there remained a minority who kept to another tradition. These were the separatists, and they missed no opportunity of drawing public attention, if only in a small way, to what they stood for. They organized patriotic protests on the occasion of royal visits, and when on the day of King Edward's funeral in 1910 a votive mass was offered in the Pro-Cathedral, Dublin, they tarred the steps leading to the church and painted in black letters on the wall beneath the railings the words 'Remember '67 McManus', a reference to the fact that in the eighteen-sixties the remains of Terence Bellew MacManus, the 1848 Young Irelander turned Fenian, had been refused entry into any church in the Dublin diocese by Cardinal Cullen, the Archbishop at the time. These separatists had painfully long memories.[74]

CHAPTER II
Home Rule for Ireland
1911–1913

WHEN the Parliament Bill reached the committee stage in the House of Lords an amendment was carried which altered its whole nature. Under this amendment any bill which affected the Crown or the Protestant Succession, or which made provision for Home Rule in Ireland, Scotland or Wales or which raised an issue of great gravity on which the judgment of the country had not sufficiently been ascertained, would not become law until it had been submitted to, and approved by, the electors in a manner to be provided by Act of Parliament–presumably by referendum. Faced with this amendment, the Government informed the King that a deadlock had been reached and, as a third dissolution was out of the question, they advised him to exercise the Royal Prerogative so as to secure the passage of the Bill. An idea had spread among the Conservatives that the Government was bluffing, and that when the moment came the Prime Minister would hesitate to invoke the Royal Prerogative. To eliminate any doubt on this score, the King's Private Secretary, with the Prime Minister's consent, informed Balfour of the purport of the pledge that had been secretly given in November, before the election. Balfour then asked for a statement in writing, whereupon Asquith wrote to him saying that when the Parliament Bill, in the form it had assumed, returned to the House of Commons, the Government would be compelled to ask the House to disagree with the Lords' amendments. In those circumstances, should the necessity arise, the Government would advise the King to exercise his prerogative to secure the passing into law of the Bill in substantially the same form in which it left the House of Commons, and the King had been pleased to signify that he would consider it his duty to accept and to act on that advice. The receipt of this information sparked off a fantastic scene in the House of Commons. Asquith, when he rose to speak, was met with a roar of interruptions and with shouts of 'Traitor', 'Let Redmond speak', and 'Who killed the King?' The uproar continued until the Speaker suspended the sitting.

At the earliest opportunity Balfour moved a vote of censure on the Government on the ground that the advice given to the King was a gross violation of constitutional liberty. This was defeated, but a similar motion was carried defiantly in the House of Lords. A few days later, however, the Lords, under pressure from the Conservative leaders, changed their tune and gave a first reading to the Parliament Bill, but only by a narrow margin. There were many men who preferred to 'die in the last ditch', men who preferred to listen to Carson and F. E. Smith rather than to the party chiefs. So offended was Balfour by this behaviour that he surrendered the leadership to Bonar Law.

On the 18th of August 1911 the King was able to sign the Parliament Bill in the normal way. He did so to his great relief. The need for the creation of peers had disappeared and he was spared the necessity of exercising his prerogative in circumstances which he believed would have done damage to the prestige of the Crown. The Conservatives had suffered a humiliating defeat in having to reverse engines. On the other hand the Irish Party by their uncompromising attitude had enabled the Liberals to score a great victory, a victory, too, for parliamentary democracy because until the enactment of the Parliament Bill it could not be said that Westminister was a democratic institution. It was now possible for Bills that were certified by the Speaker of the House of Commons as money bills to become law within one month of having been passed by the Commons and sent up to the Lords, whether or not the Lords had consented to them within that time limit. What was of more concern to the Irish Party and to Birrell and other Liberal Home Rulers was that other Public (as distinct from Private) Bills which had been passed by the House of Commons in three successive sessions (whether of the same parliament or not) could receive the Royal Assent despite their rejection by the House of Lords, provided that two years had elapsed between the second reading in the Commons in the first session and the third reading in the Commons in the third session. The way was now wide open for Home Rule.

2

There happened to be a parliamentary vacancy at this time in North Tyrone and Birrell was most anxious that it should be filled by T. W. Russell, the Vice-President of the Department of Agriculture, who was a doughty fighter in the political arena and who knew the Irish problem inside-out, particularly the Ulster aspects of it. There were difficulties in having him nominated, however. He had quite recently been defeated in South Tyrone. He was a Protestant and an ex-Unionist; and there was some local feeling in favour of another possible candidate who was both a Catholic and a Nationalist. But Birrell knew the short-cut through the thicket, and that is the significance of the following letter to Bishop Patrick O'Donnell of Raphoe, later the Cardinal Archbishop of Armagh. O'Donnell, in Birrell's eyes, was 'frankly a Nationalist politician' who could carry a constituency convention in favour of any person of his choice.

Very Confidential

August 21

My dear Bishop,

I am anxious to consult you confidentially about N. Tyrone. Redmond Barry (subject to the King's approval) will become Lord Chancellor, [James] O'Connor will I presume become Attorney General and there is then a vacancy in the solicitorship. Unluckily there is nobody now on our side at the Irish Bar likely to be of *any use* to me next year in the House of Commons when the great Tussle–and a great tussle it will be, comes on. Neither Ignatius O'Brien nor [Thomas] Moloney have either parliamentary experience or aptitude. A mere lawyer is not of much use. I want experience, knowledge, courage, and a man who will be listened to!

T. W. Russell has these qualifications to an unusual degree. Now, would he be acceptable to the convention? I know there are difficulties in his way. He also knows them. Supposing it were made known that the Government particularly wanted T. W. R. to help them with the Home Rule Bill and attached *great importance* to his being in the House to assist them, would that have the necessary effect? Of course T. W. R. would stick to the seat till the end of all things, whilst no lawyer can be expected to give any such pledge. I don't think there will be any question about money or expenses.

I am sorry the Bishop of Derry is abroad, but I felt sure I could rely on your advice confidentially given. It really is a most important matter at this crisis. I assure you that neither of the two legal gentlemen would be anything but a hindrance to me at Westminster–they or whichever of them is selected, can stay and do the legal work in Dublin and draw the salary. I want a fighting man and except T. W. R. *I can think of no one.*

Pardon my troubling you,

Yours most sincerely,

Augustine Birrell

The bishop did all that was expected of him. The convention, the largest and most representative held in the division for many years, unanimously adopted Russell as the Nationalist candidate, and did so on the proposition of one of the local Catholic curates.[1] And when Russell, who was hailed as the Grand Old Man of Ulster Liberalism, a man who through many weary years had fought the battle of the Ulster tenant-farmers,[2] came before the people of Strabane, the principal town in the constituency, he was introduced by the parish priest, Father O'Doherty, V.F. Father O'Doherty, who was a skilled performer, made it clear, when the election was over, that he had not supported Russell so much as the principles he stood for, neither had he opposed Mr. Herdman, the Unionist candidate, a respected local employer, because he was who he was but because of the bad company he was in. At nomination day, Father O'Doherty proposed Russell, while one of his curates led the list of seconders.

The contest, which was short and superficially polite, ended in a result that could hardly have been narrower–a mere eighteen votes separated the candidates–but Birrell telegraphed Russell to congratulate him on a great victory. Russell was not sure that it was a great victory but he had the seat and he rightly gave credit for his success primarily to Father O'Doherty, the Bishop's man. At this point the politeness that had characterized the election evaporated. The Nationalists blamed their poor poll on Russell–his great zeal as a temperence reformer had drawn down on him the wrath of the licensed trade–while the Unionists ascribed their defeat to gross clerical intimidation, particularly by Father O'Doherty whom they charged with having said that 'any nationalist who voted for Mr. Herdman, or abstained from voting, would be a recreant to his country, he would not be acting according to the dictates of his own conscience which every man was bound to, and for which he would be held responsible on the day of judgment'. The local Nationalist paper answered this charge with examples from the Unionist side in recent Belfast elections that were considered equally bad. Father O'Doherty also counterattacked. A Catholic priest could not move his foot, or open his lips without being accused of 'spiritual intimidation'. They had been blamed for leading voters to the poll with the aid of the clerical lash. He only wished to fling these insults back in the teeth of those who threw them. If the people who made allegations of that kind against Catholic clergymen had looked about them and watched their own clergymen before they began to talk they would have seen what he had seen. He had seen the Protestant rector of Strabane 'arming' voters to the poll out of their own homes. If these people saw the way ministers roped in the Unionist voters they might call that voting with the aid of the clerical lash. He could tell them that they were as active as bees throughout the whole constituency.[3]

Birrell did not get involved in this post-election controversy. There was nothing new in it anyway. But speaking at Ilfracombe shortly afterwards he said something that was relevant and worth saying. Two difficulties were always raised in connection with Home Rule, namely money–the cost of governing Ireland–and religion. 'It was a very odd thing', he said, 'about money and religion, that the people who got the most excited about money were the people who had the most of it–and the people who got the most excited about religion were the people who had none of it. Religion was based on love, not on hatred.'

3

With Home Rule now a probability the Irish Unionist clubs and Orange Lodges began to bestir themselves. In late September they conferred in Belfast and, having expressed their alarm at the threat to the Empire and absolute ruin to Ireland involved in the establishment of a Parliament in Dublin, they called upon their leaders to take any steps they considered necessary to avert this threat. They also appointed a commission, one of whose duties was to prepare, in consultation with Sir Edward Carson, a constitution for a provisional government for Ulster, which would come into being on the day the Home Rule Bill became law. Few people at the time took this resolution seriously, nor did they pay much attention to Carson when he stated his belief that, if necessary, the men of Ulster would march from Belfast to Cork and take the consequences, even if not one of them ever returned.

On the other hand, a feeling of hopefulness pervaded Nationalist Ireland, and some people began to wonder what was in Home Rule for them personally. The Gresham Hotel, where Redmond usually stayed when in Dublin, was beset with a swarm of office-seekers. The public elation was increased by an announcement that a Government-appointed committee of experts under Sir Henry Primrose had reported in favour of fiscal autonomy for Ireland. Birrell, however, when he sent Redmond a copy of the report intimated that 'for political considerations which lay altogether outside the purely financial aspect of the Irish problem it would be impossible with any good hopes of ultimate success to adopt the report as a whole'.

How genuine, how serious, was the opposition of Ulster to Home Rule, backed, as it was, by the Conservative Party under its new leader Bonar Law, a dour, Presbyterian Scot with Ulster connections? Was Carson's threat of civil war, of an Ulster army marching to the South, just bluff? Winston Churchill was the first to suggest publicly that it was bluff. He did so in October 1911, about the time he left the Home Office to become the First Lord of the Admiralty. Carson, he said, was the Commander-in-Chief of only half of Ulster. There was another half, consisting of Liberals and Irish Nationalists, that could not be overlooked; so, full of zeal as he was for the Home Rule cause, he agreed to take part with Redmond and Devlin in a counterblast on Ulster soil; in other words, to speak at a public meeting in Belfast which was to be held under the chairmanship of Lord Pirrie who was both head of the shipbuilding concern of Harland & Wolffe, and the leader of the Liberal Party in the North of Ireland. A date was fixed for the meeting—the 8th of February, 1912—and a booking was made of the Ulster Hall. This was the place where, in 1886, Churchill's father, Lord Randolph, had produced the slogan 'Ulster will fight and Ulster will be right!'—in opposition to Gladstone's first Home Rule Bill.

The Unionist reaction to the anouncement of the meeting was immediate and violent. For Churchill to cross the floor of the House of Commons to become a Liberal, as he had done, was bad enough, but to speak in favour of Home Rule in the Ulster Hall was sheer filial impiety. So the Ulster Unionists hired the hall for the evening before the meeting and made it known that they would pack it to the roof with men who would resist all efforts to put them out the next day.

Birrell, at his office in Dublin Castle, had to assess the strength of the Ulster opposition. He had the usual police and military reports at his disposal, supplemented by information that Sir Henry Robinson, the head of the Local Government Board, was able to obtain for him from one of his inspectors. This was Edward Sanderson, the son of a former leading Orangeman, who was in a position to find out what was going on in the Orange underworld. What he had to say was not altogether reassuring. There might be no trouble, as the Orange forces would be kept in camp, but it was feared that Devlin, if he got to hear about this, would bring out his crowd, and, if this happened, there would be a counter-demonstration from the shipyard workers who were Orangemen to a man. And the effectiveness of what they could stage might be gauged by the fact that, since Churchill's meeting was announced, nearly five tons of nuts and bolts, to be used as missiles, had disappeared from the shipyards, while the number of revolvers, known to be in the hands of the people, was enormous.

There was danger, too, of an eruption any evening between 6 and 8 o'clock. Robinson's inspector wrote colourfully about this possibility. 'The factory girls', he said, 'who are of all religions turn out at this time and are met by their young men, mostly a rather bad lot, as religious rancour is tuned up to a high pitch. . . . A very harmless remark from one girl to another such as, 'Go along, you papist bitch', which would ordinarily pass unnoticed, would set them at one another; the young men would join in, and word would be sent to the forces of both sides that Protestants and Catholics were killing each other.'

Fifty thousand pounds had been subscribed or promised to the Ulster Unionist funds and the bulk of this was to be spent on sending Presbyterian lecturers to England, which Sir Henry Robinson saw as an extension of the grossly insulting and provocative terms of recent Presbyterian speeches. Religion, said Robinson, in a commentary on his inspector's report, was a total failure in this country. He did not believe in Ulster's so-called loyalty. At the root of it all was a firm determination not to be under the rule of a Roman Catholic Parliament. England was Protestant and the Ulstermen would not be torn away from their Protestant Parliament. That was the whole thing.[4]

The situation was so highly explosive that the organizers of the meeting began to have second thoughts. If the Orange crowd defied the soldiers that were being brought into the city, there would be bloodshed. On the other hand, if they submitted to force, it would prove the argument that Home Rule could only be imposed on Ulster by bayonets.[5] At this stage Birrell gave Churchill the benefit of his views, and took the Liberal Chief

Whip, the Master of Elibank, to task for interfering in other people's business. We give his letter in full:

My dear Churchill,

I have now had the opportunity of going into the whole case about the Belfast Meeting with the authorities here –civil and military– upon whom a great burden has been thrown–and I will cast my observations in a series of propositions which I hope you will place before the Master of Elibank.

First, as the Minister responsible to the Cabinet for Irish Affairs, I think I ought to have been consulted before any arrangements whatever were made with either Devlin or the Ulster Liberals for the meeting in Belfast. My advisers here and the police Authorities in Belfast, if consulted, could and would have prevented all the agitation and trouble. I know you had really nothing whatever to do with the business, beyond loyally consenting to do whatever was demanded of you, however disagreeable.

Second, upon being informed that the meeting was to take place and in the Ulster Hall, the Authorities here, civil and military, set to work to consider and prepare plans to maintain peace and repress disorder, and they are satisfied that if the Ulster Hall was on the evening of the 8th February unoccupied and available, they could have accomplished these ends. The idea that the Protestants of Belfast, however excited, would begin by fighting the soldiers is absurd. In Belfast two mobs are necessary, a Catholic mob and a Protestant mob–it is they who fight, and it is the military who seek to prevent them from murdering each other. In this case there would have been no Catholic mob and consequently, though the excitement would have been intense and the risk of course not to be disregarded altogether, still peace could probably have been maintained. On the other hand, it is quite possible and even probable that, by trickery, the Ulster Hall would be beforehand have been filled with Protestants, and in that case the meeting could never have been held at all.

Third, the Ulster Hall being given up and (as I understand from Lord Pirrie) the St. Mary's Hall being repugnant to the fine susceptibilities of the Ulster Liberals, it is (I am told) now suggested that no evening meeting should be held, and that you should make your speech somewhere in the middle of the day. The abandonment of an evening meeting is a proof of how lightly and how inconsiderately the whole matter has been treated. I have no doubt there is much less chance of disorder in the middle of the day than at night, and personally I approve of the suggestion.

Fourth, the Belfast Police report to me this morning that the excitement is still intense, having been judiciously worked up, and that it would be rash to assume that the altered plans will greatly reduce it, and that consequently it is of much importance that I should be informed as soon as possible what is going to happen–i.e.– when and where is the meeting to be held? If in a building, what building? If in a tent, where the tent is to be pitched? In Belfast all depends on locality and the character of the surrounding streets.

Fifth. Both sides are in a funk. Lord Londonderry has been greatly perturbed. The Nationalists alone look on amused: they don't much care what happens.

Sixth. My own belief is that if you hold a midday meeting in a tent, no blood will be shed. But the moral is (for the Master's consumption) Leave Ireland alone in future.

As to crowds coming in from outside, I am having this carefully looked after. Nothing so far has been done. If anything is done on a scale sufficiently large to create danger, I would consider what can be done to prevent it. It now all depends on what the final arrangements for the meeting may prove to be, and as to this I hope I may be fully advised without delay.

Yours always,
Augustine Birrell[6]

The final arrangements envisaged the holding of a ticket meeting in the afternoon in the Celtic Football Ground, in a marquee to be brought over from Scotland. The barrier round the ground was to be strengthened so as to secure complete control of the meeting. Churchill and his party were to come over by boat arriving at Larne in the morning, and were to leave the same evening. Churchill hoped that no great display of military force would be necessary and greatly preferred the employment of extra police. He asked Birrell was he sure that all *his* people would play fair. Birrell was not sure. He shared Churchill's distrust of the Tory-minded police and military chiefs.

Tension eased considerably when the change of venue was made known. 'I am glad this ridiculous siege of the Ulster Hall is at an end,' Robinson wrote. 'The spectacle of the First Lord of the Admiralty at the head of an army of police and soldiers trying to evict two thousand religious fanatics from their sacred temple would not have been very edifying.' The arrogance of the Orange leaders did not surprise him, but he was surprised at the stupidity of the Liberal leaders in turning the limelight full blaze on the Belfast Orangemen. No one was taking much notice of them in England, he said, and the sound policy was to have ignored them and to have let them screech and yell till they were tired.

He did not know if the trouble was over yet, though 'the Catholics', he said, 'are really well under the control of Devlin and the priests who can keep them in their houses or out of the way. But the Unionist leaders have no control over the Protestants although they pretend they have.' The declarations of John Redmond and others that the Orangemen were not serious, that it was all bluff and stupid bellowings, was the one thing needful to keep up the bad blood. Robinson thought that Churchill was in very serious danger, and if something could happen to postpone the visit till the excitement had died down, it would be a very great blessing.[7]

The visit was not postponed, and the meeting was held in a moderately filled marquee. On the Churchill party arriving at Larne they faced a menacing mass of humanity singing 'God Save the King'; and later on they were exposed to whirling, bustling, flag-waving crowds who booed or cheered them as they moved through the Protestant quarters of the city or the Catholic ghettoes. No harm befell them, however, although at one point some men from the shipyards tried to turn Churchill's car over and would have done so had it not been for the presence of Mrs. Churchill by her husband's side. Cries of 'Mind the wummin' saved the situation. That incident apart, the police and military were not called upon for any duty out of the ordinary. But at the end of the day the firm impression remained that a move intended to expose a bluff had had the opposite effect.

It is relevant to the current demand from the nationalists of Scotland and Wales to recall that, in the context of the Irish Home Rule debate, the Asquith government gave consideration in 1911 to the idea of devolution all round. Churchill actually put forward as a basis for discussion a proposal that the United Kingdom should be divided into ten areas, devised with an eye to geographical, racial and historical factors; that for each of these areas a legislative and administrative body, separately elected, should be created, and that in Ireland, Scotland and Wales these bodies should be clothed with Parliamentary form; while the Imperial Parliament and Imperial Executive, which would remain, would deal with specifically English business. He could not see how an English Parliament, and still more an English Executive, could exist side by side with an Imperial Parliament and an Imperial Executive, or how in practice Imperial affairs could be separated from English party politics.[7a]

4

The Government, having earlier decided that careful and confidential enquiry should be made as to the real extent and character of the Ulster resistance, may have been convinced by the Belfast meeting that it was both widespread and deep-seated, and not likely to be bought off. A former Under Secretary, Sir David Harrell, who, in Birrell's opinion, was 'one of the best heads in Ireland' had suggested that the Ulster men were too shrewd and practical to come to final conclusions about Home Rule until they saw the Bill. They would look at the Bill primarily to see whether they were going to be excessively taxed to make up for the shortcomings and ineptitudes of their fellow countrymen in the other provinces.[8] Birrell circulated these views for the benefit of the Cabinet who, on the 6th of February, decided that the Bill should apply to the whole of Ireland as Gladstone's Bills of 1886 and 1893 had done, but that it should be made clear to Redmond that it might become necessary, during the progress of the Bill through Parliament, to provide some special treatment for the Ulster counties. As Roy Jenkins has put it, they decided to present the Bill in a form which would be acceptable to the Nationalists, but to leave a line of retreat if Ulster proved adamant. Early in April Birrell was able to give Redmond a rough draft of the Bill, and when it was introduced in the House of Commons a few days later Redmond became the recipient of congratulatory messages from all over the world.

The first reading of the Bill was taken on 16th April and Asquith, in the opening speech, reminded his listeners that from the first moment the Irish had been granted an articulate political voice they had pronounced by a majority of 4 to 1 in favour of Home Rule. There was no avoiding the implications of that pronouncement. He did not deny the existence of an Ulster problem but, taking the province as a whole, it was represented at that moment by 17 Unionists and 16 Home Rulers, figures which showed the misleading character of the pretence that Ulster would die rather than accept Home Rule. They could not admit the right of a relatively small minority to veto the verdict of the vast body of their countrymen. He pointed out the relevance to the Irish situation of the changes that had taken place within the Empire since 1893, the formation of the Australian Commonwealth, the grant of self-government for the Transvaal and the erection of the Union of South Africa. He also made a strong case for the devolution of business from the Imperial Parliament in the interests of greater efficiency all round.

The Bill was intended to confer upon Ireland, in regard to Irish concerns, local autonomy, subject to certain reservations and safeguards. The Irish Parliament was to consist of the King, and two Houses, a Senate and House of Commons, with power to make laws for the peace, order and good government of Ireland. As in the 1893 Bill, matters affecting the Crown, the making of peace and war, the Army, the Navy, treaties, dignities and such matters were excluded from the authority of the Irish Parliament. Five Irish services were likewise reserved to the Imperial Parliament and the Imperial Executive; these were land purchase, the Royal Irish Constabulary, the Post Office Savings Bank, public loans, and the collection of taxes other than duties of postage. The Irish Parliament was to pay the cost of all unreserved Irish services and would do so from a sum transferred every year from the Imperial to the Irish Exchequer, the amount to be determined by a Joint Exchequer Board.

Under Gladstone's first Bill of 1886, the Irish members were to be entirely excluded from the British House of Commons. In his Bill of 1893 they were retained to the number of 80, that number being fixed as Ireland's proportion, according to the population, compared with the other parts of the United Kingdom. The new Bill provided similarly, although as regards numbers the Irish representation was to be reduced to 42. This would give a member in the Imperial Parliament for roughly every 100,000 of the population. The justification for continued representation in the Imperial Parliament was that all the constituent parts of the United Kingdom had certain common business to transact, and were responsible for the discharge of a joint and corporate trust to the Empire as a whole.

The Parliament to be set up by Asquith's Bill was later described–fairly or unfairly–as being closer to a glorified county council than a sovereign assembly. A deferment for six years of control over the police force and the stipulation that all persons, matters and things in Ireland would remain subject to the supreme authority of the United Kingdom Parliament may have justified the description. But, in the setting of 1912, Redmond believed it was the greatest charter ever offered to Ireland and he warned a National Convention to keep their amendments in their pockets. To the House of Commons, he said that the Bill would result in the greater unity and strength of the Empire. It would put an end once and for all to the ill-will, suspicion and disaffection that had existed between Britain and Ireland and would have the ultimate effect of turning Ireland into a happy and prosperous country with a united, loyal and independent people. When he spoke these words he knew he was authorized to do so in the name of Ireland by the Convention which was unparalleled in numbers and enthusiasm.

Outside the Party some few people criticized the financial clauses of the Bill, and Arthur Griffith condemned it in its entirety. 'If this is liberty,' he said, 'the lexicographers have deceived us.' But what the Sinn Feiners said was not taken seriously. Redmond explained to the House of Commons that they belonged to the small section who desired separation as an alternative to the system the Home Rule Bill was about to change, but with the management of purely Irish affairs in Irish hands even that small feeling in favour of separation would disappear. There were no separatists in his Party, he insisted. They were no more separatist than Parnell was when he told the Times Commission in May 1899 that he had never gone further, either in his thoughts or actions, than the restitution of the legislative independence of Ireland. Parnell had specifically accepted as a final settlement the concession of a strictly subordinate Parliament for Ireland, and that acceptance by him was endorsed by the mass of the Irish people.[9]

The important question whether the Bill would lead to the separation of Ireland from the United Kingdom was uppermost in many people's minds. Birrell had scouted the idea in 1911 when helping to carry a motion in favour of the Government's policy in the Oxford Union—the Irish people were keen for business; they wanted money, but not for dreadnoughts—and Winston Churchill dealt at length with the point in the debate on the Bill in the House of Commons. He said that Ireland had so diminished in importance relatively to Great Britain that old fears of a hostile Ireland in peace or war had lost their force. The Irish claim had become steadily more moderate. The Irish were not asking for separation or even for repeal of the Union; and, anticipating a famous phrase of later years, he said of the Irish demand that 'never before has so little been asked, and never before have so many people asked for it'.[10]

National Library of Ireland

Arthur Griffith

Municipal Gallery, Dublin

John Redmond

risk, he said, of being lynched in London than the loyalists of Ulster ran of being shot in Belfast. And, at a spectacular Unionist demonstration held on the Duke of Marlborough's estate at Blenheim, he said he could imagine no length of resistance to which Ulster would go which he was not ready to support, and which would be supported by the overwhelming majority of the British people. The Government was a revolutionary committee which had seized despotic power by fraud!

That was the leader of the Conservative Opposition on the 27th July 1912. Some months earlier, a Major Crawford, who was planning to run arms into Ulster, declared that if they were put out of the Union—his own phrase—he would infinitely prefer to change his allegiance right over to the Emperor of Germany. Earlier still, Sir James Craig, later Lord Craigavon, told a London newspaper that Germany and the German Emperor would be preferred in Ulster to the rule of John Redmond. Stimulated by outbursts like these nearly half a million men and women throughought Ulster signed a Solemn Covenant, pledging themselves to defend their cherished position of equal citizenship in the United Kingdom, to use all means necessary to defeat the Home Rule conspiracy, and to refuse to recognize the authority of a Home Rule parliament in the event of its being forced upon them. They signed on Ulster Day, 28th September, at meetings which were opened by prayer, for this was a great Protestant occasion; and to underline the serious nature of the business that lay ahead the gun-runner Major Crawford signed in his own blood. The guns were for the Ulster Volunteers, a force that had come into being to support the Ulster resistance, and the emergence of this body had an important impact on political opinion outside Ulster. It induced a young Liberal M.P. to try to have the Home Rule Bill amended by excluding the four Ulster counties that contained Protestant majorities. His amendment was defeated but it drew from the Government an acknowledgment that the exclusion of Ulster had been fully considered before the Bill was framed, and it impelled them to ask some questions. Would the Opposition say what their demands were? Were they seeking autonomy for an Ulster area only or were they trying to veto autonomy for the rest of Ireland? The response was Carson's proposed exclusion of the whole of Ulster from the scope of the Bill. Redmond and the Government, as we saw, combined to reject this, but there was obviously more to be said on the question. Churchill suggested to Redmond that he should be thinking of some way around the only obstacle that he saw in the way of Home Rule, namely the opposition of three or four Ulster counties.

Redmond's position was unenviable. All his speeches stressed the Unionists' exaggerations while he constantly promised to increase their representation in the Dublin Parliament, and to accept any other safeguards they might consider necessary. At the same time he was aware of the Government's intention to watch the course of events and to negotiate some sort of compromise, and this he feared might betoken a surrender of principle. He was particularly afraid of Lloyd George who had proved unreliable when his People's Budget was being discussed and who was vulnerable to pressure from the nonconformist element inside his own Party.

Birrell had his worries too. There were times when he felt keenly the lack of information about what was happening in the Orange underground. The monthly pieces of information he received from the police were almost entirely concerned with the Secret Societies in the South of Ireland, those that had their origin in Fenianism or agrarianism; they shed little light on what was happening in the North of Ireland where all his present trouble was centred. Taking a hint from his Under Secretary, Dougherty, therefore, he wrote on this subject in July 1912 to the Inspector-General of the Royal Irish Constabulary: 'I have read for more than five years these reports about Secret Societies and their goings on in different parts of Ireland and have occasionally succeeded in extracting useful information from them as to the state of feeling and habits of life in one or two affected areas. These reports are necessarily largely concerned with the local intrigues and dissensions of a number of ruffians and bullies whom I wish could be forcibly deported to some distant land. It is most

played an overture they started a fire which, fortunately, was speedily detected and put out; otherwise lives might have been lost. Undaunted by this failure the ladies turned their attention to the Prime Minister's procession the next night. The centre-piece of this, of course, was the open landau carrying the Prime Minister himself, Mrs. Asquith, their daughter, the Lord Mayor and John Redmond. Asquith and his wife stood for most of the way, he red-faced, his white hair ruffled and untidy, and self-conscious, she waving her arms gaily to the crowds, obviously enjoying every minute of it, while, as an unfriendly reporter observed, Redmond sat, heavy and squat, like some great spider enjoying from the corner of his web the struggles of two trapped flies.[13a] Alongside the carriage walked O'Brien, the Chief Marshal, dressed out resplendently in a Robert Emmet costume of green and gold.

Before the Suffragettes put in an appearance the procession had been given a somewhat exotic character by the participation in it of a body of horsemen carrying torches. These were Dublin jarveys, members of the Anti-Taxi League, who some time previously had thrown a motor car into the Liffey as a protest against the owner's intention of starting a taxi service in the city. This was an unexpected contribution to a colourful occasion but nothing compared with what was to come. For as the procession reached the General Post Office in the very heart of the city and where the crowd was densest, a young woman of twenty-two or twenty-three rushed forward and, clinging to the back of the Prime Minister's carriage, flung a brand new hatchet at him. This was Mary Leigh. The hatchet missed its distinguished target but, passing over the Lord Mayor's head–he was a little man–, it struck Redmond in the ear, cutting him slightly. O'Brien grabbed the young woman and she, turning, beat him in the face and pulled the epaulettes off his gorgeous jacket. Despite being roughly handled by some of the crowd Mary Leigh made her escape, but was subsequently arrested in her lodgings. She had a black eye. In the police court she confessed, amongst some hisses, that she was the woman who had done the deeds with which she was charged to which O'Brien, the Chief Marshal, retorted that of that there was no doubt. 'Only you're a woman', he said, 'you wouldn't be alive today.' O'Brien was expressing a common view. That night, while Asquith's meeting was in progress in the Theatre Royal, a gathering of the Irish Women's Franchise League at Beresford Place found the audience noticeably unsympathetic. The speakers were heckled about the hatchet affair and one of them felt obliged to make it clear that her organization had nothing to do with anything of that kind, at which a voice from the crowd asked, 'Why do you allow yourselves to be ruled by an English organization?' Later apples were thrown at the speakers and there were shouts of 'Throw them into the Liffey'.[14]

In jail Mary Leigh and her companions proved a real handful. They went on hunger strike, and the problem this set the authorities kept Birrell's mind fully occupied. His sense of humour, however, was equal to every eventuality. Writing from the Lake of Geneva, he told his Private Secretary that his holiday had been gravely interfered with by daily telegraphs in cipher both ways about the pigheaded heroines in Mountjoy Prison who were being fed artificially, 'I hope', he wrote, 'that they may not continue their fight, but I fear they will. When Holy Mother Church ruled the roost, she was wise enough to burn her martyrs right away, and to crush their obstinacy in the only possible fashion. I see no way out, but either to kill these ladies by continued torture or to let them out to kill me. But in the meantime my rest cure is destroyed. Foot and mouth adds to the horrors, and a bad harvest impends. Fortunately civil war in Belfast has been most politely postponed by a request of Bonar Law and his troop of braves, so for the present at all events we may sleep in our beds, although mine is guarded every night by Scotland Yard.'[15] Mary Leigh had been given a sentence of five years' penal servitude for attempting to burn down the Theatre Royal but she had to be released in a short time because of ill health brought on by her refusal to take food.[16]

citizens, who on the passage of the Home Rule Bill would desert their homes, and flock to Belfast to fight all and sundry. I found it very difficult, believing as I do that there are grave possibilities of riots, bloodshed, and even worse incidents of religious strife and hatred in north-east Ulster to stem his torrent of hearsay, but I think I partially succeeded in putting forward the following point of view: that it was the plain duty of these potential rebels and advocates of civil war, mutiny, and the setting up of an independent government which must involve the commercial ruin of Belfast, to place before parliament, the country, and the civilized world a proposal of their own for their future government. . . . This seemed a novel point of view. I further went on to say that the fact that we did not see our way to cut Ireland in two, did not relieve the dissentients from the responsibility of stating their case in support of which they proposed their readiness to go to war.

'I then proceeded to observe that the reason why these men had not already taken their obvious course was because they more than half believed that somehow or other, by the act of God or the devil or somebody else, a general election would intervene before the Home Rule Bill got on to the Statute Book; and that at that general election there was at least a good chance, because of extraneous causes, that the Liberals would be defeated and would disappear, and with them would disappear Home Rule for any part of Ireland . . .

'His Majesty said a great deal about the awkwardness of his own position; and his determination to look at it from his own point of view as King, and left in my mind the clear impression that he was being pressed to entertain the idea, though not able quite to see how it could safely be done, of forcing a dissolution next year.

'He has been told that the Home Rule feeling outside Ulster is not very strong, that it is dying out, and that all the people really want is more money and continued prosperity. I tried to combat this idea, but as the dissolution point was not clearly raised in our conversation I did not feel myself at liberty to deal with it. Had it been otherwise I would have said that, though it might be that if the Home Rule cause was in the ordinary course of political events in England postponed for a few months or years, there would be no great disturbance in Ireland, yet if it were defeated by an unconstitutional or unusual action, risking its speedy ultimate success, the rage would be universal. . . .'[18]

It is interesting to summarize what the King took out of this interview. He gathered that the situation had been artificially created by Carson; that while it was serious, the seriousness was in danger of being exaggerated; that there would be no fighting, as there would be no one to fight, and that a provisional government would not last a week; and, that if the Opposition tabled a scheme for Ulster to contract out of the Bill, say for ten years, at the expiration of which a referendum might be taken as to whether they should come under Home Rule or not, Birrell would accept it. But, said the King, Mr. Redmond would never agree to this plan, to which Birrell replied that Redmond would have to agree. 'But he would turn you out,' said the King. 'Let him,' said Birrell, 'a damn good thing if he did!' In waiting for the Opposition to come forward with proposals the King suggested that the Government was drifting and that with this 'drift' his own position was becoming more and more difficult. This Birrell admitted, but he insisted that it was for the Opposition to move first.[19]

Following the interview, the King asked the Prime Minister whether there was any chance of settling the Home Rule problem by consent, and suggested a conference of all the parties to consider the whole policy of devolution, of which Asquith had said in April 1912 that Irish Home Rule was only the first step. Asquith took pains to answer fully his Sovereign's doubts about the constitutional position of the monarch in the crisis that was developing. These doubts had been lodged in the King's mind by Bonar Law who said the royal veto on legislation had been revived by the removal of the buffer of the House of Lords. If the Liberal ministers did not resign, the King could dismiss them, and choose others who would support him in exercising the veto. However, Asquith told him that while he was not in favour of an actual conference with the leaders of the Opposition, he was prepared to encourage a settlement by consent.

own, naturally puzzles and confuses the mind – Winston, Grey, Harcourt, myself – none quite the same, so it rests with you to reduce your colleagues, as I used to do draft affidavits in Chancery suits, to a harmonious whole. When I first came it was all Conference, but was the Conference to be confined to the exclusion of Ulster, a Parliament and Executive being conceded to the rest of Ireland? He seemed to think yes. I said "neither Carson nor Redmond would take part in any such Conference". Would Lansdowne? Stamfordham says Lansdowne is very stiff against the exclusion of Ulster. I knew this before. Lansdowne is a Kerryman and everything in Ireland is geographical. Just as Dublin could not assent to the exclusion of Ulster from the Bill, Lansdowne would not consent to the inclusion of the Protestants of the South without the support of their Northern co-religionists. . . .'[22]

While this debate went on, the position in the north of Ireland declined further. Carson and F. E. Smith availed of every opportunity to inflame the Orangemen though Birrell noted the sub-vocal refrain to all their speeches: 'You have only got to show fight and there will be none'. 'This isn't bluff,' Birrell told Asquith. 'Many of them would fight like heroes, but it is politics, and they are almost all deeply persuaded a dissolution will intervene, and until that is over they needn't make their wills or say more prayers than usual.'[23] Meanwhile the Irish Liberals were getting restless. They were tiring of all the noise being made on one side, and were wondering whether there was anything they could do to offset it. Their leader, Lord Pirrie, asked his English friends what effect it would have if he and some business associates closed down the linen trade and the Belfast shipyards. Birrell did not know that the lock-out of some thousands of fighting men would confer peace on the city of Belfast, but the very suggestion, he pointed out, showed what a dangerous game was in contemplation. It was becoming a grave question how much longer the Government could stand aside and allow rebellion to be prepared for. Should Carson be allowed to preach and practise sedition right up to the passage of the Home Rule Bill, and then to seize the Belfast City Hall and introduce, under the name of a provisional government, anarchy, disorder and bloodshed? If the Government did not think fit to interfere before that stage was reached, was not a dissolution of parliament a duty? If a dissolution was out of the question, should not the Government face all the possibilities and prepare to deal with them?[24] But, when Birrell looked more closely at the matter he agreed, as the Irish National-ist leaders did, that any prosecution of the Ulstermen was not on the cards. Apart from the practical difficulty of securing convic-tions against them, a Liberal Government, that had abandoned coercion for agrarian crime, could hardly, with consistency, apply coercion to people who did not wish to have Home Rule forced upon them.

7

Towards the end of September 1913 Birrell went over to Dublin on what he called a gloomy visit. He still adhered to the opinion that civil war in the North was unlikely but riots and disturbances on a great scale beyond the powers of the police to cope with was a serious possibility.[25] His concern for the time being was with the industrial situation. He expected to find Dublin in a horrid state for it poured with rain, it sulked with misery and discontent, its Corporation was a pack of cowards with an admixture of knaves, and a generous allowance of fools, and the executive–Birrell's own responsibility–was unpopular and not over-respected. There had been serious industrial unrest, strikes followed by a lock-out, during which the police had established a wholesome fear, not to say terror, in the minds and bodies of the mob. Birrell excused the police for acting in this way: they were only a small force, and were it not to regain even momentarily its courage, there might be no end of a row. The whole thing was rotten, however, he said.[26]

The Cabinet, on a number of occasions, had given serious attention to the growth of unrest among the working classes, particularly in Great Britain. Asquith told the King this in Sep-tember 1911. The King was afraid that the disturbances which

Hall, 'that your Mr. Birrell is a joker. But we don't want jokers in Ireland. We have had too many of them cracking jokes while the dockers and their children starve.'[30] David Garnett, who was present when this contemptuous reference was being made, considered Larkin the greatest orator he had heard until Winston Churchill began to voice the thoughts of the British people in June 1940.

The fight began in January 1913, on the docks. By the end of May, Larkin was virtual dictator of the Port of Dublin. He then organized the agricultural labourers in the county, called a strike as the harvest came in and forced the employers to surrender. He next turned his attention to the Tramway Company whose Chairman, William Martin Murphy, was also the owner of the largest daily newspaper in Ireland and other important concerns. There was no love lost between these two men, and Larkin, hitherto unsuccessful in efforts to organize Murphy's employees, made use of his own weekly, the *Irish Worker*, to denigrate Murphy himself, calling him, among other things, the 'industrial octopus', 'the tramway tyrant', a 'capitalist sweater', 'a blood-sucking vampire', 'a whited sepulchre'. And, as might be expected, the effect of these extravagances was to increase Murphy's determination to break Larkin's swelling power. Forestalling a demand for an increase in wages, the Tramway Company refused to recognize Larkin or his union and began to dismiss suspected Larkinites. Larkin met this move by calling a strike of his members, about half of Dublin's tramwaymen, and relied upon his pickets to paralyse the service. With the help of the police, however, the trams were kept running. Larkin then extended the strike to distributors of Murphy's newspaper, and Murphy retaliated by inducing 400 employers to lock-out all members of Larkin's union. This was done at the beginning of September, and soon some 25,000 men were affected, and the city had become a place of wild disorder. Attacks on police-protected 'scabs' and on employers' property led to baton charges, in the course of which some lives were lost and many people injured. Larkin's speeches became wilder and wilder, and his paper declared that if

F

the British Army was justified in shooting deserters then they were also justified in killing a scab, who was a deserter, and a traitor to his class. Larkin, in his utter disregard for the law, met a Government decision to prevent a monster labour meeting being held in Dublin's principal street (Sackville Street, now O'Connell Street) by publicly burning a proclamation in which the King's name was invoked. 'People make kings', he shouted, 'and people can unmake them. If the police and soldiers stop the meeting let them take the responsibility. . . . I recognize no law but the people's law. We are going to raise a new standard of discontent and a new battle-cry in Ireland.' The meeting was not held, but Larkin turned up in disguise on a hotel balcony in Sackville Street and was arrested as soon as he tried to speak. The windows of Clery's emporium underneath were smashed, and the police furiously set about dispersing the crowd that had gathered in defiance of the proclamation. The rioting spread through the city. Baton charge followed baton charge, and by nightfall the casualties ran into many hundreds. It was Dublin's first 'Bloody Sunday'.

Next day the Lord Mayor led the Dublin Corporation and the four members of Parliament for Dublin City in a protest about the behaviour of the police, and Birrell, recognizing that the Dublin crowds had received 'undoubted rough treatment', told the Prime Minister that he had already decided on a public enquiry. He was also contemplating a second enquiry into the state of the Dublin slums, but he conceded priority to a Board of Trade court which was set up under the Conciliation Act of 1896, to enquire into the facts and circumstances of the labour dispute and to take such steps to effect a settlement of the dispute as might seem desirable. He did this although, as he said, it was rather dreadful to be wrangling about conciliation machinery in the midst of such squalor.

While the personnel for these enquiries was being assembled, the English Labour Party, who were independently trying to settle the strike, decided to hold a meeting in Sackville Street to assert the right to free speech and to expose the methods employed by the police in the recent rioting. This meeting might also have been banned, but Birrell saw that to do so would be a blunder and, after the event, he was able to tell the Prime Minister that 'the meeting you were unnecessarily twitted about passed off quietly, not to say tamely . . .'[31]

He was convinced that the issues in the dispute were not unionism, collective bargaining and so forth but—as he said— 'only about Larkin and his methods which everybody in all ranks, outside the anarchical party, agree are impossible'. At the same time he recognized that the Dublin employers had put themselves in the wrong by demanding from their men signatures to declarations forswearing Larkin's Union, and this not only from men who belonged to it, but from men who never belonged to it at all. The enquiry would clear the issues but as to whether any *modus* for the future could be worked out he was not so sure. 'The whole atmosphere is still charged with gunpowder', he told Asquith, 'and the hooligans in the city are ripe for mischief. From the Redmond point of view this state of things is very awkward. The *Irish Times*, very kindly, is always rubbing in the impotency of the four members of the city, and of the Catholic Church, and quotes what Larkin is fond of saying that "Home Rule does not put a loaf of bread into anybody's pocket". Larkin's position is a very peculiar one. All the powers that are supposed to be of importance are against him; the party, the whole Catholic Church, and the great body of Dublin citizens, to say nothing of the Government, and yet somehow or another he has support and is a great character and figure. The fact is that the dispute has lifted the curtain upon depths below Nationalism and the Home Rule movement, and were there to be an election in Dublin tomorrow, it is quite likely that two of the four gentlemen I have just referred to would lose their seats. I should not be surprised if Carson holds out some sort of a hand to Larkin as a brother rebel against nationalist tyranny!'

The police, he added, were very overworked, and he had had to release a number of them from the duty of guarding tram depots by substituting soldiers. The hours of the other members of the force would remain as before—quite intolerable. A ship laden with food, and Larkin probably standing waving on the bridge, would arrive in the Liffey in a day or two, and as a counter-blast there was a threat to import free labourers from another ship. This would undoubtedly lead to renewed rioting.[32]

Buxton's chief industrial commissioner, Sir George Askwith, with representatives of English employers and labour, conducted the Board of Trade Enquiry and on the 6th October they de-livered their report which embodied a draft scheme of concilia-tion committees for the settling of differences. On the circum-stances that had brought about the particular dispute they were investigating, their report substantially took the same line as Birrell had done. It condemned 'the sympathetic strike' and like-wise 'the sympathetic lock-out'. No community could exist, the report declared, if resort to 'the sympathetic strike' became the general policy of trade unionism, while the document the employ-ers had insisted upon their workmen signing imposed conditions that were contrary to individual liberty such as no workman could reasonably be expected to accept. The representatives of the men indicated they were prepared to enter into discussions where the report left off, and to avail of the proffered help of the court of enquiry and Birrell encouraged this attitude. From the outset he had supported the police while endeavouring to hold the ring as between the opposing parties. He now worked hard to secure to the workers the fullest rights of trade unionism, and to this end he made it known that every legitimate pressure was being put on the employers to assist a settlement on the lines of the Enquiry's report.[33] The employers, however, refused to enter into any talks until Larkin's Union was reorganized and new officials appointed.

At this stage the tide turned strongly in favour of the strikers. George Russell (A E), in a famous open letter, accused the em-ployers of falling back upon their devilish policy of starvation, and told them to cry aloud to heaven for new souls. 'The souls you have got cast upon the screen of publicity, appear like the horrid and writhing creatures enlarged from the insect world and revealed to us by the cinematograph.' And the London *Times* said it was about time that Dublin employers learned their lesson.

Larkin ruined his chances, however, by intemperate action. He attacked the British Labour Party; they were about as useful, he said, as mummies in a museum. And when they quoted arguments about contracts, he replied 'To Hell with contracts'. He abused their leaders–J. H. Thomas, the Secretary of the National Union of Railwaymen, he said, was 'a double-dyed traitor to his class'– and particularly those who dared to say that the state of affairs in Dublin would not have lasted twenty-four hours had Larkin shown a little more commonsense. It became increasingly clear that the British unions, though willing to continue to supply Larkin with the sinews of war, did not want the war to spread to their side of the Irish Sea, and a special Trades Union congress in December closed the matter once and for all by rejecting by a large majority a proposal to stage a national strike in sympathy with their Dublin brothers. Taking the hint, the Dublin men commenced to drift back to work on the employers' terms, and by the end of January Larkin had to acknowledge defeat.

Birrell had foreseen this collapse three months earlier, when Larkin blundered by arranging to have some of the strikers' children sent to English homes 'for the duration'. This provoked the Catholic Archbishop of Dublin, Dr. Walsh, into making a statement about the danger to the faith of the children, and led to religious demonstrations on the quays. These were followed by the arrest of Larkin's sister and two English and American social workers on charges of kidnapping. Birrell, in a not altogether accurate report, told the Prime Miniser that 'the kidnapping of the Dublin children created no end of a revival. It certainly was an outrage. For in the first place there are no starving children in Dublin, and in the second place, the place swarms with homes for them. It was a new advertising dodge of a few silly women, but it has broken the strike.'[34]

Before the strike ended Birrell released Larkin from prison where he was undergoing a seven months sentence for a seditious speech. He had not wanted to do this but a large majority of the Cabinet was of opinion that the prosecution was impolitic and unnecessary and calculated to do more harm than good. So

Asquith told the King. 'Mr. Birrell', he said, 'defended it in view of the dangerous condition of affairs at that time in Dublin. The Chancellor of the Exchequer and the Attorney-General commented severely on the manner in which the jury was 'packed', and on the tone in which the prosecution was conducted by the Irish Law Officers. After much discussion, the Cabinet came unanimously to the conclusion that, in view of the fact that Larkin was acquitted on the two most serious counts in the indictment –those of inciting to larceny and riot–the sentence of seven months was grossly excessive' and should be reduced.[34a]

Birrell having done this, had to give an explanation for his action, and indeed for ever having sent Larkin for trial. He did so in the Colston Hall, Bristol, in his own constituency, and was greeted when he rose to speak with shouts of 'Tell us about the hundred thousand starving in Ireland.' He promised to comply with this request but suffragette interrupters created a prolonged disturbance before he could proceed. As the stewards rushed forward to deal with one interrupter in working garb another man seated nearby sprang to his feet and, with a cry of 'Torture that instead of women', hurled a dead cat at Birrell. The carcass struck him in the chest and fell to the platform. Immediately the hall was in an uproar. Blows were struck at the interrupters by members of the audience.

When he could at last be heard, Birrell spoke about 'the very happy release' of Mr. Larkin; justice had required that the clemency of the Crown should be exercised. And he tried, not very successfully, to dispose of the widely accepted view that the Government's poor record in recent by-elections had something to do with Dublin's industrial crisis. He was more convincing when he explained his own role in the affair, which was to bring employers and employees together and to implore them to act like Christians, one to the other. In fulfilling this role, in upholding the civic authority, namely the police, he was keeping the soldiers in their barracks.

On the same day he spoke on the function of the police to an angry deputation from the Bristol Trades Council. The duty of the police, who were honest working men themselves, was to keep the peace. If Mr. Murphy were to break the peace his head would be broken with as much pleasure, probably more, than that of anybody else. But Mr. Murphy did not expose himself in that way.

Larkin travelled down to Bristol to answer Birrell. He appeared to have been offended by the exercise of something he insisted he had not asked for, the royal prerogative. Mountjoy Prison, where he had been incarcerated, was in any event, he said, a palace compared with the hovels in which the Dublin strikers and their families were compelled to live. But apart from the usual admixture of vituperation he did little more in his speech than call on Birrell to resign and stand for re-election against a worker Larkin would nominate. At the Albert Hall meeting in London he had already suggested that Birrell should be dismissed from the government. 'He is a loafer, an idler, a trickster, a joker, and he wants shifting out of the pack.' Birrell met this tirade by saying that anyone who occupied the position of Chief Secretary to the Lord Lieutenant of Ireland carried, he would not say his life, but his character in his hands. People said he did his job badly. He dared say he did, but it was none the less his job, and his job it must remain until the welcome hour when someone else was good enough to take it from him. He had not discovered many aspirants for the office. Nobody had ever hinted that he would like it.[35]

As the strike ended the Report appeared of the Commission that had been appointed to enquire into the riots and disturbances of the previous August and September, and into the allegations of the use of excessive and unnecessary force by the police. In the Commissioners' opinion the police on the whole had discharged their duties during a trying period with conspicuous courage and patience. They had been exposed to great dangers and treated with great brutality. 'Had it not been for their zeal and determination . . . the outburst of lawlessness . . . would have assumed more serious proportions and been attended with far more evil results.'[36] The Report was widely seen as a whitewashing job but this was hardly fair to the eminent lawyers who conducted the enquiry or to the two hundred-odd constables who sustained personal injuries. They had had to face crowds of half-starved strikers who, driven on by Larkin's cries, made a hell of many a Dublin backstreet.

On the other hand, the Report omitted to make even an incidental reference to the Irish Citizen Army, which came into being during the strike for the express purpose of protecting the strikers against the police. It owed its initiation to Captain Jack White, a son of the defender of Ladysmith, who had won the D.S.O. in the South African War, and was organized and trained by him. It also owed much to Larkin's incitement. 'Carson is arming in the North,' was a typical cry of his. 'If he can arm, why shouldn't the Dublin workers arm? Arm yourselves, and I'll arm. You have to face hired assassins. Wherever one of your men is shot–then shoot two of them.' At the beginning the Citizen Army shot no one: they had no arms and were reduced to using wooden staves. But within three years they became, under the command of James Connolly, a potent revolutionary force and a competent wielder of rifle and revolver. They were never more than 300 strong. Nevertheless, Connolly, a mixture of Marxist-Socialist and advanced nationalist, was quite prepared to lead this tiny force out alone to fight the British and had to be restrained until a co-ordinated effort with other national groups could be arranged.

CHAPTER III
The Ulster Question
1913–1914

A<small>SQUITH</small> had told the King that he was prepared to encourage a settlement of the Ulster Question by consent, and
thus remove a danger to the peace and security of the United
Kingdom. In October and November 1913, therefore, he had
two secret meetings with Bonar Law at a place that was about an
hour's drive from London. The Unionist leader was frankness
itself; he admitted to doubts about his extreme commitments to
Carson: he said that most of the English Conservatives cared
more about preserving the Welsh Church establishment than
about the Home Rule issue. And he made no attempt to conceal
the electoral importance to him of the Orange card, without
which he thought the Unionists would lose the next election.
These admissions cheered Asquith, so that he, too, spoke sanguinely about his own strength *vis-à-vis* the Irish Nationalists. He
understood that Bonar Law would accept Home Rule with an
Ulster exclusion, provided Lansdowne, as the spokesman of the
Southern Irish Unionists, did not protest too strongly. Both of
them agreed it would be difficult to define Ulster. But when they
discussed, on a hypothetical basis, the existence of a Home Rule
Parliament and Executive for Ireland minus an area to be at least
temporarily excluded, it emerged that, while Carson would stand
out in the first instance for the whole province of Ulster, Bonar
Law would insist on six counties only. He dismissed, however, as
unacceptable any idea of giving the excluded area a local legislature
and executive of its own; and the area should be excluded from
the beginning with the option of voting by plebiscite for inclusion.
He repudiated immediate inclusion with an option of exemption.

The two men then went their separate ways to report to their
colleagues, and in one important respect they reported differently.
Bonar Law thought that Asquith had entered into a commitment

to urge upon the Cabinet, and then upon the Nationalists, an exclusion scheme on the conditions that he [Bonar Law] had outlined. Asquith reported what had been said as merely indicating the bargaining possibilities. The result of this misunderstanding was that Bonar Law believed that Asquith had broken his word to him. He hoped the Nationalists would not accept a settlement on the lines he had suggested, for this would improve the Conservatives' prospects at the election. On the other hand, if Asquith came up with a definite proposal on these lines, the Conservatives could hardly take the responsibility for refusing them.[1]

On the day (16th October) that Asquith and Bonar Law held their first talk, Birrell had a visit, in the Chief Secretary's Office in Dublin Castle, from Redmond who looked well and cheerful. It was the first time the Irish leader had crossed 'this Rubicon'; formerly he and his colleagues had kept strictly away from the Castle as the centre and symbol of British domination. Birrell availed of the occasion to say that the Prime Minister and the Cabinet would like to know 'what sort of things' Redmond had in his mind when he spoke of the willingness of Nationalists to do anything, short of a renunciation of their demand for a United Irish Parliament and Executive, to meet the fears and forebodings of the Protestants of Ulster; and Redmond replied that, although he had not discussed the matter with his colleagues, and was not sure that the time had come for him or them to enter into details, he always had in his mind the possibility of a Council without legislative powers for Ulster or some parts of it. This Council, subject to some guiding principles, would have administrative authority, and autonomy over important branches of the public service. Birrell got the impression that these were Redmond's 'honest opinions', though he was not disposed to formulate them for the moment nor did he think they should be more than adumbrated by anybody.

At the mention of autonomy over the public service which implied control over appointments, Birrell could see that Devlin and company were on Redmond's mind–for, as he told the Prime Minister when reporting the visit, 'whilst all Irishmen are jobbers, the Northern Irishman, of whatever hue, is the quintessence of jobbery'.

'It is an odd country,' he continued. 'I have just had a visit from the Tory Lieutenant of County Sligo who wants troops sent at once to Sligo to protect the Protestant minority. I asked what risk they ran. He replied quite simply: if the Catholics are handled roughly in Belfast and its neighbourhood, there would be reprisals in Sligo. I said he might rely upon it that if the Catholics of Belfast were ill-treated, H.M.'s government would dispose their military forces throughout the North of Ireland in such a manner as would enable them to crush disorder with so stern a hand as would ensure protection to all law-abiding citizens. Thereupon he became very angry and wanted to know how people who flew the Union Jack could be treated as rebels! Fortunately he had to catch the five o'clock train to Sligo.'[2]

Shortly after this, Birrell gave the Prime Minister an account of a little tour he had made in Ulster in the company of Sir James Dougherty, 'who knows the climate of every manse in Antrim and Down and introduced me on our rounds to several of them, thin-lipped, bitter-black, teeth-neglected, Presbyterians, with queer old churches and session houses, and services without a squeak of music or a hymn, and then in the towns, you found quite a different sort of parson, glib of speech with a choir squalling an anthem!

'It is a splendidly prosperous province in the Protestant parts with mills and factories by the side of the rivers and plenty of employment for the young. The farmers are not so well off or satisfied, as Land Purchase has worked very slowly. And then if you wind up, as we did, in Belfast, which is really a great Protestant effort, with a Town Hall as fine as Glasgow or Manchester and shrewd level-headed business men managing its affairs, you realise what a thing it is you are asking these conceited, unimaginative Protestant citizens to do, when you expect them to throw in their lot with such a place as Dublin, with its fatuous and scandalous Corporation and senseless disputes about the Irish language! The new Belfast University has already spent its £60,000 on new buildings and I never saw anything better done, or money more wisely spent, and this over a job they didn't much care for. They have already made it a great success, not on romantic lines, but still for all that a fine Protestant thing. I had what is called a mixed reception from the students but all good-humoured.

'It was easy and interesting to get any number of sidelights but on the great questions—what is Protestant Ulster going to do? and what can she do? it was very difficult to get any real light. Some people living in the very thick of it all don't take it very seriously—"street rioting and no more"—one or two ministers—Presbyterians—the Rev. J. Armour—a warrior of many fights takes this view. Personally my instinct tells me these people are wrong. The Chief Police Inspector in Belfast, Smith, an officer of great courage but morally timid and closely allied by ties of friendship to the Carsonites, thinks nothing of their Provisional Government, and altogether denies their power to keep order in the green sections of Belfast (and the Catholics now exceed 100,000 in number out of a population of 400,000) but believes they will attempt in Belfast and one or two urban places great things; unless cowed beforehand by great forces. He thinks the fanatics will wag the dog. Others say no. He thinks, bar accidents, nothing can happen for a good while, and that both sides will continue to exercise their extraordinary influence on their respective mobs as long as possible, up to the passage of the Bill. Then, if so much as a single dog barks triumph, blood will flow.

'At the bottom the moving passion is hatred and contempt for the papist as a papist: at the top it is contempt and fear of the papist as a man of business.

'I don't think it is possible to exaggerate the strength of these top and bottom emotions, and if the Protestants don't fight, it will simply be because they can't; and I don't see how they can in any tented field sense of the word, but short of the "pomp and circumstance of the glorious war" they will do whatever hatred can.

'The leaders are ready to settle if they dare. Carson can always go away. He is not an Ulster man and has always said "If you want to compromise you can, but without me". He will be very glad to be out of it. My friend Captain Craig who is I believe a Christian–odd as it may sound–is ready to listen to reason. Londonderry is a cur and his wife a clever woman.

'But how advantage is to be taken of this willingness, I don't at present see.

'But I must stop.

'The state of the R.I.C. is very serious. There are practically no recruits and the resignations are pouring in. They are undoubtedly worse paid than any other police force in the three kingdoms and we simply must however disagreeably increase their pay. Whether this will stop the leakage I don't know. For the moment it is the most serious question there is. I am preparing a memo. It is a question of some £80,000 a year.'[3]

After Asquith's second conversation with Bonar Law, the Cabinet reviewed the whole position. They were all agreed that the temper of the Party outside was strongly opposed to any form of compromise, largely, no doubt, because they wholly disbelieved in the reality of the Ulster threats; and Birrell explained that the exclusion of Ulster, in whole or part, was universally opposed by all sections as a bad and unworkable expedient. A good deal of support, however, was given to a suggestion from Lloyd George to exclude the Protestant counties of Ulster for a term of five or six years, with a provision for their automatic inclusion at the expiration of that time, and Asquith was empowered to discuss this with Redmond. Lloyd George saw in his proposal distinct advantages–no one could support the violent resistance of Ulster to a change which would not affect her for years to come, and before the automatic inclusion took place the British electorate, with experience of the actual working of Home Rule in the rest of Ireland, would have had two opportunities of continuing the exclusion if so minded. Thoroughly dissatisfied with this decision, Birrell made up his mind that he could not remain as Chief Secretary; so after the meeting he wrote (13th November, 1913) as follows to the Prime Minister:

My dear Asquith,

I am just off in no very exalted frame of mind to meet the mob at Bristol.

Now that I have broached the matter to you and having regard to the decision of the Cabinet today that *pour parlers* should be at once exchanged with Redmond I feel convinced that in the real interests of peace and party, I ought at the earliest possible date to be relieved of my present office, which all of a sudden has become extraordinarily distasteful to me. I don't mind a bit how it is to be done or what people say. I hope, therefore, amidst the pressure of other things, you won't overlook this, which I don't think can stand over until after Xmas.

I have wired to the Castle for the memoranda relative to our statutory powers to deal with incipient rebellion, and will forward them on receipt to the Attorney General for England.

Yours as ever

A. B.[4]

Not for the first time Birrell was prevailed on to stay on, possibly in the light of Redmond's reaction to the Lloyd George proposal which was, that if it were put forward at the last moment by Bonar Law as the price of an agreed settlement, he might look at it but otherwise he could not entertain it for a moment. When asked by Asquith what concessions he was prepared to make, Redmond offered what Bonar Law had already told Asquith was impossible, namely, 'Home Rule within Home Rule', which meant conferring a large degree of administrative autonomy on Ulster *within* a united Irish Parliament. Redmond argued strongly against the Government putting forward any proposals for a compromise; it was better to wait and let them come from Bonar Law. Like the majority of Liberals he believed that the Ulster threat was a gigantic game of bluff and blackmail. He said this although Asquith had told him that the Carsonites were secretly arming and that there would be a number of resignations of commissions from the army in the event of troops being used to put down an Ulster insurrection.

Lloyd George also made it his business to see Redmond, to try to get him to look favourably on his proposal. He said that the Government would move to suppress a review of armed men which they were informed was Carson's next move, but that they felt they ought simultaneously to make some offer to Ulster such as his own proposal which, he tried to convince Redmond, had the approval of the Cabinet generally. If no offer were made, he said, there would be resignations from the Cabinet and a great political débâcle, which would be a very serious thing for Home Rule and for Redmond personally. Redmond replied that the consequences would be more serious for Lloyd George himself and that the débâcle might finish the Liberal Party for a generation, perhaps indeed for ever. Lloyd George admitted this. 'The disgusting thing about my interview', Redmond recorded, 'was the impression left on my mind that Lloyd George thought that, in the last resort, we would agree to anything rather than face the break-up of the Government. In view of this I spoke to him more strongly and more frankly than, perhaps, was absolutely necessary. But I think I made an impression on him. . . .'5 Birrell, when Redmond hurried to see him, pooh-poohed what Lloyd George had said. The Government had not even considered adopting Lloyd George's proposal, but only to try it out. Indeed there was very strong and bitter opposition to it among Ministers. It was ridiculous to suppose that Lloyd George's proposal would lead to any settlement by agreement. Something would be done as regards the arms situation in the North, but he did not agree with Lloyd George that this necessitated any offer being made to Ulster. Redmond found Birrell in the best of spirits and quite confident. He had had two enthusiastic meetings in his constituency and he seemed to have quite got over his state of nerves about the Larkin incident.6

The Cabinet duly received from Asquith an account of his conversation with Redmond, and decided to tell the Nationalist leader that there was no question of an immediate offer being made to Bonar Law but that they must be free, when the critical stage was ultimately reached, to take such a course as then, in all the circumstances, seemed best calculated to safeguard the fortunes of Home Rule.

Urged by the King, Asquith saw Bonar Law for the third time. Nothing came of the meeting, however, except that it enabled Asquith to say that there could be no settlement of the Ulster problem on the basis of indefinite exclusion, while Bonar Law made it clear that Lloyd George's proposal of temporary exclusion, which he was told about, was unacceptable to him. The negotiations finally ended by the two leaders agreeing to make it known that they had met but had failed to reach a settlement. Carson had already rejected a fresh compromise that Asquith had put forward tentatively. It was that a 'Statutory' Ulster, whose boundaries remained to be defined, should have powers of veto in the Irish Parliament over fiscal, religious, educational, industrial or land tenure matters. When the Prime Minister, with a very silent Birrell along with him, saw Redmond, the Leviathan, as Asquith privately called him, on the 2nd of February 1914, he put this proposition to him, having first emphasized that some concession was essential if they were to deal with the unfavourable situation that had developed; an uneasy Liberal Party in the House of Commons, and the Conservatives planning to hold up the annual Army Act until they first saw how the Army was going to be used in Ulster. This tactic, Asquith feared, might force a general election on them. 'I developed the situation with such art as I could muster', he wrote, 'until the psychological moment arrived for discharging my bomb. My visitor shivered visibly and was a good deal perturbed, but I think the general effect was salutary.'[7] The bomb, though it perturbed Redmond, was considered ineffective in advance by the King who told Asquith that Ulster would never agree to send representatives to an Irish Parliament in Dublin, no matter what safeguards or guarantees might be provided. The King himself believed that the Six Counties that now constitute Northern Ireland should be allowed to contract out, without a plebiscite and for an indefinite period.

Still looking for a settlement by consent the Cabinet decided that a concession along the lines of Lloyd George's earlier pro-

John MacNeill

The Earl of Oxford and Asquith

posal would have to be sought from the Irish Nationalists, and Asquith, Lloyd George and Birrell discussed the matter with Redmond. Redmond had always made it clear on behalf of his Party that he was prepared to support any reasonable attempt to have the Ulster Question settled by agreement and, now, under pressure, and very reluctantly, and as the price of peace, he agreed to a six years exclusion, by option, of the counties of Ulster. A detailed White Paper was thereupon prepared in consultation with him and was released to the public on the 9th March 1914, when Asquith moved the second reading of the Home Rule Bill on one of its circuits of the House of Commons under the provisions of the Parliament Act. The terms of the announcement were received in nationalist Ulster with bitter disappointment, and with a sense of betrayal, and yet they failed to satisfy the Orangemen. Their parliamentary representatives contemptuously rejected the idea of a time-limited exclusion. As Carson put it: 'We don't want a sentence of death with a stay of execution for six years'. They were holding out for permanent exclusion.

2

No notice had been taken of the formation of the Irish Citizen Army in October 1913, but within a few weeks another organization, the Irish Volunteers, got under way in Dublin and to this Birrell and Redmond were compelled to pay very special attention. A primary moving force in this development was Professor John MacNeill who, in the twenty years since he had co-founded the popular movement for the revival of the Irish language, had won a wide reputation both as a scholar and as a genial leader of men. He was a steady supporter of John Redmond but the only political speech he had ever made was at the great Home Rule meeting of 1912 when, with Pearse, he spoke in support of Redmond.[8] Affected by what he now saw happening in the north of Ireland he wrote for the Gaelic League paper an article entitled 'The North Began', advocating the formation of an Irish Volunteer force in Nationalist Ireland. It appeared, he wrote, that the

British Army could not now be used to prevent the enrolment, drilling and reviewing of Volunteers. There was nothing, therefore, to prevent the rest of Ireland following the North's example by calling into existence citizen forces to hold Ireland 'for the Empire'. It was precisely with this object that the Volunteers of 1780 were enrolled, and they became the instruments of self-government and Irish prosperity. And he explained that it did not matter for what or for whom Ireland was to be held; what mattered was *by whom* she was to be held.

This explanation was too subtle for some people. Indeed, in Cork, MacNeill nearly produced a riot when he called for cheers for Carson, the man who had brought a new courage into Ireland. The generality of nationalists regarded a Volunteer Force as the means of defending whatever Redmond had secured; the old physical force men, whose organization was the I.R.B., had more radical uses for it. Within a fortnight they had contrived to bring a Provisional Committee into being which, while representative of all shades of national political opinion, had a majority of I.R.B. men on it. Within a few weeks more an Irish Volunteer Movement was formally launched in Dublin and the first three thousand men were being drilled either by I.R.B. men, who had been drilling secretly themselves for years, or by officers of a youth organization that the energetic Bulmer Hobson and the no less energetic Countess Markievicz had set up in 1909 as a counterblast to the earlier formation in Ireland of branches of the Baden Powell boy scouts. As the Volunteer idea caught on throughout the country there was no shortage of instructors. Men with police, military or naval backgrounds were plentiful in Ireland and were only too willing to do what was asked of them.

The police had been reporting regularly, district by district, on the strength, armament and training of the Ulster Volunteers. They now began to do the same for the Irish Volunteers, a name that, as Birrell explained to the Cabinet, was full of historical significance, and touched the national sentiment in all parts of the country. Although these Irish National Volunteers were so far composed of somewhat ragged, ill-equipped and not particularly well-disciplined regiments they were daily increasing in number and might become a formidable force in the future. They had established a newspaper called *The Irish Volunteer* in Dublin and, although he did not think it would have a long life, it was for the time being an interesting document.[9] To their reports on this new body the police added notes about the character and standing of the men who were organizing or joining it. The named organizers included Sir Roger Casement who had welcomed as 'good and healthy' the formation of the Irish Citizen Army and had hoped it might initiate a widespread movement of drilled and dis- ciplined Irish Volunteers who would assert Irish manhood and uphold the national cause. He was elated to see his hope so quickly realized, although the Irish Volunteers were, and remained, a separate body from the Irish Citizen Army and were somewhat critical of it.

The main organizers of the Volunteers, as distinct from those mentioned by name, were I.R.B. men variously described in the police reports as 'the local suspects', 'the secret society men' and 'the extreme nationalists'. As an organization the I.R.B. had be- come something of a joke; if there was a dangerous organization in the country it was the United Irish League, whose meetings to deal with land-grabbing and the eviction of tenants were fre- quently proscribed even with the Liberals in power. The I.R.B., with its roots back in Fenian days, had fallen into the hands of in- competent men, and police agents had no difficulty in keeping Dublin Castle informed as to what was happening at their meet- ings. Dougherty, the Under Secretary, told Birrell in 1908 that they had become 'monstrously ineffective', and that whenever they exerted themselves 'the result was an increased consumption of porter and whiskey.'[10] But, even as he spoke these contempt- uous words, a change was on the way. A group of reformers in the north of Ireland, including Bulmer Hobson and Sean McDer- mott, began to purge and galvanize the organization, in collabora- tion with a man who Birrell usually referred to as 'the tobacconist'. This was Thomas J. Clarke alias Wilson, an ex-Fenian prisoner who had a little shop in a Dublin side-street. Clarke was on the

Castle's 'B List', which meant that his movements were tele-graphed by the police from place to place.[11] In other words, he was a major suspect and was not allowed out of sight. By December 1911 the reformers had full control of the I.R.B.[12]

The formation of the Volunteers, under any auspices but parti-cularly at the instigation of the I.R.B., horrified Redmond. The Home Rule Bill precluded the formation of an Irish Territorial Force; but this restriction had been negatived by Carson's action in the north. Now North and South had armies in the making which brought the possibility of civil war nearer than ever before. Yet while he would have liked nothing better than to see an end to further drilling and arming, Redmond was unable to utter any public discouragement to the nationalists in face of the military preparations in Ulster.[13]

The Government was also alarmed by the new development and met it by proscribing the importation of arms on 4th December 1913. This action set nationalist Ireland ablaze with resentment. The Ulster Volunteers had been openly drilling for a year, and had imported substantial quantities of arms and ammuni-tion without serious restriction, whereas within about a week of the public inauguration of the Irish Volunteers the Government had moved to render them impotent. The Government also contemplated action to deal with the existing arms situation in the North but they dallied and before they had done anything they had been stripped of much of their power to act by what has been called the Curragh Mutiny or the Curragh Incident. A Cabinet Committee consisting of Birrell, Churchill, Seely, Simon and Crewe which had been set up in March 1914, to consider threatened action by the Ulster Volunteers against local military arms depots, recommended moving troops from the South of Ireland and England to reinforce the guards on these depots. Churchill simultaneously ordered some warships to Northern Ireland waters. He had already publicly issued a stern warning to the men who sought to challenge parliamentary institutions; the grave matters that were being raised would be put to the proof, he said. These moves provoked a scene in the Commons, where

Carson, having attacked Churchill, and called Devlin a liar, walked out of the House to the accompaniment of ringing Tory cheers. It was assumed that he was making for Belfast to proclaim the long-threatened Provisional Government.

In the meantime, the Commander-in-Chief of the Army in Ireland, General Sir Arthur Paget, had been to the War Office, and on his return to Dublin had called a conference of his senior officers at which he spoke of the instructions he had received from 'those swines of politicians' and of the likelihood of the whole country being ablaze within twenty-four hours. He then said he would require, from the officers likely to be involved, an assurance that they would do their duty in the Ulster operation, and made it clear to them that if they did not they would be dismissed. When this information reached the Curragh, fifty-eight of the cavalry officers stationed there said they would prefer dismissal rather than be involved in active military operations against Ulster. This was the signal for widespread alarm, and the King was grieved beyond words at the disastrous and irreparable catastrophe which had befallen his Army. The trouble was quickly patched up, however, but in favour of the rebel cavalry officers. It was all a misunderstanding they were told. So they retained their commissions, while the resignations came from Seely, the Secretary of State for War, and some members of the Army Council. The episode proved the weakness of the Government's position, and what had often been forecast, that the Ulster Unionists could rely upon the support of the Army in an emergency. All the determination was on the Unionist side.

Birrell was necessarily involved in this affair both as Chief Secretary and as a member of the Cabinet Committee. He saw, as the Prime Minister did, that the crisis had been brought about by 'Paget's tactless blundering and Seely's clumsy phrases'. On the evening the story broke he happened to be speaking in London at a dinner organized by the National League of Young Liberals, and he warned his listeners not to be flurried by exciting headlines or articles in the Press. 'The forces of the Crown', he said, 'would never be used in Ulster except for their legitimate purpose of maintaining unbroken the integrity of the King's dominions, of assisting the civil power in the maintenance of law and order, and of securing to every minority, be it large or small, be it Catholic or Protestant, the protection to which it was entitled against alike the fury of the religious bigot or the savagery of the political partisan.'[14]

The Ulster Volunteers, now estimated by the police to be over 84,000 strong, were arming themselves with great deliberation, as the events of the night of 24th April 1914 demonstrated. On that night about 800 of them, armed with truncheons, drew a cordon around the harbour at Larne, excluded the police and customs officers, disrupted telegraph and telephone communications, and proceeded to unload the contents of two steamers that had arrived in the harbour into large numbers of motor cars that had simultaneously appeared on the scene. What they unloaded was 35,000 rifles and 5,000,000 rounds of ammunition, and this very substantial cargo was then rapidly dispatched to Volunteer units throughout the province or hidden away near at hand in places where the police could not find it. It was, in the Prime Minister's words, 'a grave and unprecedented outrage', but Carson proudly accepted full responsibility for it, and coolly waited to see what were the appropriate steps the Government promised to take in order to vindicate the authority of the law.

The Sunday following the landing of arms, Birrell wrote to the Prime Minister from Dublin. He had hurriedly crossed over to assess the situation for himself, and in his company he had an officer he esteemed highly, General Sir Nevil Macready, the Director of Personal Services in the War Office, who was on his way to Belfast on a special assignment. This gave him authority over military and police alike, and he was superseding General Gleichen who had advised against sending extra troops into Ulster. This was an unneccessary step, in his opinion. The main object of the Unionist leaders was to preserve order, and the Ulster Volunteers were not only quite willing but quite capable of putting down every disturbance.[15]

With his letter to Asquith, Birrell enclosed copies of police reports which gave interesting details of 'the great smuggling coup' which, he said, certainly reflected great credit on its organizers; 'as plotters they beat us hollow'. It was extraordinary, he said, that the military had been given no warning of what was going on within six or eight miles of them, and the telephone service had not apparently functioned. The only casualty–'Winston's first victim',he called him–was a coastguard who died of heart failure. He could not imagine a more impudent and successful business but he was not surprised. The authorities, police and customs, were completely overwhelmed and surrounded on every side by hosts of well-organized and high-spirited volunteers. The head of the R.I.C. had admitted the obvious truth that outside Belfast there were only a few places where his men could be expected to do much more than to defend their stations for a short time. The only remedy he could propose was more soldiers, and Macready should be authorized to take some measures for the protection of the scattered police force.

'I wish we could locate the arms with any degree of precision', he said, 'so that the police with a force of military might seize them, but we have literally no information, only surmise where they are. It is very difficult to get this information, and I really don't know that it is anybody's fault. Very few people know the secret, and those who do are neither traitors nor blabbers, people who abound in the South in greater numbers than in the North of Ireland, more's the pity.' Nevertheless, he did not anticipate immediate trouble in Belfast where everything for the moment was very quiet, and where the Volunteers, cheekily, were saying: 'Keep out of this, leave it to us, and all will be well'. But the situation might easily break down and fighting in the streets begin. Of this possibility Macready was very conscious.[16]

The big question, of course, was how the Prime Minister's declaration of the Government's determination to vindicate the law was to be carried out. On the Monday following the gun-running and for three or four days after the Cabinet considered the matter. The Lord Lieutenant, Aberdeen, had recommended the arrest of all the ringleaders, and Birrell had had sent over from Dublin the drafts prepared by the Irish law officers of Informations affecting a long list of persons, including doctors, parsons and schoolmasters—quite a representative Ulster rabble, as Birrell called them. It was a question of how many the Cabinet wanted to pursue. He was not at all happy himself about prosecutions. While the facts could hardly be disputed, each case would be defended by Counsel and was entitled to be heard at length. He did not even know whether the culprits would appear to plead, and he hoped they would not shoot any officers of the King's Bench who had the audacity to approach their sacred persons to serve summonses on them.

In a sense it was more of an English and House of Commons question than an Irish one, he pointed out, doubtless meaning that it was there, on the Opposition front bench, that the provocation had arisen. In Ireland it was a question of the Army and Navy, of soldiers and ships. Nothing else would affect the Ulster Volunteers; but soldiers and ships, if available, would do all that was required. Soldiers and sailors would have to be protected, however, against the wiles of the Volunteers who were very confident they could win them over to their side by giving them enthusiastic receptions and hospitality. He had passed on to Winston Churchill a strange but well-supported tale of a party of Orangemen who were entertained aboard the *Pathfinder*, and of the actual removal of a quantity of ammunition whilst dinner was being served to them. 'I really can believe anything,' he said, 'so complete is the isolation of society in these parts.' The less soldiers and sailors saw of the inhabitants, therefore, the better, for the atmosphere was demoralizing.

However, if the Government were going to move in the courts they would have to move quickly. He did not think legal proceedings would accelerate the date of the wonderful Provisional Government which had been held over them as a threat for so long. But one never could tell. A landed class at the top and the Orange Lodges at the bottom were ripe for treason, but the farmers were by no means anxious to be involved an hour earlier than they must.

A senior army staff officer to whom he had spoken was very gloomy indeed about the morale of the army both in Dublin and in the Curragh. They were all asking questions and expressing doubts. General Paget was more sanguine, however, and thought that all the troops except the cavalry regiments would move if ordered but he was by no means confident, though he was ready to go to the North himself if only with a single battalion. A message from the King wishing them to go would settle the business. Then they would all go, barring the committed cavalry-men. Birrell, whose sense of humour rarely failed him, ended this message by saying that their Excellencies, Lord and Lady Aberdeen, were giving a dance that night; it was like an early chapter in Carlyle's *French Revolution*.[17]

Ultimately nothing was done: Birrell was directed by the Cabinet to hold his hand. The King was against action, so also was Redmond. He told Asquith that he did not believe that any Irish problem could be solved by the application of the Criminal Law. Asquith likewise felt that prosecutions would not improve the situation; and as he thought he had detected a note of moderation in a speech of Carson's, he was anxious to explore once more the possibility of an arrangement with him. So, a further secret meeting took place, and this time Carson joined Bonar Law. Once more nothing was achieved except that, on a point of procedure, it was agreed that if any changes were made in regard to the Ulster issue, they should be incorporated in a separate Amending Bill which would receive the Royal Assent on the same day as the Home Rule Bill itself.

The Government proceeded accordingly. An Amending Bill was drafted containing the proposals as to voting for exclusion by county option already made. It was introduced first in the House of Lords because it was obviously desirable to see what the peers would do with the Bill before wasting the time of the Commons upon it. Within little more than a week they had re-fashioned it so as to make it accord with the most extreme Unionist demands. All the nine counties of Ulster were to be excluded, without plebiscites and without a time limit. This brought

Asquith up against a complete impasse. Within a month the Home Rule Bill, protected by the Parliament Act, would be ready for the Royal Assent. Assuming no further difficulty with the King, how was it to be implemented? It would have been difficult enough to enforce it on parts of Ulster in any event, but once the Government had publicly declared in favour of some form of exclusion, this became simply impossible. Yet the Lords would only allow the Bill to be amended in a form that was unacceptable to the majority in the House of Commons. A settlement by negotiation had therefore become an urgent necessity for the Government. Asquith could only hope that the Opposition, as the critical moment approached, had become equally worried by the dangers of continued deadlock.[18]

3

All this time a great revival of nationalist spirit was taking place in Ireland, particularly in the Northern counties. The Curragh Mutiny, the gun-running at Larne, the obvious helplessness of the Government and the growing truculence of the Ulster Unionists had convinced many people that they would have to rely upon themselves if the worst came to the worst. The army certainly could not be counted upon to defend them and the senior officers of the police were equally doubtful. The result was an enormous increase in the strength of the Irish Volunteers. Their numbers rose from about 10,000 at the beginning of 1914 to over 100,000 by the middle of May. This development, which was not at all to Redmond's liking, compelled him to urge Birrell to have the military and police in Ulster centres strengthened, while simultaneously he moved to secure control over the Irish Volunteers. He had a letter published in the Irish newspapers on the 9th June in which he asked that the provisional committee be enlarged by the addition of twenty-five persons to be nominated by him. As the alternative was to split the movement in two, this ultimatum was accepted under duress and with considerable misgiving inside the I.R.B. Indeed Hobson, who advocated acceptance, was ac-

cused by Tom Clarke of being in the pay of Dublin Castle and
resigned or was removed from some of his I.R.B. functions.

Redmond was delighted that the transfer of control to him was
effected so easily. He took it for granted that the few remaining
Sinn Feiners on the committee would very soon separate themselves from it. 'We have thought it wiser to let this happen', he
told an American correspondent, 'than to expel them from that
body. This latter course would inevitably have led to their
establishing a counter-organization, and this, no matter how small
and unrepresentative, would have been a source of weakness to
us at the present moment. . . .' The one pretext on which the Sinn
Feiners had been relying would disappear when the Home Rule
Bill received the Royal Assent. They really had no following in
the country and would be steam-rolled by public opinion.[19]

4

Birrell visited Ulster in June and subsequently gave his colleagues
the impressions that remained permanently in his mind following
serious conversations he had had there with representative men
in most of the walks of life. The whole position was still good, he
said, but affected by the firm conviction of Unionists everywhere
in Ireland that before anything of real political consequence
happened with regard to the Home Rule Bill there would have to
be a general election. 'If you ask who tells them this, they reply
"our political instincts". If you go on to enquire what effect
upon Ulster opinion would be produced by a general election,
the answer is that they are content to wait and see. They have of
course been told by the British members of their Coalition that a
general election, which may get rid of this Home Rule Bill altogether, is a likely event, and until this contingency is removed
from the realm of probability, it is impossible to measure the full,
fighting force of the Covenanters.

'From all accounts the Ulster Volunteers are already sick unto
death of drilling, even under the present, and to many of them,
profitable conditions of the last two years. Their leaders are

perceiving that their men must either fight soon or company by company dwindle away and disappear.

'Of the pluck of all the Ulster Volunteers and the religious fury of many there can be no question—and that they are now well drilled and well armed is also certain—but signs are visible that the talk about the separation of Ulster, either as a whole or in parts, from the rest of Ireland, has made all save the most furious "No Popery" men very uneasy. The feeling is universal throughout Ireland that the exclusion of any part of Ulster is both hateful and impossible, and I am certain that, but for the belief that a general election may get rid of the Home Rule Bill altogether, this opinion would in Ulster itself have been publicly and vehemently expressed.

'The legal profession in both its branches, in Belfast no less than in Dublin, are as bitterly opposed to the exclusion of Ulster, in whole or in part, as were their predecessors to the original Act of Union. The Bank of Ulster, and in a lesser degree the other Northern Banking Companies, are in alarm as to their future. Men of business, both in wholesale and retail trade, cannot much longer conceal their real opinion, which is that however bad Home Rule may prove to be, exclusion is and must always be worse.

'I am therefore convinced that however useful the proposals of our Amending Bill may be (1) as a means of keeping the door open, and (2) as an answer to the cry that we are "coercing" Ulster, they present no solution to the difficulties of the situation. Neither an Ulster Convention sitting in Belfast nor a National Convention sitting in Dublin would consent to a partition, even for a short period. Probably the Irish Nationalist leaders would demur to the latter part of my statement, but if so, they would base their demurrer on the assumption that at the end of the six years excluded Ulster *must* come in, whether it wants to do so or not.

'The National Volunteer Movement has had a great effect on the minds of all Irishmen. The Irish have a great facility for hating and admiring each other at the same time. The recent gun-running exploit of the Ulster Volunteers excited as much admiration amongst the lodges of the A.O.H. as in those of the Orange faction, "Well done, Ireland!" was the general verdict. And the fact that among the 80,000 already enrolled National Volunteers, there are to be found thousands of old soldiers ready for action, and tens of thousands of the finest young fellows of the South and West makes many a pious Presbyterian in Antrim and Down more than half-inclined to breathe the prayer "Would that once more we could *all* be United Irishmen".

'The practical dangers of the immediate situation may have been increased by the existence of this new force, owing, as it is said, to their lack of responsible leaders. This perhaps may be so, but I am not sure of it by any means.

'The common talk of the heads of the Ulster police is that at any moment some trifling incident of everyday Irish life, where whisky is an ingredient, may begin troubles which would spread "like wildfire" from county to county. It is rash to express an opinion but I was not much impressed by the "wildfire" argument. I think outside Belfast disturbances can be localized. Inside that city the present discipline is wonderful, but, were it to give way at any point, a great conflagration cannot be avoided.

'I could not find out anything certain as to the date of the hoisting of the standard of rebellion, but the general view was that the Carsonite leaders would find it very difficult (failing an agreement, in which nobody I met believes) to postpone doing something whenever the Bill becomes Statute Law. What overt acts would accompany this "something" nobody I met knew. The usual talk about seizing the Customs and the Post Office, policing the streets of Belfast, and so on, was the most they could say. Rebellion has no secret methods, and it is far easier for us to guess, than for the Ulster leaders to devise, what their particular sort of rebellion will prove to be.

'I have no doubt that the nearer the day of action approaches, the stronger will become the influences that will still urge postponement, but unless some agreement as to the date of a dissolution is arrived at, I am certain that Sir Edward Carson will be compelled (unless a compromise has been obtained) to raise the flag somehow or another in Belfast whenever the unamended Home Rule Bill becomes law.

'What the effect of this would be on the British electorate, and what consequences might flow therefrom are considerations outside the scope of this memo'.[20]

5

The Irish Volunteers, like their northern counterparts, had to be armed somehow if they were to be the defensive force they liked to consider themselves to be, and arming meant defying the Government prohibition and following the stimulating example of the Larne gun-running. Guns of course could not be bought without money, however; and the Irish Volunteers were a poor man's organization compared with the Ulster Volunteers who had a defence fund of one million pounds, one-tenth of which had been subscribed by a handful of peers and by out and out Imperialists like Rudyard Kipling. In Britain, however, there were Liberals and Home Rule sympathizers who, alarmed at Asquith's inability to reduce the Orangemen to order, were willing to help, and Sir Roger Casement, on a visit to London, made contact with a few of these through his friend, Mrs. Green. Between them £1,500 was subscribed on loan, and with this sum 1,500 old German Mausers and 45,000 rounds of ammunition were bought in Hamburg by Darrell Figgis and Erskine Childers and subsequently brought to Ireland on two yachts. One of these put in in broad daylight at Howth, a few miles to the north of Dublin, on Sunday the 26th July, 1914, and the other a week later in the early hours, at Kilcoole, about twenty miles to the south of the city. In both cases Volunteers met the yachts and removed their contents.

The landing at Howth had a sensational sequel. Some 800 of the Volunteers–each of them carrying a rifle–were marching back to Dublin when an attempt at disarming them was made by a combined force of police and military under the command of W. V. Harrell, the Assistant Commissioner of the Dublin

Metropolitan Police (D.M.P.). And while a struggle was taking place at the head of the column, in which some Volunteers were bayoneted and two soldiers wounded by revolver shots, the main body of Volunteers dispersed, taking their rifles with them. Later that day a detachment of The King's Own Scottish Borderers under a Major Haigh, some of whom had taken part in the earlier incident, was boohed by a crowd as they marched through the streets of Dublin and pelted with stones and other missiles. To warn off the crowd, Haigh from time to time directed his rear-guard to face them and make feints with their bayonets, and, when this was unsuccessful, he halted his men in Bachelor's Walk on the north quays and got thirty of them to form a line across the road with fixed bayonets. Then the soldiers opened fire, killing three people and wounding at least thirty-eight others. The major said he had given no order, and in any event, in the words of the popular song, he did not know the guns were loaded.

A tremendous hullabaloo followed, and a demand for the punishment of the person or persons responsible for allowing the soldiers to fire upon the people. The stark contrast with what happened when the Orangemen landed a vastly larger consignment of arms did not go unnoticed. When the Commons met the following afternoon, the Prime Minister promptly accepted a motion from Redmond for an immediate discussion and willingly agreed that there was an unanswerable case for a full judicial enquiry into the circumstances of the shooting. He was genuinely dismayed and sorrowful. So, of course, was Birrell. It was about dinner-time on the Sunday when he, in his London home, had his first news of what had happened and between 11 and 12 o'clock that night he telegraphed to Dougherty as follows:

1. Did the police requisition the military entirely on their own responsibility, and, if so, what were the reasons that induced them to take that course?

2. Why did the military fire on the crowd? From the telegrams which have come, it would seem that the soldiers were boohed and that there were some stones thrown, but this would not

justify firing on the crowd. I should be glad to know why no police accompanied the military on the return journey.

On the Monday morning he received a telegram in reply from Harrell, in which he stated that the military were requisitioned by him entirely on his own responsibility. On that report Birrell had no doubt in his own mind that his duty was to suspend Harrell pending an enquiry, but he did not take this step until after placing the Prime Minister in possession of all the facts of the case so far as they were known to him and obtaining his concurrence.[21]

While many people, particularly among Tories, believed that Harrell was being made a scapegoat, a Royal Commission, which was set up without delay, established that the employment of the police and the military was not in accordance with law, that military intervention was not warranted by the circumstances, and that Harrell was personally responsible for calling out the military. This was an unanimous decision on the part of the three judges who held the enquiry and at which there was a conflict of evidence. The judges found that Dougherty was in the Under-Secretary's lodge when Harrell told him over the telephone of the landing of the rifles and of the orders he had given the D.M.P. but did not tell him that he had called out the military. Dougherty said he would go to the Castle at once to take over the direction of affairs, but Harrell was not able to recall this fact, and said that the telephone seemed to be indistinct. When Dougherty reached the Castle and found how the land lay, he had a word with the Lord Lieutenant, in the absence in London of Birrell, and sent this note to Harrell:

The Assistant Commissioner

As regards the steps which you have taken on your own responsibility to deal with the arms landed at Howth this morning, His Excellency is advised that forcible disarmament of the men now marching into Dublin with these arms should not in all the circumstances be attempted, but the names of the men carrying the arms should, as far as is possible, be taken, and watch should be kept to

Sir Mathew Nathan

Thomas J. Clarke
(National Library of Ireland)

ascertain the distribution of the arms illegally imported. His Excellency cannot authorize any further steps in this matter at present.

J.B.D. 27. 7. 1914.

On the strength of the Commission's report Harrell was removed from the public service and his Chief, Sir John Ross, who had been away on leave at the time of the incident, insisted on sharing the blame with him. He did so in dramatic fashion; he stormed into Dougherty's office and, having 'dusted the floor' with him, resigned. He was particularly irate because some words of Birrell's in the House of Commons were open, he thought, to the construction that he had shirked his responsibility and left his assistant in the lurch. Birrell was not worried by the resignation. As an official Ross had not a high reputation and Birrell was pleased to boast afterwards that he had played a part in getting rid of him. Tempers were high all round. 'I am tempted to regret', the Prime Minister wrote, 'that I didn't make the "clean cut" six months ago, and insist upon the booting out of Aberdeen . . . and the whole crew. A weaker and more incompetent lot were never in charge of a leaking ship in stormy weather', and he added 'the poor old Birrell's occasional and fitful appearances at the wheel do not greatly improve matters.'[22] He regarded the calling out of the military as 'a most improper proceeding, one that converted a minor incident into a massacre'. He also obviously retained an unpleasant memory of how the Castle authorities had handled the 1913 strike. His reference to the 'poor old Birrell, however, was not a reflection on the Chief Secretary but an indication of sympathy with him in a prolonged domestic tragedy of which we shall hear later. On account of these 'occasional and fitful appearances at the wheel' Birrell had already offered to resign and had been turned down.

6

From early in July 1914 the Government continued their efforts to secure an agreed settlement of the Ulster problem. They consulted the leaders on both sides separately and concentrated on the permanent exclusion of an area of Ulster to be determined by reference to the strength of the Nationalist and Unionist elements inside the electoral divisions. By the middle of the month, although everything was still tentative, Asquith thought that he was in sight of his goal and that the time was now ripe for a formal conference that the King had suggested should be convened at Buckingham Palace. The Conference was held between the 21st and 24th July under the chairmanship of the Speaker of the House of Commons and the participants were Asquith and Lloyd George, Redmond and Dillon, Bonar Law, Lansdowne, Carson and Captain Craig, later better known as Lord Craigavon. Birrell was a notable absentee. Nothing, Asquith said later, could have been more amicable in tone or more desperately fruitless in result. Two subjects were tabled for examination–area and time limit–and taking area first the Conference lost itself in not only, as Churchill suggested, the muddy byeways of Fermanagh and Tyrone but in the almost equally muddy byeways of Down, Derry and Armagh. Redmond and Dillon defended the thesis that, so far as practicable, those districts only should be excluded in which the population was predominantly Unionist and those districts included where the population was unquestionably Nationalist. There was no agreement on this proposition, or on any proposition put forward by the other groups, including the suggestion that the matter should be settled by an arbitrator.

The Conference having broken down, Asquith, Lloyd George and Birrell brought Redmond and Dillon over to Downing Street and told them that the Amending Bill with its provision for voting for exclusion by county option would have to go through without a time limit. To this the Irishmen agreed after a good deal of demur, subject to the approval of their Party, which was to be obtained before the Bill was taken in the House of Commons on the following Tuesday. By that time the Bachelor's Walk affair had occurred and the Nationalists were not in the mood to discuss anything else. The second stage debate on the Amending Bill was therefore deferred. It was never resumed. On the day the Buckingham Palace talks ended, Austria issued an ultimatum to Serbia in consequence of the murder in Sarajevo of the Archduke Franz Ferdinand. A world war, the bloodiest in all history, was about to erupt, and the political leaders on all sides speedily concluded that it was in the highest interests of the United Kingdom and the Empire that their domestic dissensions should cease. The Germans, who were to side with Austria against all comers, were well informed about the trouble in Ireland, and recognized that this was bound to have a crippling effect on British initiative in a continental war. The new urgency did not produce a settlement of the Ulster Question, however, although elements in the British Cabinet tried hard to secure it. What was achieved, in mid-September, was a decision to postpone the dissension. The Home Rule Bill was to become law immediately but its operation was to be suspended until the end of the war.

There was great delight in the Nationalist camp when the Royal Assent was given on the 18th September, but the Ulster Unionists were equally sustained by Asquith's assurance that, when the war was over, the fullest opportunity would be given to them to seek to alter, modify or qualify the provisions of the Home Rule Act in accordance with their wishes. Carson bade his followers not to worry. The Act, so far as they were concerned, was nothing but a scrap of paper. 'When the war is over, and we have beaten the Germans, as we are going to do', he said, 'I tell you what we'll do: we will call our Provisional Government together, and we will repeal the Home Rule Act, so far as it concerns us, in ten minutes. We are never going to allow any Home Rule in Ulster, and I tell you why; all our Volunteers are going to kick out anybody who tries to put it into force in Ulster.[23] There it was: both sides left looking to the end of the war, but neither of them foreseeing that the war would last more than four years, and that long before that time the Home Rule Bill on the Statute Book would become a subject of derision.

Birrell did foresee, however, that the war would have the most serious long-term consequences, as indeed it had. After a Cabinet meeting, held a few days before the declaration of war on

Germany, he said to his private secretary, A. P. Magill: 'It is still doubtful whether we shall go into the war or not. If we don't go in we shall be dragged in when it is too late, and in the meantime we shall earn the contempt, and justly so, of every nation in Europe. If we do go in it may mean the end of the British Empire.'[36a]

7

As the war began, something like a competition in loyalty developed between Redmond and the Ulster Unionist leaders. Its object was the Empire, which no doubt they saw in different perspectives. Redmond was moved by considerations of honour. He believed that Ireland would be dishonoured before the world if, at the moment England fulfilled her promise of passing the Home Rule Bill into law, the response was to stab her in the back. If this happened, the Home Rule settlement would not be worth an hour's purchase. It would be torn up by the whole of the English people and the chances of Ireland's constitutional freedom would be destroyed, perhaps for ever. Any other course would be insane in the extreme.[24]

His emotions were deeply involved in the defence of France, and of Catholic Belgium, a country smaller even than Ireland, that had been brutally assailed by pagan Prussian hordes. He likewise saw the war as providing an opportunity for welding north and south together; the Government could withdraw their troops and leave the defence of Ireland to the Irish and Ulster Volunteers. But while he might well have stopped there, he went on to declare that it was the duty and honour of Irishmen to take their place in the firing line. 'From the lowest point of view, namely, self-interest,' he said, 'we are bound to see that the west and south of Ireland respond to the call for recruits.'[25] This was well received in many quarters but Aberdeen quoted to Birrell a 'ghastly' reaction from a local Unionist Group. 'We are making garments and bandages', their spokesman said, 'but they will all be sent to London for I would not like to think that any of our things would be used by Nationalists.'[26] A more rational Protestant view was that the comradeship for purposes of defence would do much to destroy the old hatreds.[27]

Redmond, in his zeal for the success of British arms, welcomed the Bill suspending the operation of Home Rule. When everybody is preoccupied by the war, he said, and when everyone is endeavouring – and the endeavour will be made as enthusiastically in Ireland as anywhere else in the United Kingdom – to bring about the creation of an army, the idea is absurd that under these circumstances a new government and a new parliament could be erected in Ireland.[28] He wanted to demonstrate that, as in every other part of the Empire, and notably in recent years in South Africa, disaffection would give way to friendship and goodwill, and that Ireland would become a strength instead of a weakness to the Empire. He threw himself with enormous vigour into the recruiting campaign, and was supported by a united Party. Such was his assurance that he could speak for the nation that, without consulting anybody, he told a parade of Irish Volunteers near his home in County Wicklow on 20th September that it would be a disgrace forever to their country, and a reproach to her manhood, and a denial of the lessons of her history, if young Ireland confined their efforts to remaining at home to defend the shores of Ireland from an unlikely invasion, and shrank from the duty of proving on the field of battle that gallantry and courage which had distinguished the Irish race all through its history.

This speech produced an immediate split in the Irish Volunteers. At a special meeting of the original founders of the movement, among them all the I.R.B. representatives, the speech was repudiated and a statement to that effect, prepared by John MacNeill, was signed by those present and issued to the Press. The Volunteer companies throughout the country thereupon decided where their allegiance lay. The vast majority of them followed Redmond and were thereafter known as the National Volunteers, the minority – a few thousand men only – continued as the Irish Volunteers. A month earlier a committee of the American Clan na Gael told the German Ambassador in the

United States that it was their intention to organize an armed revolt in Ireland and asked for military assistance. This decision was communicated to the Supreme Council of the I.R.B. who agreed that a rebellion should take place before the war ended.[29] And Sir Roger Casement had made his way from the United States into Germany despite all attempts to stop him. The British Minister in Norway conspired with Adler Christensen, Casement's manservant, to lure Casement to a point on the coast where a British ship could run in to get him or, better still, to knock him on the head. Photographic evidence of a letter written on British Legation paper in the Minister's handwriting was produced in which Christensen was promised £5,000 for the capture of Casement, as well as personal immunity and a passage to the United States should he desire it. Christensen was also said to have in his possession a key to the backdoor of the Legation given to him by the Minister in order that he could slip in and out unobserved during the negotiations. This is an extraordinary story and when it first appeared in the English Press, having been received from German wireless stations, Birrell thought it 'absurd'.[30] It is difficult, however, not to accept it in its essentials.

8

Redmond's recruiting campaign was highly successful, notwithstanding the Minister for War, Lord Kitchener of Khartoum, who had an unconcealed contempt for the mere Irish of the South and who raised every conceivable difficulty to the formation of a distinctive Irish division like the one he sanctioned without demur for Ulster. Redmond also had to contend with the counter-propaganda of what increasingly came to be called the Sinn Feiners. The Gaelic League was turning political; in 1915 Douglas Hyde was replaced as President by MacNeill as the result of a decision to add national independence to the avowed objects of the organization. The I.R.B. were active as usual behind the scenes in effecting this change of policy which was summarized in Pearse's phrase of 'Not Gaelic only but free as well; not free only but Gaelic as well'. MacNeill, in speeches and in the columns of *The Irish Volunteer* which he edited, poured scorn on the policy of sending Irishmen out to die in the expectation of favours to come. For Irishmen, he insisted, there was one paramount allegiance, allegiance to Ireland, and one treason, treason against Ireland. For Imperialists, and he ranked Redmond among them, the highest allegiance was to the Empire, and the worst treason was to be against the Empire. Empire, in MacNeill's eyes, meant English predominance.

The official Nationalist papers resented this sort of talk and questions were asked in Parliament. Surely something should be done to control MacNeill, this occupant of a State-subsidised university post. There were hints of intrigue with the Germans, based probably upon a letter from Germany that MacNeill's friend Sir Roger Casement had sent him and that had been intercepted. The letter enclosed an official German declaration of goodwill towards Ireland, warned against British intrigue at the Vatican, and asked that the Germans and Casement himself should be trusted. He wanted MacNeill also to let him know what rifles, officers and men he required. Mrs. Green, on whom Casement relied for the delivery of this letter, was horrified when she heard about it and, fearing the worst for MacNeill and hoping that he would be induced to give up the volunteers and return to his own work, she offered to speak to the Senate of the National University on his behalf. 'He had no part in any pro-German movement at all', she said, which was true. 'He had no letters from Roger Casement and used to ask me for news. . . . What an appalling waste if an Irish scholar is thrown out. Redmond is horribly vindictive and will persecute to the last.'[31] Convinced that MacNeill was 'being pursued with the utmost bitterness'[32] she asked Birrell for an interview which he reluctantly gave her on the 1st December, 1914. He gave it reluctantly because he had grown to distrust 'the widow Green' as he called her. Somehow she had initiated herself into Casement's hierarchy of treason though rather low down in it. MacNeill 'the professorial gentleman', he wrote, 'might I think remember that he fattens on public money and has no claim to pose as a rebel, but he picks his words very carefully as befits a man who has a good deal to lose besides his head'.[33] He meant that both MacNeill's chair and liberty were in danger. This was the perplexing line he took with Mrs. Green, and afterwards he thought, optimistically, that MacNeill would mend his ways. 'He is more a donkey than anything else', he told Nathan, 'and once he grasps the idea that he may lose his head surgically or at all events be sent away for three years leaving "a long family" penniless he will I expect bray very gently. As however I told the House of Commons that the University were taking his case into consideration I had better write a confidential letter to the Archbishop of Dublin who is the Chancellor on the subject and leave it there for the present. . . .'[34] His letter is here reproduced in full:

Confidential

Dec. 10'14

My dear Archbishop,

I don't know whether your attention has as yet been directed to a Question asked me in the House about certain extra-professional utterances made by a learned Early Irish Historian who holds a Chair (value £600 per ann.) in the National University. I replied that Professors were not Civil Servants, that I had no control over them, but that I believed the attention of the University Authorities had been called to the matter. But has it? This is the Question I now ask myself; being naturally (if a man who carries my Christian Name about the world can be good naturally) a truthful Chief Secretary—and if it has not—it is my duty by this letter to do so.

Personally I am all for leaving Professors, *qua* Professors alone; and I certainly do not urge any action of a Corporate character. I have already endeavoured through a private channel to bring to the man's mind that it is not his Chair but his head, or at all events, his liberty, that is in danger. We now live under martial law, authorized by statute, and foolish, outrageous speeches which may in the opinions of soldiers, imperil the State or encourage the enemy, may easily conduct a Professor into prison—these are considerations to which it is only friendly to call attention and I hope they may teach the Professor to take Dr. Johnson's advice and

'pause awhile from letters to be wise'.

Pray pardon my troubling you, but in your cancellarian capacity I feel in writing to you I am calling the attention of the Authorities (though in a private manner) to the conduct of the Professor in question.

Believe me,

Always most sincerely yours,

Augustine Birrell

His Grace the Archbishop of Dublin

Nothing came of this move and MacNeill retained his Chair until after the 1916 Rising. In *The Irish Volunteer*, which he was editing, MacNeill dealt with the attempt that was being made to deprive him of his livelihood. 'It does not disturb my peace of mind', he wrote, 'to find that I have earned the censure of anti-Irish Unionists or of treaty-breaking Whigs. In all these matters I find only one cause of regret, and that is to see Irishmen who, as I thought, had some standard of national principle, so far carried away by a wave of factious rancour that they are actually engaged in supplying the ammunition for the Whigs who have sold them and for the Tories who are waiting, as they say themselves, "to send Home Rule to the Devil".'[35]

The police view at this time was that the Irish Volunteer organization had shown itself to be 'disloyal and seditious and revolutionary if the means and opportunity were at hand'.[36]

CHAPTER IV
The Rise of Sinn Fein
1914–1915

FROM October 1914, Birrell had a new Under-Secretary in place of Sir James Dougherty who retired in his seventieth year, and was shortly afterwards elected unopposed to a vacant Liberal seat in Derry city. The newcomer was Sir Matthew Nathan who came to Dublin Castle from the Board of Inland Revenue of which he had been Chairman. Before that he was the Secretary of the Post Office and before that again he had had a distinguished military and colonial career. In his early fifties, Nathan was a pleasant, rather good-looking man, with an unequalled capacity for hard work. Politically he was a Liberal but, being a Jew, he was a religious neutral so far as Ireland was concerned, and that was an advantage. When it was bruited abroad that he was coming to Dublin, the Tories there took fright and inspired Walter Long to warn him off a reorganization of the Irish Civil Service, if that was in his mind. This fear was due to the recollection of Lord MacDonnell who, when appointed Under-Secretary, openly expressed his contempt for the Irish Civil Service and his determination to reform it root and branch. He had not succeeded in doing this, but he did succeed in destroying confidence in the permanent chiefs and causing a profound feeling of irritation.[1] Reform of the higher Civil Service was commonly talked of in Nationalist circles; it was a recurrent topic, for instance, in Moran's *Leader*. Nearly all the Irish Departments were stuffed in the top storeys with men of the Ascendancy, Moran said, but he did not believe that 'the jocular and eloquent Mr. Birrell' was capable of tackling this 'sour, anti-Irish gang'. 'He comes over, and a plausible, Unionist jobocrat takes him round in a motor car, then he goes back to London and talks nicely and quite humorously in the House of Commons, leaving the anti-Irish top dogs to run the show.'[2]

Nathan had advice from other quarters on a variety of subjects. There was, for instance, the question of women, an important subject for such an eligible bachelor. 'I give you the freest of free hands in dealing with the women of Ireland from Her Excellency [Lady Aberdeen] downwards', Birrell told him,[3] but Sir Henry Robinson thought that some counsel in specific cases would not go amiss. In advance of a meeting with a Women's Employment Committee, he warned Nathan that his position would be akin to that of a super-dreadnought surrounded by submarines. He might expect an explosion whichever way he turned.[4] 'Probably you may not be aware of it', he told Nathan on another occasion, 'but the fact remains that there is among Irish ladies a most perfect and outspoken unanimity as to your personal charm and sterling worth. Hence these interviews and deputations will grow and increase until some Dark Rosaleen ultimately annexes you for her very own. . . . Mrs. Noel Guinness is a rather clever and attractive lady and she knows it. It is my firm conviction that her chief reason for her visit to you is that she intends you to know it also.' A Miss Mellone was 'a tartar', a real fighting suffragette. 'Be careful of her', he said. 'She'd chuck an inkpot at you as soon as she'd look at you.' Then there was Miss Fitzgerald Kenny, a lady inspector of nurse children. 'She knows her job thoroughly, tho' a little too drastic in her methods which have formed the subject of an Abbey play *The Shuler's Child.* Go and see it the next time it is on: it is clever and dramatic. She is a very smart lady and what she lacks in efficiency she makes up in gush.' His advice to Nathan when dealing with these deputations was 'to sit tight and hear what they have to say and don't believe everything or promise anything until you have verified it'.[5]

This well-intentioned advice was superfluous. Nathan had much experience of handling women without getting too emotionally involved with them. He also speedily showed his capacity as a peacemaker among conflicting departmental interests. 'The Chief [Secretary] should see your memo on your interview with Glynn, Stafford and Biggar', Robinson told him, 'and I can only say that you are a magician. I had given up Glynn in despair as a bad job. I found him so peevish and unreasonable but your *via media* which he seems to have accepted should put an end to all difficulties between his Department and mine, and I hope he will now shake hands.'[6] Glynn was the head of the National Health Insurance Commission and Birrell did not like him any more than Robinson did. 'Glynn's head', he told Nathan, 'has been turned by being removed from an attorney's office in Galway to the free society of Lloyd George and (more particularly) Masterman. I had a rare fight with him on his outrageous schemes for a whole time medical service, but with the assistance of the permanent Treasury officials I crushed it, to Glynn's dismay and Masterman's chagrin'.[7]

With the Cabinet meeting so frequently Birrell only came over to Ireland now and again. But Nathan wrote to him practically every day to tell him what was going on, and Birrell replied almost as frequently to give decisions or to make a general comment. At the beginning he felt obliged to give the new boy a certain amount of instruction about Ireland. 'It is at once a hateful and a fascinating country,' he said, 'and so are its inmates.'[8] Nathan would have much to do with Ulstermen and Birrell told him what he thought of them. 'I had a champagne luncheon at the City Hall, Belfast, with all the worst of the crowd–devilish clever fellows, hard as nails, and as sympathetic as a rhinoceros, but splendid at doling out money in the smallest possible sums. They were on the verge of rebellion over the Prince of Wales Fund but I think I have soothed their feelings in the only way possible, with a dole of cash.' They were people 'wholly untinged by romance' who left him completely sceptical of the possibility of arriving even on the threshold of agreement with them on the outstanding political issue.[9]

He told Nathan about Redmond and the desperate fight he had on his hands at that time in trying to get recognition for a distinctive Irish Brigade. He ought to be fully supported. 'I had a talk with the dreaded Kitchener of Khartoum yesterday', he said, 'and he assured me almost with emotion . . . that if approached, as Head of the War Office, on specific and proved heads of complaint there is really nothing he is not prepared to do for his Irish Brigade inside his Army. What he will do with them then, it is better only guessing. . . .' Kitchener of whom, quoting Burke, he said, 'a great Empire and a small mind go ill together',[10] had been putting all sorts of obstacles in the way of recruiting in nationalist Ireland, while the Unionists were being treated preferentially. 'Captain, now Major, Craig,' Birrell said, 'goes about with his pocket full of commissions which he has great difficulty in disposing of. Our side have to fight as hard to get a commission as ever they will have to do against the Germans. One or two, well bestowed, would create a considerable demand for them amongst the Catholics, both gentry and simple'. He thought it would be a very good thing if a few of the Irish M.P.s went to the front. He mentioned 'Young Lundon,' the member for East Limerick, 'who had a great hold on the hurlers of Ireland, and who could take a troop with him, if he were allowed to collect one'.[11]

Nathan, when he had surveyed the scene, proceeded to tighten up the Administration by dealing with Sinn Fein and pro-German civil servants. He got Birrell to lay a memorandum before the Cabinet on the subject, to which was joined a police report that stated on good authority that the American Clan-na-Gael had taken over the military control of the Sinn Fein section of the Irish Volunteers. All matters of policy would be determined by the Clan-na-Gael Executive, on which the I.R.B. Council would have a representative. An agent from America was expected to travel to Ireland soon to carry out the terms of the alliance. Nathan, however, could see but little confirmation of this, except perhaps that the anti-British literature that the Sinn Feiners were attempting to circulate emanated from New York and not from Dublin.[12]

Nathan also took a personal interest in police appointments, a move that Birrell commended, blaming himself for his own inaction previously in this regard. He had no sort of confidence, he said, in Neville Chamberlain, the Inspector-General of the R.I.C., whose judgment was nil.[13] The men under him were not wizards either; a blunder by them would be worse than all the sedition that was ever spouted. There had been 'an absurd incursion into Hobson's house and his pockets searched'. This was 'babyish nonsense' whoever did it.[14] He had not much use, either, for the Army chiefs led by their General Officer Commanding, General Friend. They were great blunderers in his opinion, and needed coaching and assistance at every stage. 'I have complete lack of confidence in General Friend's and Neville Chamberlain's capacity to avoid tumbling into every ditch, dry and wet, that lies in their way.'[15] This feeling increased with the passing of time.

In November 1914, Birrell circulated to the Cabinet a careful summary of the state of Ireland which had been written, he said, at a time when, for her very life and national honour, England was fighting a war, the outbreak of which synchronized with a great forward step over the prolonged, complicated and still dubious Home Rule controversy. The historian Froude, comparing the rebellion of 1798 with an earlier one, had observed that the Irish were the most unchanging people on the globe. The phenomena of 1641 repeated themselves in 1798. This reflection, he said, could no longer be made. 'The Irish *have* changed, and their attitude today, north, south, east and west, towards England in her tremendous struggle with Germany and Austria is, speaking of Ireland as a whole, one of great friendliness. This may not strike Englishmen as being odd, but it is none the less unprecedented, and therefore calls for notice. The loyalty of Ireland, whether Catholic or Protestant, has always been a carefully conditioned loyalty. It is so today both in Ulster and elsewhere, but much less so than it has ever been before.

'There is an actively disloyal minority who proclaim their position after the old-fashioned Irish fashion, whilst there is another minority who find it hard all at once to become fluent loyalists, and whose fervour it would be unwise too eagerly to stimulate.'

He quoted some figures for the purpose of attempting an estimate of the forces of Irish sedition. The Ulster Volunteers, whose loyalty could be depended upon so long as the war lasted, amounted to some 60,000 men fully equipped with rifles which still continued, with other munitions, to be supplied to them. The National Volunteers numbered 170,000 men who had no more than 10,000 rifles, many of them of an old pattern. Of this number possibly 12,000 belonged to the ranks of the Sinn Feiners, but to what extremes these might be ready to push their opinions he could not say, but probably not very far. Whatever dimensions the figure of 12,000 might assume in one's imagination, it did not represent a fighting force. 'The old Fenian strain, though capable still of some reinforcement from the States, is worn very thin indeed in Ireland.' Amongst the Parliamentary Party not the slightest sedition or opposition to the war was noticeable; in fact, the extent to which the contrary spirit had been exhibited was very remarkable.

Amongst the ranks of the lower clergy a few outrageous orators were to be found, although he did not think they had said worse things than were said by some of the Orange parsons previous to the declaration of the war. One or two of the Catholic bishops had called these curates over the coals, but one bishop to his knowledge had refused to interfere. Generally, the bishops were friendly, but indisposed to take a leading part in the controversy, if controversy it could be called. Whether they were restrained by any hint from the Vatican he had no way of knowing. In England Cardinal Bourne was very outspoken on the subject of the war, but he was not a prelate of influence in Ireland.

German money was talked about a great deal but no proof of its actual entry into Ireland was forthcoming. Suspects, who a short while before had no money, seemed now to have plenty. 'The notoriously impecunious Larkin, who is in America and I hope carefully watched, just before he sailed was able to put down £6,000 in cash as purchase money for some house adjacent to Liberty Hall, and newspapers without real circulation are in some cases well and expensively produced, and find their chief purchasers among the loyalists of Ireland, who buy them in order to transmit them to horrified friends in England.' That money was coming into Ireland for seditious purposes was certain, that some treasonable communications were taking place between Berlin and crack-brained Irishmen in Dublin or elsewhere was also certain, and evidence of such trafficking with the enemy should be sought with vigilance, and acted upon with promptitude wherever possible.

He told the Cabinet of the dissemination of sedition through newspapers, in leaflets and in speeches. The general character of the weekly *Sinn Fein* was outrageous; this was controlled and edited mainly by Arthur Griffiths [*sic*] who was 'an extraordinarily clever journalist'. The *Irish Volunteer* edited by William Sears was also outrageous. The *Irish Worker* nominally edited by James Larkin, gave an industrial air to what otherwise was plain treason; while *Irish Freedom* edited and managed by John MacDermott and Bulmer Hobson was a newspaper of a most violent character, and bore the most evidence of imported money. None of these papers could be considered to supply news, and any attempt to censor them would be absurd. They were simply treasonable from beginning to end in their statements, though it would be difficult to prove that they conveyed any military intelligence to the enemy. Regulations that were contemplated under the Defence of the Realm Bill before Parliament would render it quite easy, however, for the military authorities to suppress these newspapers and close their premises wherever this became necessary.

Some of the speeches which were being made in Dublin could no longer be overlooked. They were creating, he thought, an entirely false impression of the powers and intentions of the Government in the minds of the Dublin mob, many of whom were organized into what was called the Citizen Army. Most violent speeches of the kind indicated had been made at a recent public meeting in St. Stephen's Green and soldiers had been held in readiness to deal with the crowd if that had been necessary. Some of the men who spoke at that meeting should be tried at court martial. Civil procedure for such purposes in Dublin was of no avail. A very good effect had been produced by the military deportation of a clerk called Monteith in the Ordnance Department. Suspected clerks in the public offices were being closely

Lord Carson

John Dillon

watched. Most of them would prefer their salaries to the Kaiser.[16]

Birrell had asked for a report as to why James Larkin had gone to America and as to how he was being financed; if he trafficked with the enemy, he was to be arrested on his return. (Larkin did not in fact return until April 1923 by which time there was an Irish Government in charge of Irish affairs.) The information available to the police was limited, however. Since the outbreak of the war Larkin had been making pro-German and anti-recruiting speeches. At meetings in Cork, one of which drew an audience of 1,000, he called the King's Own Scottish Borderers hired assassins and thanked God that they were now lying dead on the battlefield. Kitchener was a murderer. This was characteristic Larkin stuff. What was more interesting and potentially valuable was a report that Larkin had been visited in Liberty Hall on the 9th September by the I.R.B. men T. J. Clarke and John McDermott with a view to arranging an alliance between the Citizen Army and the Irish Volunteers. He had spoken later on the same platform with these and other extremists. He had told a Labour meeting that part of his pilgrimage to America was to collect money to pay off the mortgage on Liberty Hall and to cover the cost of rebuilding the premises, but, from a source considered reliable, the police had learned that he was receiving £16 a month from the 'German Socialists' via America. The funds of his own union were not in a flourishing condition, so that it was common belief that the Germans were paying for his mission to the United States.[17]

A few days after Birrell's document was circulated, Nathan found the Irish leaders in two minds about the contemplated suppression of the seditious magazines. Redmond told him that the decision was a splendid one but Dillon did not agree. Nobody in Ireland, he said, paid any attention to those 'rags'.[18] Birrell was impressed by what Dillon said. He personally regarded drink and firearms as more serious than seditious newspapers, but he could not overlook English public opinion, which was in favour of suppressing the papers, so he allowed Nathan to open fire on them. He did this although he did not think that the ordinary

Englishman had either the knowledge or the insight to understand what was at stake. *Irish Freedom*, *Sinn Fein*, and *Eire* (Ireland) were therefore suppressed early in December, and a few days later military raided the offices of the *Irish Worker* and seized the machinery and plant. This looked like real business, but in fact Nathan, as much as Birrell, almost immediately began to realize the need for discretion, in other words, that action should not be in excess of what was absolutely necessary to prevent these troublesome movements from becoming actively harmful. Birrell could work up no enthusiasm for suppressing 'a ridiculous little paper' called *Scissors and Paste*. If they followed the rigid doctrine the Attorney-General was laying down, even an Anthologist would be exposed to prison.[19]

Home Rule being round the corner, as it were, Nathan, helped by Greer, the Irish Office's draftsman, began to discuss with Redmond, Dillon and Devlin—the Irish Trinity as Birrell called them—the organization of government under the new dispensation. Birrell's first reaction was one of pleasure at this development. He was glad, he said, to see the Irish leaders devoting their ample leisure to the consideration of this vast and unwieldy subject. The more their heads were occupied the better. But the dread secrets of the Castle, when unfolded to them, would seem very flat. A supply of good administrators would be vital to the Home Rule Civil Service and he wondered whether there were a dozen good ones available in Ireland. But when he thought it over, he became rather fidgety about the need for secrecy.

'If it gets about', he wrote, 'and what does not get about in the most babyish of cities, that a secret committee has been constituted and is in weekly session to arrange for Home Rule, there will be the same silly rumpus as when I, in oratorical stress at the Oxford Union, let out the formation of Sir Henry Primrose's Committee. You never heard such a farmyard row, gruntings, cacklings, and shriekings, all the young idiots on the make vomiting questions, and though things are quieter now, owing to the real row in Europe, we might still have trouble akin to that over the Welsh Bill. So I hope it will all be quite informal, and, at the most, casual conversations between interested parties and that the records of the conversations will be kept in as few hands as possible.' Nathan would find Clancy, one of the Irish participants, a very nice fellow and the soul of honour but the most soporific talker he had ever slept under, and quite unfit to be trusted with the custody of documents. He once left a most secret paper on one of the London buses.[20]

The *Daily Express* in January 1915 put out the story that Birrell was about to retire and go to the House of Lords. Birrell's reaction was that he would gladly become Baron Brian Boru if Starkie and the other Commissioners of Education had their way in a matter in which he was in conflict with them and which was before the Treasury. But he would not be beaten, though he had pertinacious enemies pulling all kinds of strings against him, so that there would be no resignation on that score, or on account of the pressure Lloyd George was putting on him to have Land Purchase suspended for the duration of the war.[21] The chronic illness of his wife was a more serious reason for resignation.

His continuing dislike of Starkie showed up again when Mahaffy, the provost of Trinity College, was suggested for a vacancy that occurred on the Protestant half of the Board of National Education early in 1915. Mahaffy was a 'Facing Both Ways' gentleman who would not, even if he could, take up a strong line against the Government. 'But', said Birrell, 'he loves mischief and cannot deny himself the pleasure of a gibe. He and Starkie hate one another—which is a good argument for putting him on the Board, if he will go. But have a chat with Dillon about it.' We do not know what Dillon said, but when the filling of a vacancy on the Catholic side of the Board arose, he said that the Castle was leaving to the future Nationalist Government too much clerical rule in the country. This so impressed Nathan that he suggested to Birrell that they should begin to diminish rather than increase the clerical element in governing bodies and especially in those to do with education.[22]

The war was not making the filling of vacancies of this kind any easier. When Bishop O'Dea of Galway was suggested for one on the Congested Districts Board Birrell thought it would not be a wise appointment 'just now when we most particularly need a man who understands England and English sentiment. We need this, not in the vain hope or even wish to turn Ireland into an English province, but to get the use for a little longer of English or British credit. Prelates don't like having their mouths shut by laymen. But I have no personal interest in the matter as my days must of necessity be numbered. . . .'[23]

2

An important centre of strife and contention at this time was the Viceregal Lodge, where the Aberdeens were anything but happy. Aberdeen was already the Lord Lieutenant when Birrell was appointed. He had got on splendidly with Bryce, largely because of the personal relations which had been maintained between them since they were at Oxford together. He felt he would get on 'very comfortably' with Birrell also, but he recognized that the Chief Secretary was the guiding authority, so far as knowing and carrying out the mind of the Cabinet was concerned.[24] The position of the Lord Lieutenant *vis-à-vis* his Chief Secretary, for that was their theoretical relationship, was well known to be anomalous. Lloyd George picturesquely described the office of Lord Lieutenant as a sinecure and its occupant a man in buttons who wore silk stockings and had a coat of arms on his carriage,[25] the implication being that the effective head of government was the Chief Secretary. This was not the position under the Liberals only. Balfour, when he was Prime Minister, coached Wyndham, when Chief Secretary, to exert himself similarly as the real ruler of Ireland. Aberdeen would have liked things to be different, of course, but he had to accept the situation of fact and only asked that he should be given more information about what was going on. Campbell-Bannerman passed his remarks to Birrell who said he was glad to know the state of His Lordship's mind. Knowing nothing in advance about the practical difficulties it seemed reasonable to him that a more or less redundant Lord Lieutenant should be told as much as was possible whenever mischief was afoot, and presumably something much less in normal times.[26]

The Aberdeens were an earnest, well-meaning pair who looked rather grotesque when they appeared together; he, bearded and small and polite, she disproportionately large, matronly and masterful. They were sympathetic to Irish national aspirations, and were indeed regarded in some quarters as more Irish than the Irish themselves. Lady Aberdeen even managed to learn a few words of Irish, but the acclaim this won her was neutralized by the action of the police in prosecuting people for having their names in Irish only on their carts.

They were never quite accepted. The Loyalist 'garrison', otherwise known in Dublin as 'the quality' would have nothing to do with Home Rule Lord Lieutenants and even went so far as to impose something like a social boycott on persons appointed to office by them. In doing this they unwittingly put themselves alongside separatists and advanced nationalists who had other reasons for boycotting the Viceregal court. The Nationalist *Leader* admitted that Aberdeen meant well, but he was a representative of the British Government and was surrounded by a gang of oily sourfaces, freemasons and the like, and when he made a speech it was of the 'all creeds, all classes' kind. The Aberdeens ignored these criticisms and went ahead with their mildly gaelicizing ideas. The result was that 'strong silent Unionists gnashed their teeth when they heard of jigs and reels being danced in the Castle, while shoneen Catholics and nominal Nationalists also shuddered, unless they chanced to be among the dancers'.[27]

A story that went into circulation concerned an occasion when Aberdeen, who had a pleasant light tenor voice, was asked to entertain the company. This he was perfectly willing to do, but Lady Aberdeen, assertive and punctilious as she was, raised a difficulty. If he did sing, the whole company would have to stand up during the song, as it was improper for anyone to remain seated while the King's representative was on his legs. To this the very kindly little Lord Lieutenant demurred, and it was ultimately arranged that he should sing *sitting down*, which he proceeded to do. In the middle of the song he saw with horror that he was approaching a high note, which he would never be able to reach while seated. When the moment came, he half rose from his chair, still singing, motioning with his left hand to the company to show that they should remain as they were.[28]

The ballad makers enjoyed themselves at Lady Aberdeen's expense, her pioneering child welfare and anti-tuberculosis activities providing them with excellent material. One very popular ballad began:

> *Says Lady Aberdeen*
> *I'm a step below your Queen,*
> *She lives beyond the sea*
> *   and loves you dearly;*
> *I love you just as well,*
> *And I've come with you to dwell,*
> *For the paltry sum of twenty*
> *   thousand yearly'.*[29]

In her anxiety to get things done she interfered in public matters for which she had no responsibility and in a manner which led to unpleasantness. It had always been accepted that Viceroy's wives were to be 'ornamental rather than departmental', but Lady Aberdeen, in disregard of her position, lobbied ministers and departments relentlessly. This gave offence in some official quarters. When she pressed Sir Henry Robinson to make certain appointments, he refused; when she sought a subsidy for the Women's National Health Association (W.N.H.A.) he protested to the Treasury against a grant being handed over to an association of irresponsible women. And he was particularly angry when to bolster up the W.N.H.A. Sanatorium at Peamount she entertained in the Lodge the Council Chairmen of Counties remote from Dublin and induced them to send up consumptives who would have preferred to have been treated near their friends and homes.[30]

Birrell, though always most polite, could not stand either the lady or her lord. To the Prime Minister in October 1913 he wrote: 'The Aberdeens are back and fussing about, attending deputations, which are waiting *on me*. They can't be left out of anything for a moment. It is a capital disaster their being here at this critical time, but as I have no suggestion to make I ought not to send this agonized cry of acute misery.'[31]

This was the time of the Great Lock-Out when Aberdeen was reported to have entertained Larkin in the Viceregal Lodge, and to have put pressure on the Under Secretary to invite the labour leader to see him in the Castle. Larkin was no respecter of persons. When he arrived in Dougherty's room with some of his fellow organizers he is said to have stretched himself out on a sofa and to have filled the room with odours of plug tobacco.[32]

Lady Aberdeen described the atmosphere of one meeting she had with Birrell and Robinson as that of 'war open and declared'. She was sorry for Birrell personally. She believed he was on her side while at the same time acting on his instructions from Robinson who made no pretence of concealing his hostility, and would not yield an inch.[33] A civil servant who was present at this meeting saw seated at one side of the table Lady Aberdeen's ample form and at the other the sharp-witted, lean and wiry Robinson, and both of them equally implacable and unyielding. Placed at the point of impact between the immovable mass and the irresistible force was Birrell, 'the compromising minister, desperately anxious to secure the peace by agreement which he was pathetically incapable of achieving by either persuasion or authority'.[34]

This particular tussle, and many others, went in favour of Lady Aberdeen, who later tried to induce Birrell to get rid of Robinson, suggesting that his long and valuable services might be rewarded by the governorship of some distant island. Birrell did not oblige her though he managed to conceal his feelings regarding the Aberdeens themselves. But he was increasingly displeased with their behaviour and we can be sure he had a hand in the Prime Minister's decision in October 1914 to dispense with their services. On the 7th of that month in a 'very confidential' letter to the Countess he said that unless he had greatly mistaken the signs of the heavens it would not be long before '*we* have disappeared'[35] – meaning the Aberdeens and himself. This was for her private ear alone. He would be coming over shortly, probably on his last visit, he said. But he remained in office, while the Aberdeens went. They would have gone in any event, we feel, as the result of a critical situation which Lady Aberdeen now provoked. She wanted people of all political persuasions to join the British Red Cross Society whose activities in Ireland were under her patronage, and wrote to the newspapers commending the idea. To Brayden, the editor of the *Freeman's Journal*, the organ of the Irish Party, she added a private note asking for publication of her letter in a prominent place, because, as she said, 'I'm afraid there is a bit of a plot among Unionists to capture the Red Cross Society in Ireland and to run it in such a way from London and through County Lieutenants and Deputy Lieutenants that it will be unacceptable to the Irish Volunteer people, etc. You will understand I am sure. I believe that ultimately we may be able to have an Irish Red Cross Society directly under the War Office without the intermediary of the British Red Cross. . . .' She added a postscript praising an editorial he had written and suggested that they could exchange heartiest congratulations on the consummation of their hopes about Home Rule and on the part Brayden had played in helping to bring this about. Brayden did what he was asked to do, but the private note to him mysteriously disappeared–rumour has it that it was taken from Brayden's desk by a young Sinn Feiner who in later life became one of Ireland's leading political figures–and a copy of it fell into the hands of Arthur Griffith who printed it in facsimile in his paper, *Sinn Fein*. The letter was also printed in the *Irish Worker*.

Griffith and Brayden were old enemies, and Griffith had no compunction in getting at him through Lady Aberdeen whom everybody knew, he said, was the real Lord Lieutenant. Her letter, which from a national point of view, should really have earned credit for her, spoke to Griffith in trumpet tones that the curse of a British-kept Press was upon Ireland, the worst curse that could happen to a nation struggling towards freedom.[36] The disclosure of the letter greatly offended the directors of the British Red Cross Society in Ireland. They called upon Lady Aberdeen to disavow its authenticity which, of course, she could not do. Neither, she said, could she discuss the letter in any way, having regard to the circumstances attending its publication; and, when the directors said they proposed to publish their correspondence with her she raised no objection, although she was afraid it would do more harm than good to the work of the Red Cross Society. She expressed surprise, however, that it should be thought fitting and in accordance with the recognized standards of fair dealing, that any notice should have been taken of a communication the knowledge of which was acquired in such a manner.

The correspondence was duly published and The *Irish Times*[37] took Lady Aberdeen severely to task. As the wife of the one man whose strict duty it was to stand aloof from party politics, she was holding a large body of Irishmen and Irishwomen guilty of the use of a great public calamity for political purposes. The members of the Red Cross Society, men and women of all creeds and political opinions, resented passionately this charge. Their sole concern was with the English and Irish soldiers who were lying wounded and maimed in Irish hospitals, and it came ill of Lady Aberdeen to suggest anything else. Whatever his real feelings were, Birrell told Lady Aberdeen that the 'scandalous article' in *The Irish Times* was 'the parting kick of the Jackass. I don't think we shall hear anything more of it in public–a few grumblings and bumblings and perhaps a Question in Parliament will be the last of it. It is all part of the jealousy of your and my House of which I see so many traces. . . . They [the Unionists] like running shows of their own and if their private correspondence were stolen and published we should see some singular utterances.' On the subject of the pending changes in the Irish Government, affecting the Aberdeens in particular, he agreed with her that it would never do just then to make any public comment about them, though nothing could be kept secret in the Whispering Gallery she inhabited in Dublin. It was incredible the gossip that went on there.[38]

The letter terminating the Aberdeen era was already on its way.

In it Asquith pointed out that on the 5th December 1914 it would be nine years since Aberdeen was appointed Viceroy; a term, which considerably exceeded in duration that of any Viceroy since the Union; it was from no lack of appreciation of his work, which had been crowned with so much success, that he proposed it should now come to an end.[39] This implied that Aberdeen would send in a letter of resignation which would be accepted as a matter of course.

The Aberdeens did not want to leave Ireland and doubtless made it known to their wide circle of friends and acquaintances that they were being victimized. In any event, when the news got out, voices were raised in protest especially from among those who had witnessed Lady Aberdeen's genuinely impressive humanitarian efforts. Redmond is said to have regarded the decision as a stupid blunder, and one of those who protested most was Margaret MacNeill, a sister of John MacNeill, the President of the Irish Volunteers. 'You have worked day and night', she wrote, 'for a country you have loved, and for a country that has loved you no matter what stupid or malignant or disappointed persons may have said.'[40] But D. P. Moran, the editor-owner of *The Leader*, adopted a typically individualist standpoint. While recognizing that there was a considerable amount of genuine regret and indignation throughout the country at what was regarded as the casting out of the Aberdeens, he felt that in Ireland's half-slave state sympathetic Viceroys were undesirable. The Aberdeens had been indirectly responsible for a lot of toadyism and flunkeyism – the daughters of local bungs presenting flowers, tame ladies wagging their skirts and decent men who ought to know better getting into silk hats which they had not worn since their wedding day. Top-lofty and exclusive Lords Lieutenant would be less harmful to the national character.[41]

When the campaign to keep them in Dublin was well under way, the Aberdeens thought they could rely on Birrell to make an approach on their behalf to the King and the Prime Minister. But Birrell said: 'I am not likely to see His Majesty and I am sure he would not mention the matter to me but neither I am sure would it be wise to mention the matter to him for I do not suppose he knows more than that His Excellency has sent in his resignation which has been accepted. As for the Prime Minister—when once he has made up his mind it is hard to alter it—but he may find it difficult to lay hands on a successor. My advice would be to do nothing. A new postponement would not be dignified. ...'[42]

That seems to have kept them quiet for a while but around Christmas time they wrote directly to the King, drawing his attention to the popular clamour for their retention, and suggesting rather crudely that if they were not retained it would look as if His Majesty was not so keenly alive to the wishes of his Irish subjects as had increasingly been thought. The clamour, which they could do nothing to repress, they said, was a reaction against those people who for a long time in a mean underhand manner had misrepresented them and succeeded in giving the impression that their continuance in office was undesirable.[43] The King interrupted the Prime Minister's holiday to let him see this letter and sent the putting-off reply Asquith suggested.[44]

The Aberdeens did succeed, however, in securing a postponement of their departure till the early part of February 1915, and a bid they made to have a new Irish dukedom created for their benefit was met by the award of a marquisate of the United Kingdom.[45] This gave some satisfaction to them and Birrell, quoting Bacon, made the comment to Nathan that it would have been too cruel to refuse His Excellency a single ostentatious feather with which to glorify his sunset.[46] A howl of protest and derision, however, went up when the Viceregal pair sought to be known as the Marquis and Marchioness of Aberdeen and *Tara*. 'It shows how little Aberdeen knows Ireland', said Birrell's private secretary Sam Power, 'when he thinks he can blend "the harp that once thro' Tara's halls" with the Scotch bagpipes.'[47] The Aberdeens compromised by substituting Temair for Tara. This fooled some of the opposition, for Temair was an old Irish language form of the same word; but they did not fool people like Mrs. Green who considered this move as a last insult to the ignorant aristocracy.

'Can you imagine anything more Jesuitical?' she asked, 'if it were not so silly . . .'[48] Birrell considered 'the Tara business' . . . pathetically absurd. The poor dear innocents are flouted and disgraced and what might have been quite a respectable, a trifle soiled, but still flamboyant apotheosis.* What a thing is man, and what a spectacle sister woman when sense is dethroned! I'm really sorry—'[49]

Lady Aberdeen maintained the pressure on Birrell right up to the end. When she heard that it was intended to publish the name of the new Lord Lieutenant on New Year's Day she thought the announcement could be postponed, but Birrell, to whom she again turned, told her plainly that this could not be done and that she and her husband should accept the inevitable. 'It is impossible for me in the course of the next two or three hours', he wrote, 'to do what would be equally impossible had I three weeks, viz. to procure any postponement. I was always convinced that the best thing to do was to have made public *at once* the fact that you were going in February. Your Excellencies would then have had the glorious apotheosis I had predicted for you. You are having it now in a manner which must be some reward for your long and unparalleled labours and toil—but over here [in London] its effect is spoiled by the underlying effort to induce His Excellency to withdraw his resignation and by the suggestion that in reality he does not want to go and is waiting to be pressed by a friendly and affectionate population to remain on, and yet I do ask you to believe me when I say that any more postponement of your hour of departure would only prolong the agony, and make the Viceroy's position very difficult and indeed undignified. As for the political consequences of the impending change it would be hard to predict what they may be. So much, if not all, depends upon the duration of the war which certainly does not seem to be even approaching its end—and anyhow it is plain that we have all of us to live through such tremendous events as to make everything else insignificant in proportion. . . .'[50]

From then onwards Birrell watched with anxiety to see whether any fresh move would keep the 'outgoing tenants', as he called

* The sentence appears to be unfinished.

them, on the shores of Ireland. On the 11th of February he wrote to Nathan: 'the fateful Saturday approaches "when the parting genius is with sighing sent" (Milton). I could easily weep but I won't.'[51] And four days later: 'I understand that the outgoing tenants have disappeared to-day but I await confirmation of the tidings, for the advent of wounded soldiers must have been a sore temptation to stay.' He quoted Matthew Prior:

> 'Now fitted the halter, now traversed the cart,
> And often took leave, but was loth to depart.'[52]

There was no further hitch. Aberdeen, who in the words of *The Leader*[53] had opened everything in Dublin except the Parliament House in College Green and the safe containing the Crown Jewels, left the Viceregal Lodge with his lady and was played out of Dublin by the band of the Royal Irish Constabulary. The tune they played was 'Hold your hand out, naughty boy' which was said to be their way of revenging themselves on the Marchioness for declaring, without the faintest blush of shame, that her favourite band was that of the Artane Boys' Industrial School.[54] As the procession passed through the streets a Dublin gutty was heard to shout: 'There they go, microbes. Crown Jules an' all.'[55]

The filling of the vacancy was not easy. Birrell pooh-pooed Nathan's 'sublime' suggestion that he should take the job himself. 'I would sooner be Provost of T.C.D. than that', he said.[56] His own first choice for the job would have been Lord Powerscourt of whom he thought highly but a non-political appointment at that time was impossible. It would be thought, he said, that the Aberdeens had been got rid of, in order to lower the national flag.[57] He also wanted to keep out the Kildare Street Club type of man. 'They crop up with their suggestions at critical moments and always with the same object, to cripple the Home Rule movement. It is hard not to feel almost as suspicious as John Dillon of these men.'[58] It was a man of this type who anonymously told the new Viceroy, Lord Wimborne, that he had watched the careers of twelve of his predecessors. Many of them looked down from their gilded frames on the walls of Dublin Castle. Amongst them

Wimborne could not find the portrait of his immediate predecessor whose career in Ireland it was to be hoped Wimborne had no intention of emulating. For what did it result in? Pandering to the disloyal, releasing the criminals, encouraging the law breakers while his good-natured, though over-zealous consort, opened baby clubs. People of all shades of opinion had grown tired of the regime at the Viceregal Lodge, where anyone who favoured Unionist views was quietly tabooed, and only those political hermaphrodites and sycophants who pretended they had no politics, were favoured by the Viceregal smile.[59]

When the appointment of Lord Wimborne was announced Birrell told Nathan that the Wimbornes in their very different way were likely to be as troublesome as their predecessors. He hoped they would be properly handled from the first.[60] If there was any difficulty about housing them while the Viceregal Lodge was being cleansed of tuberculosis and other germs, the Chief Secretary's Lodge was at their service. Birrell would gladly accept a bed in the Under-Secretary's Lodge which was the most comfortable of the three.[61] Wimborne could be as ornamental as was possible in wartime, but he was to be no more than that, and Birrell discussed with his secretary, Sam Power, who was being assigned to Wimborne's staff, the treatment that was to be applied. He kept Nathan informed. 'I spoke freely to Power', he said, 'who was quite alive to the danger and told me in effect that he would explain to his bear that he must not dance on my platform. If he exhibits any tendency to do so it must be checked *ab ovo*. But I think all he wants is "air and exercise". He can get that in one of his own go-carts. It is important not to cool his ardour. Sir Henry Robinson has already been introduced and I can see meditates a campaign of his own. A tour is always Sir Henry's recipe and very agreeable medicine it is. . . .'[62] He sketched out an itinerary, and suggested that when Robinson had finished with Wimborne, Doran and Company from the C.D.B. could take him over, and then Bailey and Company from the Land Commission. Robinson, by the time the tour was to start, began to doubt whether it would be politic for him to appear in it at all, so that, finally, Nathan was told to escort the Lord Lieutenant 'with or without such entourage of officials as appeared to him as likely to give a sunburstery atmosphere to the procession as foreshadowing the dawn of Home Rule'.[63]

Birrell also alerted Redmond. 'I had a call from the expectant new Lord Lieutenant the other day', he told him. 'I found him buoyed up with the expectation, planted in his breast, so he said, by long John O'Connor, that you and your friends were going to place your feet under his mahogany. I hinted doubt as to this and he seemed taken a little aback. The worst of it with these people is that if not backed up in one direction, they go a-whoring (it is a biblical expression) in the other and the Kildare Street Club is always there to lure them on. But he will take advice at present. . . .'[64]

Birrell also mentioned the appointment to T. P. Le Fanu, a former private secretary of his. Wimborne was the new calf in Israel before whom he hoped Le Fanu was prepared to dance. 'My dancing days are over', said Birrell, 'and I am only waiting for an opportunity to bid the world of politics good night, but the opportunity never comes. . . .'[65]

The aptness of Birrell's allusion to dancing before the new Viceroy is borne out by the diaries of Lady Cynthia Asquith, the wife of the Prime Minister's second son. She found 'tremendous ceremony maintained' in the Viceregal. Everything was 'very regal and stiff' and 'terrifying' curtseying was insisted upon as one approached or withdrew from the 'presence'. Lady Wimborne with her heaven-born manner, smile and dimple was really perfection, but her husband was 'just a fairly frank bounder', whose behaviour made one wince. He swilled brandy, was incredibly stagy, flapped his furry eyelids at women, and Lady Cynthia shuddered to think of what went on in the sitting-room to which he invited the ladies of his choice for a *tête-à-tête*. She thought he really ought to restrain himself with the natives in that lovely, glamorous land.[65a] It should be said, however, that this rather savage criticism of Wimborne is not reflected in any way in the Birrell-Nathan correspondence.

3

We have already suggested why Birrell only made 'occasional and fitful appearances at the wheel', especially after the start of the War. He believed he could meet the demands of Cabinet and Parliament better by living in London where he had all the facilities of the Irish Office available to him including direct communication with Dublin Castle. Redmond, his Irish Party *vis-à-vis*, ordinarily lived there, while Birrell was able to rely on his Under-Secretary, Nathan, to maintain regular contact in Dublin with the Irish Party's second string, John Dillon. Nathan was disappointed at times with Dillon and said so to Birrell, who reminded him that the trouble was Dillon's boundless self-satisfaction. 'He can't believe that anybody can be wiser than himself where Ireland is concerned. He is really quite unusually fond of you.'[66]

From 1913 on, Birrell had another more personal reason for not coming to Ireland as often as he might otherwise have done. His second wife, Eleanor, the widow of Lionel, the younger son of the poet Tennyson, who shared his literary and political interests, was chronically incapacitated as the result of a brain tumour in an inoperable position. They had been married since 1888, and had two children, Frankie and Tony.

In the Tennyson family the grim reception given to Birrell on his first appearance is remembered. The sight of the untidy widower barrister who was acquiring a modest reputation as a literary critic and essayist did not impress the great poet. Why should he force an entrance into the family and want to marry Eleanor who, after all, was an aristocrat, a grand-daughter of the Earl of Elgin, a Bruce who claimed descent from Robert of the Spider episode? Tennyson did not approve of second marriages anyway and he disliked Birrell's radicalism, which was mixed up with an odd enthusiasm for John Henry Newman. However, Birrell was frank and manly in his replies to Tennyson's questions and he won the old man's regard by turning the interview into a discussion of the merits of Samuel Butler's *Hudibras*. Subsequently Tennyson had no cause to regret Eleanor's choice, for Birrell

James Larkin

proved a devoted husband and a delightful father to her two families.[67]

Eleanor was a charmingly beautiful and vivacious woman, and Birrell used to twit her with having inherited her retrousée nose, which suited her admirably, from the Bruces; he called it the *Fuimus* nose, after the Bruce family motto. He was always given to mild sarcasm; he would sometimes chaff Eleanor and her Tennyson sons with their descent, as he alleged, from Don Pedro the Cruel of Portugal, owing possibly to some statement in a pedigree that was drawn up when the Poet Laureate was made a Peer.[68] He enjoyed the high spirits of the children and encouraged them; it was better, he said, for children to have a bad father as a warning than a good one as an example. Sometimes indigestion from eating too fast made him irritable and he would give vent to his feelings in what the family called a bellow. But this would not last long, and a large dose of bicarbonate of soda would restore normality. Birrell had an unshakeable belief in bicarbonate of soda. Once he got so tired of sending for sixpennyworths that he went to the chemist himself, planked down a sovereign and was seen staggering home with a glass jar of the magic powder about the size of a pillar-box.[69]

He got it into his head on one occasion that he was suffering from an incurable disease and went to see a specialist. It was a warm day and he was in a lather of sweat as he walked towards Harley Street. On entering the waiting-room he did what he always did, he went over to the book case and studied the titles. Among them was a medical directory. He took it out and found among the symptoms of the disease he feared, that a person suffering from it could not perspire. That was enough. He slipped out of the house and went home, gaily jingling his two guineas in his pocket.[70]

Eleanor's sense of humour enabled her to enjoy her husband's eccentricities and tolerate his sly references to her aristocratic nose. She was practical and efficient, just the sort of person he needed, for though his judgment in affairs, public and domestic, was of a high order he was always impatient of the ordinary obligations of daily life. He never asked the price of anything, never knew how he stood at the bank and detested petty economies. He was physically unhandy, could not shave himself, while the care of clothes, or anything other than books, never occurred to him. He was a book-hunter and accumulated 10,000 volumes by the time he was fifty, but it was Eleanor who found and fitted out the house in Chelsea where this vast library was stored and organized.

Now that she was illBirrell took her to Ireland for a change, but her giddiness, which was a feature of her illness, seemed to get worse there, and her nerves went to shreds. So he brought her back and put her in a hospital where he visited her as often as he was allowed. This pegged him down in England for months on end, so that he found his retention of an office (which implied some residence in Ireland) hard to justify to himself; he did not mind what other people thought. In December 1914, he explained the position to the Prime Minister and said he was willing to resign and thought he should. He said this though at the time he did not really want to go.[71] It was a predicament that affected his mind, will and spirits. Occasionally Eleanor seemed to be showing improvement but he always carried the fear that 'all would topple over again'. She was never likely, he said, to recover her reason though she was reasonable enough in the imaginary world in which she lived and was very quiet and sweet. He suffered bitterly on account of her and inveighed against the professionals in whose charge she found herself. 'I hate', he said, 'all operations, surgeons, doctors, nurses – a vile crowd of harpies and egoists. . . .' The specialists had spent many months diagnosing what was wrong but they unnecessarily tortured her and her husband by pulling out all her teeth and by resorting to other drastic and entirely irrelevant forms of treatment.[72] In February the end came in view, 'My long vigil here is very slowly approaching its conclusion', he told Nathan. 'The doctors relying upon their tests don't anticipate any immediate crisis, but I cannot share their view. She gets more and more shadowy every day and at any moment the end may begin. I must definitely decide not to come over this week. After all I am not wanted.'[73]

She died on the 10th March, 1915, and Birrell wrote to Maida Mirrielees, his first wife's sister: 'I have now been twice evicted and turned out on to the road. Once with our dear Maggie when I was eight and twenty, after a twelvemonth's bliss, and now at sixty-four, after six and twenty years of happiness such as seldom falls to the lot of men. We must pay a dear price for loving a mortal.' He wrote from Dublin Castle where, he said, 'I am finding more ease from my pain in this grim place.'[74] Thanking Redmond for a message of condolence he wished that Eleanor could have read it, 'for like the good wife she always was, she was more jealous of my reputation than I ever was. . . . The people who say she didn't care about politics are all wrong. On both Education and the Home Rule Questions she felt keenly and she longed to see things done and not jabbered about. The kind of politics she hated are the politics of the Lobby and the petty rivalries of politicians.'[75] He was no doubt here expressing his own feelings also about the political game. Among the friends who wrote at this time was Sydney Lee, the editor of the Dictionary of National Biography. Birrell had suggested to him once that all biographies had become alike charming to him – bawds and bishops, pimps and puritans – but now, as he thanked him for his message of condolence, he could say 'It is an old story, often told by study biographers, no one of whom, we may be sure, really knew the actual feelings he may think it his duty to describe. But each one of us, *in his own case*, knows how the matter stands with him. Fortunately, this time I am near the end of my tether.'[76]

4

'We are in a gloomy fit over the war,' he had told Nathan in mid-January 1915, 'doubtful about the Roumanians and almost equally doubtful about Italy and convinced that the batting has beaten the bowling, and that though no runs are scored, each side keeps its wicket up both East and West. The Zeppelin scare prevails and those in the know (the foreign know) are advising even their mothers-in-law to leave London at once. Unmoved and unblanched I remain at my post, only praying that if a bomb hits me it may strike a vital part, for though I am not now much of a walker, and as you see cannot write, I should not care to live without legs or hands. . . .' The weather added to the gloom, and so did the growing viciousness of party politics. 'The attacks on Haldane are intolerable,' he said, 'and I am told that that poor result of intercourse between a half-worn out Chancery barrister and a middle-aged lady of quality, Lord Selborne, openly alleges that the Lord Chancellor is a traitor! Amongst the lower ranks of the Tory ex-Ministers temper is rising. It is a pity that their abilities are as low as their tempers are high, for were any of them of any use it would be wise to call 'em in and rub their noses in the mire.'[77]

After Eleanor's death he braced himself. The strain was over, he was still feeling rather unsure of himself, but he was no longer thinking of giving up. 'I am hoping for the advent of spring when I shall once more visit my island', he told Nathan.[78] His idea was to spend a couple of days in Dublin and then disappear with Sir Henry Robinson into the country. Frankie was coming over, too, to explore Dublin's art treasures. But when he came he was nervous that in his absence his colleagues would forget that there was an Irish point of view. 'There ought to be a jackdaw in the Cabinet Room trained to say Ireland at stated short intervals. The bird would be cheaper than a Chief Secretary.' He loved to come to Ireland at this time. It was always quiet and peaceful; it was in England all the fuss was made.[79] In England the war news seemed more insufferable, and it was there, too, he whimsically remembered, that his pocket was picked and eleven one pound notes extracted that he had just triumphantly recovered in excess income tax from the Treasury. He had made over his own Lodge in the Phoenix Park for use as a military hospital and stayed with either Wimborne or Nathan in theirs. He was in the Viceregal Lodge on a Saturday night in 1915 when he told Tony, 'There is a houseful of ladies here and a good deal of giggling goes on, but I get away in the morning and go down to the

Castle and do a little work and come back in the afternoon to tea. The Great O'Leary, V.C., was here today and the ladies made a great fuss of him. But he has a twinkling eye and knows how to handle them. I took Miss Montagu and Lady Gwendoline Churchill to the Irish Plays this afternoon. We saw a piece called *The Mineral Workers* and *Spreading the News*–pretty good but not quite so good as they might have been.'[80] Miss (Ruth) Montagu was a daughter of the Minister of Munitions, and Lady Gwendoline Churchill was the wife of John Spencer Churchill, the brother of Winston Churchill. She was apparently a lady of character, for when Wimborne made an amorous advance to her in his 'parlour', she gave him a 'gifle', a slap in the face.[80a]

But even in the comparative peace of Ireland, Birrell heard on all sides of death and disaster that no acts of heroism tempered. 'It is hard for the young to be thus early battered and shattered', he told Maida Mirrielees, and he was not forgetting his own boys who were coming up to military age. 'It is our children who are called upon to bear the most excruciating of the sufferings caused by this outburst of devilry. As I never was a believer in what is called Human Progress I am not so cruelly disappointed as are some of my more sentimental friends but it is bad enough for all of us.'

The Chancellor of the Exchequer announced in March 1915 the Government's intention to restrict the hours for the sale of liquor with the object of ensuring sobriety in places where there were armament works. The Irish Party opposed the application of this decision to Ireland on the grounds that there were practically no such places in Ireland and that general conditions in Ireland were in any event different from those in Great Britain. That was what they said in public, but to the Government privately they also said that the restrictions would have the effect of making the Party incur the hostility of the vast number of licence holders throughout the country, each of whom would become a centre for Sinn Fein ideas. This would militate against recruiting, and would impair the advance the Party had achieved towards the establishment of good relations. Birrell and Nathan accepted these arguments, and promised to support the Irish Party's case but they both had strong personal views about the need for temperance measures in Ireland. Ireland was a sodden community, Birrell said. It was borne home to his mind that there had been, and still was, a superfluity of beastliness and debauchery in a certain number of the drink shops, and that their police did them a poor service in this regard. 'The beastliness of Dublin drunken men and the degraded character of the Dublin prostitutes were, and always had been beyond comparison. . . .'[81]

5

By the beginning of May 1915 it was fairly obvious that the days of the Liberal Government were numbered. The war, now nine months in being, was only beginning in Birrell's view. It was going disastrously. The slaughter of officers and men was terrible, and the effort to break through at the Dardanelles had been a pathetic failure. There was a crisis over the shortage of shells and this provided the generals with an excuse for their own limitations. Sir John French, the head of the expeditionary force in France, secretly used the British Press for complaints against Asquith and Kitchener.[82] These in turn led to accusations of intrigue and mutual recriminations amongst ministers. Fisher, the First Sea Lord, quarrelled bitterly with his political chief, Winston Churchill, over the Dardanelles venture and then locked himself up in a room in the Charing Cross Hotel as a preliminary to resigning. Asquith tried valiantly to save the Government, but finally had to submit before a threatened Tory attack in the House of Commons which, he feared, would end the hopes of enticing a wavering Italy into the war.[83] So, having consulted Lloyd George and Bonar Law, he proceeded to reconstruct the Government on a broad and non-party basis. It was clearly understood that, whatever happened, Churchill was to leave the Admiralty, and Haldane the Lord Chancellorship.

'I'm in a depressed mood about everything,' Birrell said a few days before the coalition was agreed upon, 'but, altho' the Devil is not dead, we must I suppose still cry courage, tho' it's hard to believe that if, after all the world has gone thro', its inhabitants are still the savages they are, why they should ever improve. I think even Emerson and more of his kidney would believe in hell to-day.'[84] When he was coming over to Ireland next time he might be torpedoed but he would not mind. 'Better drown in salt water', he said 'than in Irish Whisky.'[85] In this mood he awaited his fate, while the Prime Minister spent his time pole-axing his friends and interviewing his enemies. He felt that he would be asked to retain the Chief Secretaryship. 'My position is odd', he wrote, 'they cannot touch me. It is not the strength of the garrison, but the invulnerability of the position, and the irony of it is that I want to go, what some of my pole-axed friends do not want to do. . . . But a Prime Minister in making up a new com-bination is as untrusting as a young woman making up her mind whether she will have diamonds or rubies in her engagement ring. But if I remain, what is likely to be my lot in a Cabinet con-taining A. J. Balfour, possibly Carson!, perhaps, if his health permits, Walter Long? The thought is hateful to me, and suppose they begin listening to the hungry gang of excluded lawyers and honour-hunters, and pressing claims upon us, or criticising our modes and methods of administering Ireland during the next two to three years, what then? Am I to stand it? The Lonsdales and the Craigs and the Barrys scuffling round. It is the very devil. One gang was enough to make you vomit. Two will make you spit blood. 'Think of it, picture it, dissolute man. Love in it, drink of it then, if you can.'[86]

His next letter to Nathan conveyed the news that he was continuing in office. 'I have coalesced!' he wrote, 'I have shaken hands with Lord Selborne! winked at his new Under-Secretary Acland! vice my poor slaughtered lamb, Sir H. Verney, spoken to the new Home Secretary and his underling Brace, M.P., and had an interesting confabulation with the new Chancellor of the Exchequer . . . but beyond a general curse and a queaziness of stomach I have survived the first shock better than I had anti-cipated.'[87] He recognized, none the less, that nothing could be more uncomfortable, thankless and, it might well prove, impossible than to be Chief Secretary for Ireland in a Coalition Government. He had had the most hellish fortnight of his life, he told Redmond, and the outlook was bleaker. He had been fighting about the Irish Office, insisting that on no terms would he share the daily administration with anybody belonging to the Unionist side, and broadly had succeeded in having his way, although the Unionist James Campbell had effected a lodgment as Lord Chancellor of Ireland. It was a very awkward and damaging business, but Nathan and himself had the Prime Minister's qualified assurance that Irish affairs would remain in their hands. In discussing the position with Asquith, he had used language which he hoped would secure his release from the Chief Secretaryship which had become odious and hateful to him. but it had not. Later he might be more successful. He owed a double loyalty, which was always a dubious position, first to the Prime Minister who had always treated him like a brother, and second to Ireland, whose Nationalist Party had also always treated him with the utmost consideration, so that he could not see how he could properly at the moment desert either.[88]

Carson and Redmond were offered places in the reconstructed Cabinet but Redmond declined, because of the principles and history of his party, and urged Asquith not to include Carson. Carson did not want to accept the invitation either, but being the Opposition's best man, as Birrell acknowledged, he was pressed on the Prime Minister by the Conservatives and was made Attorney-General for England. 'I wish you could have come in for my sake,' Birrell said later to Redmond, 'but I am equally sure that you did right to stay out.' He, himself, was dodging Cabinet meetings, for he felt like George IV, who, when he first saw his future wife, called for a brandy.[89]

The retention of Birrell was seen by the Irish Nationalists as the only bright feature of a situation which had been made particularly horrible for them by Campbell's appointment. He was regarded by them as a miserable party hack, a man who had no Ulster connections but who had publicly counselled civil war as the path of duty for the loyalists of the North.[90] Redmond behind the scenes worked hard to have the appointment cancelled. He reminded Asquith that since the war he had kept the truce, not making a single political speech. Nationalist Ireland, in the expectation of Home Rule, had followed his lead. 114,000 Irishmen were in the Army, among them 23,000 of his National Volunteers. Now a coalition had been launched by the Liberals without serving notice on their allies. Carson, the apostle of physical force against the law, was in the new Cabinet while he, Redmond, had been offered, not a place in the government of his own country, but some unknown and unnamed English office. And Campbell was being injected into what was traditionally a thoroughly political office in Dublin. He let Asquith see a letter from Bishop Fogarty of Killaloe, a strong supporter of the Irish Party, which expressed with intense bitterness the disgust and rage which had swept the country. 'Home Rule is dead and buried', the Bishop wrote, 'and Ireland is without a national party....' He prophesied that there would ultimately be a bloody feud between the people and soldiers.[91]

Redmond's protest was partly successful in as much as Campbell's appointment to the Lord Chancellorship was not proceeded with, the Unionists getting instead the Attorney-Generalship for John Gordon who, from the Liberal point of view, was the least objectionable of the Unionist lawyers. The 'wretched Campbell' was to be consoled with some glittering prize in England which plays, Birrell said, the role Ireland used to play in the days when discarded royal mistresses were placed on the Irish civil list.[92]

Birrell was concerned about Asquith's painful isolation. His honour was involved to men who were lacking in delicacy. His rank and file were not behind him. The grand *coup* of coalition was not either popular or regarded as inevitable. He had parted, in circumstances which never could be reported favourably upon, with one or two of his closest friends. And he had a Cabinet composed of warring, uncongenial, and it might be traitorous elements. 'I think oddly enough', Birrell told Nathan. 'he has found more sympathy extended to him by Redmond! than by anybody else.'[93] In a 'somewhat emotional interview' Redmond had shown understanding of the Prime Minister's predicament but he left him in no doubt either as to how the Irish Party felt with six sworn enemies in the Cabinet, and one in the Castle. In these circumstances it was more than ever desirable that as close a touch as possible on controversial and explosive matters should be kept between Nathan, Dillon, and himself. Asquith readily agreed and spoke to Birrell about it. 'However, on the closer touch', as Birrell told Nathan, 'there is nothing more in it than to continue the cultivation of friendly talks with John Dillon as No. 2 and to keep an eye upon the new Attorney-General and avoid State trials as you would the devil . . .', and he concluded: 'You will find Dillon (if he unfolds his mind to you) full of the darkest suspicions against Lloyd George.'[94] Nathan hardly needed to be directed. Since he had been at Dublin Castle he understood that it was Government policy to play up the Nationalists as against all others.[94a] He recognized that the Nationalist leaders and their Volunteers were eventually to become Ministers and soldiers of the Crown.[95a]

From this on Birrell found the House of Commons, which the Nationalists members rarely attended now, 'a truly detestable place'. 'A bad temper prevails, bad speeches are made, bad legislation is produced, my Irish friends have disappeared, and I am left responsible for their views. . . .'[95] 'The debate last night (8 July 1915) was very uncomfortable. My only colleagues on the Front Bench were Long, Carson, Hayes Fisher and Gordon. Not a Liberal soul within call. An almost empty house, but containing all the cranks. . . . However I pitched my figures into them . . . and pulled thro', leaving only a little wool on the hedge. . . . The Ulster gang are determined, being the petty-minded babies they are, to make a great parade of their feverish loyalty as compared with the wicked indifference of the Papists.'[96] The 12th of July, the anniversary of King William's victory at the Boyne, was coming up, and as it passed quietly Birrell sent a note of congratulation to Nathan. But there was really very little to be thankful for, he said; with so huge a Butcher's Bill in Flanders and the

Dardanelles, it was impossible to wax grateful over a few hundred Orangemen and Papists not being allowed to break each other's heads.[97]

6

Bishop Fogarty may have been premature in announcing that Home Rule was dead and buried but there were signs that the Home Rule party was being displaced by the small minority group known as the Sinn Feiners. Their volunteer force was growing while Redmond's National Volunteers rapidly disintegrated. They were obtaining possession of arms by one means or another. They were actively opposing recruitment for the forces. They throve, moreover, on every evidence of 'coercion' such as the suppression of papers or arrests under the Defence of the Realm regulations. And they missed no opportunity of making propaganda such as the funeral in August of the old Fenian, O'Donovan Rossa, who had died in the United States and was brought home for interment. National Volunteers joined the Irish Volunteers in the funeral: it was the first time they had done so since they parted company the previous year and it was the last time they would march together. These national funerals were occasions the police feared but they were warned by the Castle to be discreet and there was not even a notetaker present in Glasnevin to record P. H. Pearse's dramatic graveside oration. Unknown to the authorities Pearse had risen to a position of eminence in the I.R.B. and was shortly to emerge as Commander-in-Chief of the Army of the Irish Republic and President of its Provisional Government. Birrell was, therefore, miles off the mark when, on reading the reports of the funeral, he commented on its futility. It was a melancholy spectacle, in his eyes, and the very height of unreality. As for O'Donovan Rossa, 'I do not suppose anybody in the whole concourse', he said, 'cared anything for the old fellow, who never cared for anything at any time.' The funeral had been staged to annoy somebody and to keep alive a sham revolutionary sentiment. It did, however, increase the uncomfortable feeling he had that Redmond's position was becoming more and more unsatisfactory.[98] He could see what the Sinn Feiners were up to. If there was ever a reaction against the war and trouble in some of the big centres in England there would be room for Irish fishermen in those waters; so that it was of the first importance to keep alive the always smoking embers of Fenianism and if possible to get the two bodies of Volunteers to work together. Had the Sinn Feiners any leader of first rate ability, either as an organizer or orator, there might easily in six months time, if the war dragged on, or if the British armies suffered severe setbacks, be serious outbreaks, but as it was, it seemed to him a play-acting business, without blood in it, but very disgusting.[99]

There was more 'play-acting' during September when twelve hundred Irish Volunteers marched openly with their arms through Dublin, and in October, when the Irish Citizen Army under James Connolly led a sham attack on Dublin Castle. Birrell, in his anxiety not to cause alarm, vetoed an effort of the military's to stop the collection of money for the purchase of arms for the Volunteers, but he did counsel greater vigilance over the importation of arms. He still distrusted the military mind. On the subject of the 'Banishees', for instance–a name he gave to some Irish Volunteer organizers who had been ordered to leave the country– he had no doubt that they were dangerous men, but he would not accept the military evaluation of how dangerous they were. 'I have no doubt they still think Sheehy-Skeffington and the *Spark* dangerous.'[100] 'They should, therefore, be let out immediately before any new agitation for their release took place.'[101] Sheehy-Skeffington was a pacifist whose wife Birrell had cause to remember, because in the suffragette days she had knocked his hat off at Greystones and broken windows in the Castle. The *Spark* was a one-page weekly that sometimes wrote with comprehension and light-heartedly about the Chief Secretary himself. Thus: 'Augustine was no reactionary backwoodsman. Genial and kindly he bowled over the Unionist questioner with his flippancy. The fatherly care of the leader of our race [Redmond] worked Gus, *unser* Gus, into the mystic movement of the Celtic heart. And he waxed fat thereat, beaming all the time the satisfied smile of the protuberant waistcoat. Kindly, lovable, too flippant to be serious, *unser* Gus was the man to mollify the wild Celt, to lead him from his devious ways, to paths of peace and Imperialism, to bridge the gulf, to make the British democracy to realize that the Celt, inscrutable, was not a bad fellow, if properly handled.'

There was the usual hint of unpleasantness to come as Parliament reassembled in September. Redmond and Dillon were greatly perturbed about the possibility of universal compulsory military service, and Redmond was disgusted with the stupidity and neglect of the War Office so far as voluntary recruiting in Ireland was concerned. They exaggerated, Birrell believed, but their enemies were so numerous, and the holes in their Home Rule armour so wide, that he was not surprised at their apprehensions. The Irish Unionists were also seriously perturbed for other reasons, and were pressing Birrell to disarm the Irish Volunteers and stop their parading. As usual, he pooh-poohed their fears, but by November he knew from what Nathan told him that the general situation was bad and fairly rapidly growing worse. The Nationalist Party had lost control of the country and the extremists were everywhere gaining strength. Conscription, if introduced in Ireland, would result in the immobilization of a considerable British force. The Irish Party leaders now also saw the reality of the threat of Sinn Fein, but continued to advise the Government to keep their hands off the Volunteer organizers.

Birrell was a victim of fluctuating moods 'I am depressed in spirits', he wrote at the end of August 1915, 'for whatever happens in Europe, I think the world is on the downgrade.' As for Ireland, 'doing anything there was like walking on the upturned faces of men, everybody was so sensitive'.[102] He was going over to France, but except by the round face of his son who was building houses there with what would today be called a peace corps, he did not expect to be cheered. Nor was he. From the photographs of the German lines he was shown, taken from aircraft, it seemed impossible, short of a huge convulsion of nature, to drive out the men who lay out of sight within the trenches.[103] Within a month he said, 'I am a little more hopeful than I was, but don't ask me why, for I don't know. Yet I entertain the fair goddess once more in my sombre bosom. On Sunday night I appear in the Chelsea Palace Music Hall to recruit for the London Irish Regiment. I trust my faintly reviving spirits will survive my own oratory.'[103a]

The political situation was tottering again. Carson had resigned because of the inadequacy of British support for Serbia and general dissatisfaction with the conduct of the war. Lloyd George was calling for Kitchener's head. There were demands from various quarters for Government reorganization, and Birrell thought he detected a movement directed against Asquith whose health was beginning to suffer as the result of overwork. Loreburn, the Lord Chancellor, was 'stirring in his sleep'; he had always hated the Prime Minister and missed no chance of giving him a dig. But he was too honest to intrigue with Northcliffe, the newspaper king, who was the main conspirator. Carson was being run as the strong man successor to Asquith but, in Birrell's opinion, Carson was not a Saviour, and he even doubted if he had aspirations in that direction. "He is not a cementing man but a fissiparous one, and his Ulster training and latent passions unfit him for friendly and close relations with Englishmen."[104]

The Government survived a test of strength in November when the House of Commons debated the general military and naval situation, and Birrell gave Nathan the result. 'We are still afloat. The great Carson gun has exploded without loss save to the gunner. His speech was a poor performance, almost beggarly, considering that he did not allow himself to be restrained either by public or private considerations. The truth is that, tho' a most able man and an astute advocate, his own resources are very limited, and he cannot infuse his subject with either wisdom or wit. Therefore, on a great parliamentary occasion (outside the Ulster Question) he is bound to fall flat. He had a mixed hearing, but when he sat down he must have felt conscious of failure, for he disappeared for the rest of the evening.'[105]

Redmond took part in this debate, speaking for the first time since the Home Rule Bill had been placed on the Statute Book fourteen months before. He was encouraged to speak by Carson's resignation and to express a degree of confidence in the Government that he certainly had not felt for many months. His speech made a deep impression on Birrell. 'Redmond,' he said, 'if ever man did, deserves well of the British Empire whose cause he has manfully espoused, knowing full well that he had behind him no longer that United Irish Party "who never hedge within their pledge", but a large concourse of petty-minded money-grabbers . . . who grumble at his patriotisms and would desert him tomorrow if they saw the way to stick to their £400 a year without him. The Prime Minister has his difficulties but so has Redmond. Tho' as in special duty bound to stick to my chief, I am none the less sorrowfully convinced that hard measure is being dealt out to Redmond. . . . He hears from John Dillon "three times a day", an exaggeration I hope, urging him to get up and make an Anti-Conscription harangue in the House. This . . . Redmond will not do. The situation, however, is still far from good and any bad luck abroad would have effects. Good luck on the other hand would tide us over Christmas, but where are we to look for it?'

Whether there was to be conscription depended on the figures for voluntary recruiting and on whether the risk of disunity would be justified in order to lay hands on perhaps fifty thousand shirkers, as Birrell called them. It was obvious there would be trouble in the Cabinet over this still unexploded bomb. If a decision in favour of conscription were taken, all the Irish Nationalists, Redmond included, would join hands and fortunes with the radical rump and fight the Bill in the old style with the gloves off, involving the closure and perhaps police in the House. Assuming such a Bill were passed in the Commons, he did not think the Irish could ask to be excluded from it or would be consenting parties to any excluding clause. Their cry would be 'To your tents, O Israel!' In his opinion, conscription could not be enforced in Ireland. In Catholic Ireland it would have to be enforced by the Castle or the military headquarters. Soldiers would have to enter the villages and carry off the Pats and Mikes in custody. Shots

would be fired, whole villages would take to the hills, the Volunteers would parade in force, and somewhere or another there
would be slaughter. 'I certainly would not make myself responsible for any such proceedings', he told Nathan, 'for in my
judgment, Ireland as an island has done at least as well as any
historically-minded person has any right to expect.'[106]

Nationalist Ireland's contribution might have been larger still
had fewer blunders been made. Some disreputable persons had
been employed as recruiting agents, prominent Protestant Unionists were too much to the fore, and national sentiment had been
discouraged by the waving of Union Jacks and by appeals to
patriotism, not for Ireland, but for England. Recruiting was not
helped either by some well-intentioned and nationally-disposed
people who engaged in it. Bernard Shaw was one such. He tried
his hand at a recruiting play which he called 'O'Flaherty, V.C.',
but the Abbey Theatre when they read it were so alarmed that
they sent it off to the military authorities who in turn sent it to
Nathan who told Birrell about it. Birrell's reaction was typical of
the man. 'Bernard Shaw's play is a bore,' he said. 'I wouldn't
censor it, unless really obliged. The military is not a good authority to which to submit a play. I don't think they would have
passed *Henry V*. Does it rest with them? Surely not. If it offends
both sides it cannot be very bad. Speaking without the book of
words, I say let it alone.'[107] The play was not produced. In 1909
Lord Aberdeen had tried to exercise an indirect censorship over
another Shaw Play, *The Shewing Up of Blanco Posnet*, but the
Abbey directors stood up to him and presented the play to a
crowded house in which there was a large party from the Castle.
On that occasion Birrell was said to have used violent language
when he heard of Aberdeen's action; it had made the whole
government ridiculous.[108]

The play within the Cabinet, in which Birrell himself had a
modest part, dragged on to what he called the last day of this
'*Annus Damnabilis*', 1915. There were interviews and discussions without cease between distressed souls and an angry because baffled Prime Minister.[109] Already dramatic organizational

"HIS MASTER'S VOICE."

IRISH PIG (*to Chief Secretary*). "DIVIL A TASTE OF A HOLIDAY FOR YOU, ME BHOY, IF I CAN HELP IT!"

TAKING HIS LITTLE PIGS TO MARKET

Quot porculi, tot sententiæ

MR. BIRRELL'S EDUCATION BILL TASK

changes had been made. A small War Council was set up inside the Cabinet and the absence of Kitchener from it spoke eloquently of the decline of the War Minister's reputation. Sir John French had been replaced as Commander-in-Chief in France and was brought back to take charge of the Home Forces. Winston Churchill had chucked in his hand and gone to fight in the war, on realizing that he was to be left to endure his 'well-paid inactivity' as administrator of the Duchy of Lancaster to which he had been demoted. Birrell was left alone. He was not included in the War Council for which he said '*Laus Deo*'. He was still a complete Minister of the Crown, however, 'though shaky on the legs, trembling in the hands and muzzy in the head' as a result of a cold he had picked up on the Athenaeum balcony watching Lady Scott unveiling a statue of her husband, the great explorer. 'I am not', Birrell said, 'an Arctic type!'[110]

The Ministers that were left could not agree on a Bill to compel recalcitrant bachelors to join the forces, and they were even more divided on the trade and financial aspects of the war, between the rivalry of soldiers demanding more and more men to be butchered on the Fronts, and the Treasury and the Board of Trade who said there were limits which, if disregarded, meant collapse. McKenna, the Chancellor of the Exchequer, and Runciman, the President of the Board of Trade, threatened resignation, and Birrell made it known to the Prime Minister that, if they went, he would go too. In the event McKenna and Runciman stayed on, and Birrell was relieved from the necessity of having to make a disagreeable decision. To him the thought was horrible beyond his powers of conception to have to desert a leader he loved and, what was worse, to leave him in the hands of his enemies. And if he went, how would Ireland fare under an unfriendly Dublin Castle and Chief Secretary? Who would be left to utter words of warning?

He was convinced that, apart from Ulster which had horrors *in posse* all its own, things were getting worse in Ireland. The Sinn Feiners were increasing in numbers, organization and spirit, the Home Rule Party was 'under the weather', and 'the Bill on the Statute Book' had ceased to be a cry. The disloyal section of the priesthood were becoming the leaders of the people, as they always did when a national party was waning. John Redmond was becoming more and more a detached figure and the crowd be hind him in Parliament were discontented. Dillon, his Achilles, had returned to his tent. The possibility of conscription formed a rallying group for the few who were perhaps ready to risk their lives on the hillside. Were there to be any great reverse to British arms they should have to look out for rows. 'And yet', he concluded, 'if I had been asked before the war to hazard an opinion as to the attitude of Catholic Ireland in the event of such a war as the present, I think I should have painted a darker picture than the one now on the canvas.'[111]

Nathan, at the end of October, had thought that the Lord Lieutenant's new recruiting campaign looked slightly more promising than he had first dared to hope, but a fortnight later he noted that the Sinn Fein movement had grown in strength somewhat rapidly of late. The official recruiting campaign had been answered by considerable activity in recruiting for the Irish Volunteers to fight *the* enemy. Dillon was showing himself impressed with the real danger that the Sinn Feiners were becoming to his party and to the State, and he was painting lurid pictures of what might happen if conscription were attempted. In the middle of November, however, Nathan noticed 'an abatement of the mischievious and feverish energies of the Sinn Feiners'. Birrell was glad to hear of this, but, he said, 'we must watch them carefully and hit them hard at the right moment'.[112] The right moment would occur at Eastertime 1916 – that is to say, within a matter of five months.

7

The Chief Secretaryship exposed Birrell to great pressure in the matter of patronage, not only in the filling of appointments but in the use of his official position to override or modify decisions about the misapplication of funds, derelictions of duty or other misdemeanours. These he was expected to regard as the natural vagaries of an impulsive and high-spirited race.[113] Ireland was a poor backward country and employment hard to come by, so that whenever a government job fell vacant there was no shortage of candidates for it, and political 'pull' was widely exercised. 'Have you settled the Irish Question yet?' he was asked one day, and he jocosely replied, 'I'd have settled it long ago if there were enough jobs to go round.' On other occasions he declared that any disinterested person in Ireland was a *rara avis*. It was a country in which, when an appointment was in issue, everybody thought at least a month ahead.[114] The exercise of patronage grew more distasteful to him every day,[115] so much so that he thanked God whenever he found that somebody else had the last word, as was the case at the time of the nasty scramble for jobs when the National Health Insurance Commission was set up in 1911.[116] But when he had a say in the filling of vacancies as, for instance, in the Congested Districts Board all sorts of difficulties arose the moment a name was suggested. Was he a 'landlords' man, an agents' man, a priests' man, a cattle-drivers' man and so on through and down the weary scale?'[117]

It was impossible, of course, to please everybody. The Nationalist party had to place their constituents, but the Unionists also had to get a share of whatever jobs were going. When the Government was a coalition, as it now was, increased pressure came from the Unionists, while concessions to one side brought forth protests from the other. Birrell wished that the coalitionists would trust him, for it was a nuisance having both packs yelping at his heels each time a placeman died.[118] But when a formula was suggested for dividing patronage with the Tories he would not have it: he did not want it to be thought that he had become a mere machine in the hands of unscrupulous jobbers.[119] He commented on the 'good-natured British egotism' of a letter he had received from Long. 'As if', he said, 'there was no real place called Ireland at all, only a number of honest gentlemen filling or about to fill certain well-paid posts.'[120]

Legal appointments were the most troublesome; the candidates were always numerous and strong, for law seemed to thrive on

Irish soil. The vacancies also occurred too frequently. 'I hope', he once said, 'that Ronan will prove a good judge. . . . He has ploughed a lonely furrow, reached the top of his tree, and to boycott him at the bidding of the poorest elements in the Irish Parliamentary Party would have been humiliation. And now let us pray for long life to all the judges on Irish soil. Recommendations for a solicitor called Shannon for a R.M.-ship are flooding me out as if he were the river of that ilk. . . .'[121] When he heard that a judge named Moriarty was ill, he asked Nathan–'If he dies, what are we to do? The harpies are already on the wing and are, I doubt not, in telephonic communication with the Nursing Home. . . . I wish I had some patronage in hell.'[122] There were people he would like to send there.

He was scathing about the Honours Lists. The 'shower of knights' that Aberdeen had made before he left Dublin had only added to the dishonour he had brought on the city, while the antics of T. P. Gill angered him. Gill was a former member of the Irish Party who had become Secretary to the Department of Agriculture and Technical Instruction and now wanted to be a Privy Councillor, but he said he would be satisfied if Birrell wrote him a letter saying he had recommended him for the honour and regretted he had not got it. 'This I certainly will not do', Birrell told Nathan, 'as it would be most hypocritical. I don't mind his being a Privy Councillor a bit, but to pretend that I was his backer and to be disappointed that he didn't get it is too much. . . .' Nathan showed him letters he also had received from Gill, and Birrell returned these 'impertinences'. 'You will see', he said, 'from his unseemly interfering intrigues the kind of man he is. I understand he is over here now behind Russell's back trying to cajole the Treasury into some scheme for giving the Board of Agriculture £16,000.'[123]

When he was being pestered about an anticipated vacancy among the Commissioners of Public Works, he again hoped there would be none. There would be bound to be pressuring that he would be happy to avoid, if at all possible. 'I often wonder', he wrote to T. P. Le Fanu who had once been his private secretary, 'whether your peaceful labours, I had almost written slumbers, but I know that would be a calumny, are ever disturbed by the thought that your late Chief is still chained to his Rock and his vitals daily preyed upon by Obscene Birds of both sexes. I dare say your affectionate nature recoils from the thought of such sufferings and you dismiss them from your mind.' And he passed for consideration a letter from 'a lady of fanatical temper, violent speech, but kind heart'.[124]

Mrs. Green sometimes approached Birrell about appointments as this reply about a vacancy among the Commissioners of Charitable Donations and Bequests indicates:

My dear Mrs. Green,

One of the first Acts of a Home Rule Government, after it has once got firmly seated on the saddle, will I hope be to abolish the Board in question. As it is, I am bound by the Balance of Power, the Comity of Generations and by other high-sounding phrases to fill up the vacant place by some trusted representative of the Protestant Episcopal Church; and I am already provided with the names of rival gentlemen, mostly clerical, who are alleged to possess this *sine qua non*, the confidence of the Church. No one has ever suggested to me the possibility of taking anything else into consideration. If you can in confidence give me the name of anybody who, besides this *sine qua non*, also possesses a knowledge of Irish subjects, I shall be only too pleased to see what I can do for him.

But it is too late to save the Board.

Yours very sincerly,
Augustine Birrell[125]

His forecast was wholly wrong; the Board still exists.

When Mahaffy of Trinity consulted him about a vacancy on the Intermediate Education Board Birrell explained that he had to maintain a balance between the different religious interests. 'As I understand the ethics of this appointment,' he said, 'the new Assistant Commissioner must be a Roman, and ought to be a Classical Scholar, just as the next man must be a Protestant. I can assure you I shall not interfere with so nicely-calculated an

arrangement. Any cynical humour I may have ought to be fully
satisfied with things as they are. . . . I have not had time to consider the question at all, but am ready as I always am, to listen to
those in a position to make suggestions, and who may think fit
to do so. When my days are numbered, I believe, in the matter of
jobs, I shall compare favourably with all my forty-one predecessors.[126]

He had to put up the best show he could when some of his
appointments were publicly criticized. On such occasions his wit
was a great standby. In the Commons one day he was asked was
it a fact that a particular gentleman who had been 'pitchforked'
into a job without previous experience was the son of the Irish
Lord Chancellor. He immediately replied: 'I have always heard
that he is the son of the Lord Chancellor and I have no reason to
doubt it.'[127]

In a different context he was told one day by the 'pestilent
Ginnell' that he had not said how a particular prisoner was being
treated. 'The prisoner at the present moment', he replied, 'is, I
believe, receiving closer attention than he has ever received before
in his whole life.'[128]

The Lord Chancellor was responsible for the manufacture of
Irish Justices of the Peace, an obnoxious trade about which Birrell
could be very cynical. All sorts of scallywags, gombeen men and
decayed landlords were recommended, and the R.I.C. were employed to report on them. But what they said rarely mattered.
If a candidate was backed by a member of parliament of the appropriate colour he stood a good chance of being appointed, with
the result that sometimes men who should have been in gaol
went to the bench to dispense justice. The Resident Magistrates
were likewise patronage appointments. Some of these men were
efficient enough, others were downright stupid or were just there
to claim their pay because they or friends of theirs had a pull, or
because they had rendered a political service of some kind.[129]
The Chief Secretary's staff kept long lists of applicants for these
patronage jobs up to date and religiously produced them when an
appointment arose, but they knew in their bones they were

wasting their time because there were other means of picking the winner.

But picking the winner was not always easy for the Chief Secretary, Birrell reminded Lord Aberdeen when, after his retirement, he suggested somebody for a R.M.-ship. There is always, he said, the tiresome but recognized claim of the Royal Irish Constabulary; and now the Incorporated Law Society, whose friends have been a good deal overlooked of late, are pressing for the appointment of a solicitor. I mention these points so that you may understand how difficult it is for me to say anything definite on the subject at present. A Chief Secretary is always in difficulties, and I congratulate you on your release. I have taken a note of what you say about a Knighthood for the Mayor of Waterford. . . .'130

The practice of patronage must have given Birrell pleasure at times all the same, as when he was able to secure a place for W. B. Yeats on the Civil List. The approach to him was made by Edmund Gosse, the literary critic, who urged Yeats to refrain from saying anything while the grant was being considered which might make its award difficult. Yeats, an unsworn I.R.B. man, was looking for an assurance that no political bargain would be involved if he accepted a pension, and that he would be free to join an Irish insurrection if he felt like it! He had been upset when *The Leader* took him, the author of *Caitlin Ni Houlihan*, to task for being present at 'a God Save the King Dinner'. He had been expected to speak at the dinner, but only discovered this when he arrived and found that the Aberdeens were the Guests of Honour. He explained to the readers of *The Leader* that, while he had long ceased to be an active politician, he was anxious to follow with all loyalty the general principles laid down by Parnell and never renounced by any Nationalist party.

A pension was duly approved and Yeats thanked Birrell for 'a service that sets me free from anxiety and from the need of doing less than the best I can'.131 Acknowledging Yeats's letter Birrell assured him that he had had a very easy task. 'The Prime Minister was at least as eager as I was. I know you don't much care about

Dr. Johnson but I always think *his* pension was the money best spent in England during the whole of my beloved eighteenth century. It is well that the twentieth should follow suit.'[132] Patronage of literature was assuredly to Birrell's liking; and, indeed, if the opportunities had presented themselves he might have done as much for the other arts. In the case of music, however, he would have had to take a recommendation on trust, for he was tone deaf and only recognized *God Save the King* when people stood up for it.[133]

Irishmen were not alone in clamouring for preferment. Birrell was barely a month installed 'in doubtful dignity' in the Chief Secretary's lodge when an English friend appealed to him for a favour. 'It is a world full of grievances and wrongs', he replied. 'Sending an English wrong to Ireland is a reversal of the course of Nature. I live up to my neck in them, until I can hardly suppose that anybody anywhere or at any time is treated properly.' Another Englishman asked him to speak to the English Chancellor, formerly Bob Reid, on his behalf. This Birrell found it difficult to do. He explained why. The Lord Chancellor was suspicious of his friends and preferred in matters of patronage to listen to the voice of his enemies. 'A while back "Bob Reid" was the pet of all true Radicals–now, I regret to say, he is abhorred in all such companies who, in their resentment, regret that Haldane, the Imperialist, was not placed upon the woolsack. But, to speak profanely, one lawyer's arse is very like another. . . .'[134]

Despite all his good intentions Birrell appears to have strayed from the straight and narrow path by arranging for the transfer to a better position of one of his stepsons who was a civil servant. For doing this he was accused in Parliament of 'gross nepotism'. He escaped from his embarrassment, however, with an evasive reply, and as he sank into his seat he whispered to a colleague: 'I'll never marry a widow again.'

CHAPTER V
The Unexpected Happens
1916

As 1916 opened Birrell apologized to his Under-Secretary for not taking the knock for some failing that was attributed to Nathan in the Press. 'It is a great shame and I feel a sneak but after all', he said, 'it is because you are known to be so masterful, and I so meek that nobody can believe that I ever do anything on my own account.' Nathan had been away from Dublin—now he was safe back in Castle Doleful, Birrell noted, and was at least as well off as he was in Castle Dump. 'Courage', he cried, 'for although the devil is not dead, as the editor of the *Spectator* and silly sentimentalists may have half believed, he is badly wounded both in the heel and in the head—and, tho' certain to recover, will limp worse than ever till the time comes to lock him up for a thousand years.' At a very agreeable dinner at No. 10 Downing Street he gathered that things were perhaps a little easier, but he could not believe that the Prime Minister's personal position was not weakened. He had wounded his best friends, beyond cure or redemption. The country might approve of what he had done, but he was left surrounded by men who, whilst they envied his Parliamentary gifts, had no respect for his force of character, and some of them would chuck him at the earliest opportunity.[1]

Conscription, with Ireland excluded, was legalized in January, and Birrell and Redmond renewed their efforts at voluntary recruiting in the campaign Wimborne, the Lord Lieutenant, was leading. The Irish regiments were badly in need of reinforcements. Those which had served in France had been sorely depleted, while, before the British withdrawal from the Dardanelles, the 10th (Irish) division, for whose ultimate safety Birrell had been praying daily[2] had been slaughtered by the Turks. But the supply of recruits from Nationalist Ireland was drying up, and A. P. Magill, Birrell's private secretary, told Nathan early in January that there would be a good deal of crowing in the North over the fact that Ulster's contribution was greater than the three other provinces put together. Birrell nevertheless thought they would have to give the figures,[3] and they did.

Wimborne provided relaxation from the strains and stresses of his recruiting campaign, and the form this sometimes took was graphically recorded by Lady Cynthia Asquith. Towards the end of January 1916, she was staying in the Viceregal Lodge with a party which included Birrell 'looking like a mellow old Thackeray' and which was joined for dinner one night by 'that famous charmer, Sir Matthew Nathan'. Birrell, very happy and dissipated, as she thought, flirted away with all the ladies, and showed, in a very amusing but rather coarse conversation about the English kings to which he contributed, that he was wonderfully well up in the statistics of royal bastards. He gave an imitation of King George's horror when he appealed to him to allow Lady Headfort, a most respectable chorus-girl peeress, to come to court: 'Rosie *Boote*, Rosie Boote come to my court!' He also gave an example of what Cynthia called the frivolity of his mind when asked by Wimborne if he would visit a shell factory with him the next day: 'Shells,' he asked, 'shells . . . what shells?' He was thinking, she thought, of the seashore.

One night when the Wimbornes had withdrawn, some of the guests produced *The Rape of the Lock*, in the course of which Cynthia had the audacity to sever a lovely white lock from 'dear Birrell's' head. She and Lady Gwendoline Churchill then jokingly competed for the Chief Secretary's 'nimble affections'. Birrell was 'most amusing and amused'.[4]

It was from this skittish atmosphere that Birrell went to Galway with the Lord Lieutenant and Redmond for a recruiting conference. They travelled by special train and were met on arrival by a guard of honour provided by the National Volunteers and as there was a problem of dual loyalties to be faced, there were two bands, one of which, belonging to the Industrial School, played 'God Save the King', and the other, the National Volunteer band, 'God Save Ireland'. The town was handsomely decorated with flags and bunting, and outside the Town Hall, where the conference and an overflow meeting were held, a large illuminated scroll carried the prayer 'God Save Ireland from the Huns'.

The Lord Lieutenant presented himself in his double capacity as the representative of the Crown and Director of Recruiting for Ireland. He tried to enliven a dull speech by saying that they were opposed by a ruthless and remorseless foe who did not hesitate to violate churches and non-combatants. The recent aerial activities of the Germans should remind them that even the town of Galway was not beyond the possible radius of such depredations. He knew from observation that Limerick was denuded of its cornerboys, and that the quays of Waterford were free of the usual casual people. He made no effort to describe his Galway audience, but Birrell had them sized up as we shall see.

Redmond's main effort in his speech was to remove an impression that was being created that, because conscription in Ireland was found to be unsuitable and unnecessary, Ireland was shirking her duty (cries of 'No, No.'). Such an impression would be a false one, he said, and a cruel one, and would be a deadly injury to the future interests of Ireland. The creation of the army that Ireland had sent to the war carried with it the obligation of maintaining it. It would be particularly humiliating and disgraceful if Ireland deserted her sons in the trenches. It would mean, and he assured his listeners that he spoke with every sense of responsibility and seriousness, the death-knell of all their hopes and aspirations and ambitions for the future of their country.

In a whimsical letter written a little later, Birrell described the meeting. 'It was a really huge assemblage', he said, 'and had the cause been really popular, and had Redmond been a Dan O'Connell, they should have sworn in lusty recruits by the thousand. 'But', he said, 'the cause was not popular but only interesting, and the Leader of the Nationalist Party was not a great Dan but only a plucky fellow in an odd situation. It was a curious thing to watch – all the outward signs and tokens of a friendly crowd, but the soul was not there, and how should it be? The folk who love fighting were gone or going, for the love of fighting and the lure of pay, and as for the rest, they looked on, half amused. . . . Redmond was very good and most emphatic but not inspiring, and far too long . . . he lugged in a tirade about the R.I.C. which he had better omitted. It made me rather cross and spoiled the fine unimpeded flow of my oratory.'⁵ Birrell's speech was both brief and unsubstantial.

He got away alone at 5 o'clock, and had a solitary run along the roads to Recess where he found Sir Henry Robinson and was introduced to a gombeen man named Joyce who was worrying how long the war would last, although if the truth were known he was probably making a good thing out of it. Birrell suggested two years. Joyce was appalled. 'Begor' sir,' said he, 'd'ye think we'll ever be able to sthick it?' It was a lovely day, with occasional drenching showers. Some of the hills were glistening with snow, and the bogs were a glorious red. Birrell loved it all. 'Altogether', he wrote, 'the West still tugs at my heart harder than war.'⁶ He hated going back to London, and on the way he encountered an old enemy in one of his moods. 'I had a terrible rolling on the sea', he told Nathan, 'and was nearly killed by my own bag being hurled on the bed on which I lay. But rolling no longer moves me; perhaps if I remained where I am another nine years (Oh horrible!) pitching would leave me equally unmoved. I am now cut in two by lumbago and can hardly crawl. It is painful, without being mortal. Therefore, its misery is unrelieved..⁷

It was becoming harder every day to get recruits, and Redmond had already pressed the Irish Executive to part with some hundreds of the Royal Irish Constabulary who, he believed, could well be spared from the peaceful Irish countryside. Kitchener strongly supported this view. 'I hadn't realized (as I might have)', Birrell told Nathan, 'that both these Pundits would lead a heavy assault upon me on the subject of the R.I.C. Lord Kitchener exhibited an animation to which I was a stranger and put the question–how many can you spare now? Redmond would have it (knowing very little about it) that 2,000 could go–nobody would miss them. The mice all agree the cats may go to the Front.'⁸ The result of the pow-wow apparently was that 1,000 men might be spared if they could be persuaded by Kitchener to go, but Birrell told Redmond that that was not the time to underrate the services of the police, or to draw a rosy picture of the circumstances of Ireland. They might want the police sooner than they expected. It would be another matter if the conscription issue was done with for all time, but this could not be presumed. The risk of conscription would remain so long as the war lasted. Meanwhile, there were close on 14,000 Irish Volunteers in the country, and though many of them were men of straw and wind, wherever they were organized they constituted a danger to Dublin Castle and the Government. He did not know what guns they had, some few thousand perhaps, but–and this was an unpleasant hint to Redmond–they were always trying to coax or steal guns from the far bigger number of National Volunteers who were doing next to nothing.[9]

To get as accurate an indication as they could of the number of Irish Volunteers available for mobilization, the police on St. Patrick's Day, 1916, carefully counted those who turned out on parade in response to an order from Volunteer Headquarters. The number was 4,555, of whom only 1,817 were armed, half with rifles and half with shotguns; and the attitude of the spectators to them was not encouraging.[10]

If Birrell was convinced that the National Volunteers were doing nothing, that was also how the military felt about Birrell and Nathan. Lord French, no longer in charge of the operations on the Continent, spoke to Birrell on the subject. 'O Lucifer, son of the morning, how art thou fallen!' was Birrell's first observation. He told Nathan that French showed him a letter from Friend who wanted the Irish Volunteers proclaimed and their meetings forbidden. 'We mustn't look to that quarter for inspiration, good or bad,' he said. 'Indeed I don't know where we can look for any save into our own sad hearts.'[11] To proclaim the Irish Volunteers as an illegal body and put them down by force would be a reckless and foolish act, and would promote disloyalty to a prodigious extent. Loyalty in Ireland was a plant of slow growth and the soil was still uncongenial, but the plant was growing. He did not in any event much fear that these Volunteers would resort to open rebellion. 'I am more alive', he said, 'to the chances of a dynamite explosion in the Castle or elsewhere, than to anything of a real turnout of forces. I suppose examination is made of the premises.'[12] He saw point in having as strong a military force as possible in the circumstances of the time to support the police in dealing with any contingency, but he would not allow the idea of open rebellion to enter his mind. There was, however, a heavy responsibility on Nathan and himself, he added, to be alert and watchful, and to discover as best they could what was going on, but that called for secret information, which seemed to be beyond them.[13]

On the surface there was enough going on to worry any Chief Secretary. The R.I.C. reports indicated that certain parts of Ireland were very disturbed and that insurrection had been openly suggested in the public press. On St. Patrick's Day, the Irish Volunteers held up the centre of Dublin for hours on end for a parade with arms before their President and Chief of Staff, MacNeill. Three days later, several police were injured in a shooting affair in Tullamore. How to deal with this sort of situation while one's government was on the rocks and at the same time to get recruits for the forces was a baffling business. Birrell could only think of having a show of *real* soldiers, with glittering bayonets and bands, marching through the streets of Dublin. 'Let the flatulent cowards see the Tiger's teeth,' he said.[14] But there were no soldiers available for demonstrations of this kind.

With recruiting at a low ebb Kitchener called a conference at the War Office, but when Redmond heard that conscription for Ireland was on the agenda he was furious and refused to attend. He was as anxious as ever, however, to encourage voluntary enlistment and complained that places like Fermoy were crowded, not with soldiers going to the Front, but with soldiers who had returned wounded from the Front. Birrell agreed that this was a most depressing sight. 'Recruiting in Ireland is dogged with difficulties,' he admitted. 'I wonder it goes on at all. I will always stick to it: Ireland has done magnificently.'[15]

The position of his own sons with regard to war service was a serious embarrassment to a Cabinet Minister who was actively urging other people's sons to go out and fight. Tony, the younger, was retarded while Frankie was a conscientious objector and a vegetarian. 'I have had trouble with the War Office who perpetually summon my son of unsound mind to the colours,' he told Nathan. 'This time they have done it twice after assurances that it would never be done again. My other son of unsound opinions is to have his case examined on Monday at the Town Hall, Chelsea.'[16] Frankie had no intention of joining up. He loved the French peasants among whom he was working, preferring them very much to his own countrymen, and his father thought that he would be exempted so long as he remained in France.[17] He could claim defective eyesight, but by this time they were accepting blind men quite readily, 'tho', as Birrell said, 'when it comes to the actual point they will reject them, and so he will lose his job in France and waste three or four months of valuable time, for no one of military age is now allowed to leave this land of Freedom, which is quite right but inconvenient in his case. . . .'[18] 'It was all very vexing and galling', he told Nathan, 'and I'm glad their mother is dead, which is the same as saying I wish I was dead too, but if I had been, my younger son would by this time have been in an asylum.'[19]

The military, with their special responsibilities under the Defence of the Realm Act, could not get away from the importance of anything offensive in print while Birrell, the literary man, was hard to persuade that there was anything of great concern in such flagrant nonsense. 'Of course the article is seditious,' he said. 'No defence can be made for it, but as I read it, it is far more likely to make a timid reader turn pale than to cause a bold one to turn out to be shot down, as is the fate held out in prospect for him. I don't believe such publications are dangerous, but they are scandalous, when read as they mostly are by Unionists and loyalists, who after reading them and marking them, send them on to me at my private address, with such epithets as 'coward' and 'traitor' scribbled in the margin. I am sorry to see good citizens reduced to such a state of mind; and undoubtedly it does do harm, if a large section of feeble-minded but honest men and women are induced to despise the executive.'[19a]

Nevertheless he was constrained, against his better judgment, to agree to suppressing more of the Sinn Fein papers. He also agreed reluctantly with a decision to deport a group of Irish Volunteer organizers, in order to placate the Unionists who had been pressing unceasingly for more energetic action in this direction. These decisions alarmed the Nationalists and the tension in the country was seriously increased by a spate of anti-deportation meetings, one of which in Dublin ended in an ugly scuffle with the police and the free firing of revolver shots.[20] Birrell remained uneasy about the deportations. 'The whole procedure is clumsy in the extreme', he wrote, 'and I confess I don't much fancy these men roaming about their areas in England, until disguised as women and travelling with men as their wives, they creep back again to Ireland. But we have no choice.'[21]

All his sympathy was with the Nationalists. They had been uniformly and consistently loyal since the beginning of the war, and, by reducing their criticisms to a minimum, had surrendered a traditionally popular field to the Sinn Feiners. The Irish Unionists had not shown anything like the same consideration, even to the Coalition Government. They were always making trouble. Even now an ugly irritant of theirs, which Birrell had hoped was finished and done with, reappeared. Something had gone wrong with the placing of Campbell in the judgeship that had been earmarked for him in England; he had become restless, and his party were insisting on a job being found for him at home. Nothing could be done about this while Asquith was away in Rome propping up the Italian alliance, but Birrell saw much trouble ahead. He was sick and tired of these perpetual situations of crisis inside the Cabinet, and was coming to the conclusion that a change of government might benefit Ireland - 'that mysterious island' as he called it. Redmond, he could see, agreed with him. The Nationalists would regain freedom of speech and action, and the new government would be mighty civil.[22]

THE ULSTER KING-AT-ARMS.

"THE SINCEREST FLATTERY."

GENERAL JOHN REDMOND. "ULSTER KING-AT-ARMS, IS UT? WE'LL BE AFTHER SHOWIN' 'EM WHAT THE *OTHER* THREE PROVINCES CAN DO!"

[See *Punch*, May 6, 1914.]

National Library of Ireland

WANTED—A ST. PATRICK.

St. Augustine Birrell. "I'M AFRAID I'M NOT SO SMART AS MY BROTHER-SAINT AT DEALING WITH THIS KIND OF THING. I'M APT TO TAKE REPTILES TOO LIGHTLY."

2

By the end of the first week in April the political situation seemed a little easier with the return of Asquith 'from the whore of Babylon' but some timorous or mischief-loving spirits were forecasting the collapse of the Coalition. It was in this atmosphere that Birrell told Nathan that he must prepare to have Campbell in the Castle as Attorney-General; the Prime Minister could not get out of it or postpone it any longer. He had prepared Redmond and Dillon for the event which 'fortunately, perhaps, occurs at a time when the whole crew may take to the boats . . .' over the issue of general compulsory military service which Carson was advocating. In practice Campbell might be a useful man around the Castle as Nathan thought, but Birrell reminded Nathan that Campbell had inherited a Tory tradition of his office which was very different from theirs and would have to be handled gently.

The Prime Minister was to all appearances firm as a rock, and betting was in favour of the continuance of the Coalition, but, in view of the Campbell business, Birrell wondered how the Irish Nationalists could bring themselves to support the Government when Carson's motion was debated, but he thought they would have to, as conscription was the pretended issue. Blood was bad, however. Redmond was bitterly sore, and Dillon had started to avoid Birrell like the plague. For the moment the Prime Minister was the Top Dog, but over what body was he to preside–that was the question. 'Damn all their politics,' Birrell cried.[23]

The Easter holidays were coming along and Birrell hoped to spend them in Ireland with Frankie, Tony and Tony's nurse, Miss Tattersall. They relied on Nathan to let them know if the Channel was safe from German submarines. Birrell had no wish to remain in London. In Achill he would breathe easier than in what he called 'this hotbed of dishonourable intrigue'. There were many currents stirring, the most sinister of them being a campaign to get rid of the Prime Minister in which Lloyd George was deeply involved. The Coalition had been saved for the time being by the prospect of a compromise, although that, he thought, was hardly the word. This might serve, in a secret session of parliament, to draw off the frontal attack of the Carson gang, although the cabals would begin again at once.

In the meantime he told Nathan that his relations with Redmond and Dillon were broken off. Dillon had returned to Ireland, but Redmond remained in London and would probably seek to recover his lost authority by a violent speech when the House of Commons reassembled. He was furious about Campbell and regarded his appointment as a personal affront by the Prime Minister. It was as much as to say: 'Who wants you?' Dillon in Ireland would make things lively. The pair of them would sooner abuse the Tories than the Liberals, but abuse somebody they must. Their confidence in Asquith was rudely shaken while Lloyd George was 'the accursed thing'. If they got any comfort from their colloquy with Labour and the Radical malcontents they would show fight immediately.

The prospect was not pleasing, and Birrell, unable to predict his movements, called off his Irish holiday, but Tony and Miss Tattersall travelled across. He knew that Wimborne had planned to go to Belfast on Easter Monday but his reception there would not be noticeably warm. 'To woo these brutes is impossible. They believe the war is a Protestant war and yet are angry with the Catholic Bishop of Limerick who says it is not a Catholic war.' 'Why', queried Birrell, 'should the Catholics take part in a Protestant war on the Protestant side?'[24]

So it was that when Easter Sunday came he found himself, not in Achill, but in St. James's Street, London, and consoling himself with a book he had come across 'about the Chevalier de Boufflers and his enchanting lady-mistress and wife'.[25]* This helped him to forget the political gloom. While thus engaged strange things were happening on the south-west coast of Ireland. On the morning of Good Friday, a police patrol had captured a boat which had been put ashore from a German submarine with three men on board. One of the men had been arrested, and with him had been

* Possibly *The Chevalier de Boufflers: A Romance of the French Revolution*, by Nesta Helen Webster (John Murray, London, 1916).

found three Mauser pistols, a thousand rounds of ammunition, and some maps and papers, all in German. Also, in the same area, the Navy had stopped a vessel disguised as a Norwegian and taken it into Queenstown where, at the entrance to the harbour, it had hoisted the German colours and scuttled itself. Nineteen German sailors and three officers had been rescued, but the ship's cargo of guns was at the bottom of the sea.

Nathan passed this news by telegraph and letter to Birrell, and he, in one of his understatements, commented that all of this was most encouraging, particularly if Roger Casement was the prisoner. It was indeed Casement; and the circumstances of his arrival appeared to confirm a story Nathan had indirectly heard some time previously of a projected landing of arms and a rising fixed for Easter. The Inspector-General of the R.I.C. whom he had consulted at the time, shared his doubt as to whether there was any foundation for the story. Nevertheless, for safety's sake the County Inspectors and the Chief Commissioner of the Dublin Police were put on their guard, with the happy result that the first part of whatever plan existed had been frustrated. The story Nathan heard had come to General Friend from Brigadier-General Stafford who was in charge of the Queenstown defences, and he had heard it from Admiral Bayly at Queenstown. The source and extent of the information were withheld, in order to protect British Naval Intelligence. The result was that a full month's warning of what was on foot was disregarded.[26]

During the whole of the week before Easter there had been a marked increase in tension. A general mobilization and march out by the Irish Volunteers, to take place on Easter Sunday, was widely publicized, and gave rise to disquieting rumours that made Dillon think that the Irish-American Clan-na-Gael were planning some devilish business. A threatened attack on Dublin Castle and other tip-offs kept the police busy, while a Sinn Fein alderman added to the excitement by reading out to the Dublin Corporation what was described as a decipher of an official Castle document that gave details of an Order that General Friend was supposed to have signed, for large-scale raids on buildings in the city, as part of a plan for disarming the Volunteers. An official denial that any such document existed was issued, but in the Sinn Fein camp the genuineness of the document was accepted, and it was believed that it revealed the Government's intention of provoking armed resistance and deliberately causing bloodshed. Despite all this Nathan, on Easter Saturday, repeated that he saw no indications of a rising. In any case the events on the south-west coast had revolutionized the situation. The Sinn Feiners would have been so dismayed that the menace of a rising could be considered at an end. It had probably been contingent on the successful landing of the arms and on the reappearance of Casement who was believed to be the key man in the whole business. This was what Nathan and Wimborne thought when they took stock together on Easter Saturday, and their reasoning seemed to be confirmed when, on Easter Sunday morning, they read in the *Sunday Independent* that MacNeill, the President of the Irish Volunteers, had called off the mobilization fixed for that day.

This was an hour of triumph for Birrell. His policy of cool, calm calculation, his refusal to be stampeded by police and military chiefs and by Unionist leaders, had been crowned with success. He had believed, as he once said, in letting the Sinn Fein pig cut its own throat. It had now obligingly done so. He chortled gleefully over Casement's, 'the lunatic traitor's', ridiculous effort. He had always believed that there was a Casement movement among the Irish separatists; he thought that perhaps Casement, like Henry the Eighth's bastard son, Thomas Stuckley, might have meditated an Irish Rebellion for the purpose of putting some unworthy person on the dangerous and worthless throne of Ireland. The futility of any such idea was now apparent, and he got great comfort from pondering over the discomfiture of the Irish Volunteers as they faced their mobilization and march-out. 'I think you may rely upon my being in Dublin by the end of the week'; he told Nathan, 'whatever happens I must come.' He kept this promise but in circumstances he had not foreseen.

There remained the question of taking action against the Sinn Feiners, now that a definite connection between them and the

King's enemies had been established. Wimborne wanted some-thing done right away, but Nathan was loath to move without Birrell's authority. The whole of Easter Sunday, therefore, passed in conference with the military and the police but by the end of the day Nathan had agreed that the leaders should be arrested and interned in England. It was also generally agreed that the follow-ing day, Easter Monday, would be a bad day to take action with the city full of volunteers and holiday-makers; and in any event a list of the leaders to be arrested had to be prepared and Nathan wanted to consult his Chief. He did so by cipher telegram which, however, did not reach Birrell till Easter Monday morning.

That was the fatal morning, for as Nathan awaited Birrell's fiat and prepared with Major Price, the Army Intelligence Officer, the list of men to be arrested, the Castle gate below his office was stormed, the policeman on duty shot dead and the military guard overwhelmed. Simultaneously a number of important buildings in Dublin, including the General Post Office, were seized by Irish Volunteers and the Irish Citizen Army, and an Irish Republic declared. The rising was 'on' after all. The Pig was still alive.

Nathan's telegram reached Birrell a little after 12 noon, and he sent it over to Downing Street to be deciphered, as he had not the code. He then wired his agreement with its proposals, and went over to the Home Office and saw Sir Edward Troup, the Per-manent Secretary, and Basil Thompson of Scotland Yard who had the Casement case in hand. He was scarcely back in the Irish Office when in came Lord French with the news of the rising. This was a bitter moment; the shock of the news was bad enough, but to receive it from the military whose warnings he had so fre-quently disregarded made it doubly galling. However, he com-posed himself and hurried off a message to Redmond at his London residence. Then he tried to piece together the bits of information he had received in recent days—a cable from the British Ambassador in Washington about plans for gun-running in Ireland that had been found by the American Secret Service in a raid on a German Office in New York, and the circumstances surrounding the arrest of Casement in Kerry. The telephone to

Dublin was not working but the telegraph was, and by this means he asked Nathan whether what had happened was a fit of tantrums after failure to effect a landing of the arms, or whether this was really the rising that had been talked about. He thought, in any event, that the forces available in Ireland, military and police, would be sufficient to quell the outbreak but, if not, French would send the necessary assistance. Meanwhile, he asked for a note so that he could deal with the 'I told you so' howl he expected in Parliament. He would also have to explain next day to the Prime Minister what had happened. Asquith had been out of town and only heard of the outbreak when he got back on Easter Monday night. To the man who gave him the news he had said, 'Well, that's something' and went off to bed,[27] but he may not have slept too well.

The House of Commons was decidedly uneasy at Question Time on the Tuesday and Wednesday of Easter week, and Birrell, whose information was limited, was glad to get over to Dublin to find out at first hand what precisely had gone wrong and what remained to be done to restore order. He landed from the destroyer *Dove* at Custom House Wharf at 6 o'clock on Thursday morning, and made his way to the Viceregal Lodge to the accompaniment of firing from both sides of the Liffey. There he met Wimborne and General Friend. Next day he went down to the Castle and saw Nathan, who, though the military were in control, had been doing whatever he could to help. He had not, however, left the Castle since Easter Monday morning. By this time the Irish Executive was in possession of the Cabinet's direction to proclaim martial law over the whole of Ireland, and to place themselves at the disposal of General Sir John Maxwell, who was being sent over from London with plenary powers.

Birrell wrote a sequence of letters to the Prime Minister describing what he found in Dublin, the buildings held by the rebels, the elusive snipers, the necessity of employing artillery to assault the main position in the General Post Office, and the problem of food for the population. But the rebellion, which had almost entirely been confined to Dublin, was already on the point of collapse, and he spoke disparagingly of it. It was little more than a street row, or a series of affairs like that in Sydney Street in London where a few armed gangsters had held the police and the Home Secretary, Winston Churchill, at bay for days on end. It was not, he insisted, an Irish Rebellion and it would be a pity if *ex post facto* it became one, and was added to the long and melancholy list. Yet it showed how deep in Irish hearts lay the passion for insurrection. It was staged, he said, by a small combination of the old physical force party, one or two labour men like James Connolly, plus an idle crowd that included some young fools from the National University which he had himself fathered on the Irish people. It called for immediate salutary punishment. A short shrift should be given to the leaders, both fighting men and stump orators. The others might be sent to the trenches. The disarmament of the country would also have to be attempted.

He was understandably thoroughly depressed, but his letters to the Prime Minister* were illumined nevertheless by typical flashes of wit. He described the Four Courts, which the rebels had taken, as the place that contained the Great Seal and all the historical records of Ireland since the day Henry the Second was foolish enough to do what the Romans never did, cross the Irish Channel. That Channel! And he summarized a lot of history when he said that 'nobody can govern Ireland from England save in a state of siege'.

3

In his first letter he mentioned his own position. He felt smashed to pieces as a result of 'a supreme act of criminal folly'. 'All this staggers me,' he said. 'The Thing that has happened swallows up the things that might have happened had I otherwise acted.' He wanted Asquith to tell him what he wished him to do in the general interest of the country. He was not in the least frightened of the House of Commons and could put up a good fight for himself, but he knew the general verdict would be adverse and

* These are set out at length in the author's *Dublin Castle and the 1916 Rising*.

that he could not go on. He reminded Asquith that months before he had advised him to wield the pole-axe.

Asquith read into these letters that Birrell was tendering his resignation and this he accepted 'with infinite regret'. The words were no formality. Between these two men relations were unusually intimate, and this was never more apparent than when Birrell, having crossed the Irish Sea for the last time, and in the gun-boat that had bombarded Connolly's Liberty Hall, presented himself to the Prime Minister in his room in the House of Commons. The leave-taking was painful but Lady Cynthia Asquith saw Birrell's political sun setting in a sky of soppy affection.[28] Birrell, in any event, was so upset that he could not remember afterwards what words were spoken; the Prime Minister, jingling some coins in his pocket, just stood at the window and wept. There was another moving scene in the House of Commons when Birrell came to announce his resignation there. An Irish reporter saw 'an aged and broken figure rising from a place behind the Treasury Bench, wringing his hands and with tears in his eyes'[29] whom the 'pestilent Ginnell' tried at first to prevent from being heard. 'The statement he's going to make isn't worth a snap of the finger'; Ginnell cried, 'the condition of Ireland is the important matter.' But then relenting, 'Give him a chance,' he said, 'we've got rid of him at last.'[30]

Birrell began a repetitive speech by saying that what he had seen and heard during the previous five days would never fade from his memory. He had made an untrue estimate of the Sinn Fein movement in that, while recognizing the dangers that might result from such obvious disloyalty, he had not foreseen a disturbance of the kind that had occurred. As soon as ever the war broke out with Germany he took it to be his supreme task to maintain in Ireland and in the face of Europe the picture of an unbroken unanimity. He thought of nothing else, he cared for nothing else, he wished for nothing else. He was well aware of the difficulties of the situation. He knew Ireland well enough to know that there was grave cause for anxiety. The ice was thin, yet he considered it to be his duty to run ever greater risk to maintain the appearance of a united country. In that hope and aim he had been gallantly assisted by John Redmond. He had been urged by many persons to suppress the Sinn Fein movement wherever they found it, and to take away from it its arms; and although up to the last moment, no proof was forthcoming that they were in hostile association with the enemy, it had been said to him that that ought to be done. But if it had been done, what would have been the consequences? For one thing, unanimity would not have been preserved as it still was, for he insisted that this was no Irish rebellion, and he hoped that it would never, in the minds and memories of the Irish people, be associated with their past rebelions, or become a landmark in their history. The disturbance, as he called it, would be put down, he prayed, with success and courage, and yet with humanity displayed towards the dupes, the rank and file, who had been led astray by their leaders. . . . 'When yesterday morning I drove down from the Phoenix Park through all the familiar streets of Dublin and . . . viewed the smoking ruins of a great portion of Sackville Street, when I was surrounded by my own ruins in my own mind and thought, and all the hopes and aspirations and work I have done during the past nine years, one ray of comfort was graciously permitted to reach my heart, and that was that this was no Irish rebellion, that Irish soldiers are still earning for themselves glory in all the fields of war, that evidence is already forthcoming that over these ashes hands may be shaken and much may be done, that new bonds of union may be forged, and that there may be found new sources of strength and of prosperity for that country. I at all events have done what I could for her, and although I end my connexion with her . . . in this melancholy manner to-day I can assure the House . . . that I still hope some measure of good may come out of this great evil.'

Asquith, in a few words, told the House of his ten years of close and intimate association with Birrell and said that in the whole of his public life there had been no personal loss he more acutely felt, or more greatly deplored. He was followed by Redmond, and then by Carson who spoke in a kindly way of Birrell, a man who on all occasions did his best. Redmond's speech was remarkable. The whole of 'the incident in Ireland' had been to him a misery and a heartbreak and one of the immediate consequences had been the withdrawal of Birrell. 'Deeply', he said, 'I sorrow and grieve at the severance . . . I have been for several years closely associated with him, and so have my colleagues, and we all believe that during his tenure of office he has been animated by a single-minded devotion to what he regarded as the highest interests of the country that he went to govern. We believe that he grew to love Ireland and that he has honestly done his best for her interests. He has taken blame this afternoon, and he has been widely blamed in this country already, because he underrated the dangerous situation which confronted him. Of course I had no responsibility of the same kind as he, but I do feel, and I think it is only just that I should say it, that I have incurred some share of the blame which he has laid at his own door, because I entirely agreed with his view that the danger of an outbreak of this kind was not a real one, and in my conversations with him I have expressed that view, and for all I know, what I have said to him influenced him in his conduct and in his management of Irish affairs. Therefore, I think it is only just on my part that I should to that extent share the blame which he lays upon his own shoulders. Mr. Birrell leaves Ireland under melancholy circumstances, but he has some consolations. During his term of office he has conferred some great and imperishable benefits upon Ireland. His name will always be honourably associated in the minds of all classes of the Irish people with the creation of the National University, and with all he has done for the educational interests of the country, and I can assure him that he takes with him into his retirement . . . the respect, the good-will . . . and the affection of large masses of the Irish people. . . .'[31]

A few days later, feeling that he had gone too far, Redmond availed of another debate to say that Dublin Castle had never consulted him as to policy. He had not hesitated to express a strong view to them as to how they should deal with seditious newspapers and with prosecutions but they had never given him any information, bad or good, about the state of the country. From first to last he had never seen a single confidential report from the police or from any other source. He knew nothing whatever about the Government's secret information. Commenting on this statement, Stephen Gwynn, one of Redmond's associates, says that it is fair to add that Nathan was in communication from time to time with other members of the party, who were of course in touch with Redmond.[31a] The present book, and the author's *Dublin Castle and the 1916 Rising* show the nature and extent of this communication.

The King postponed bidding farewell to Birrell apparently because of the delay in appointing a successor, but when he was called to the Palace Birrell did not welcome the prospect. 'It will not be a very gushful occasion', he said.[32]

Birrell explained to his sister-in-law, Maida Mirrielees, that his critics were those who had urged him to do the obvious, namely to take repressive action against the Sinn Feiners, and who were now saying after the rebellion 'we told you so'. His reply was that he had tried his hardest to avoid the shedding of Irish blood, in Ireland, during the war which would have been the outcome of repressive action, and had failed. 'It is always safer', he pointed out, 'to do the obvious, because whatever happens you cannot be very much blamed, whereas if you refrain from the obvious, and things don't go well, you are defenceless. The humdrum is the safest and easiest in all human affairs. That good may somehow come out of it all must be our hope, but it is dark at present.'[32] To another friend he explained how he had sought to use the passing Irish unity on the issue of the war to help recruiting for the forces. 'As soon as this terrific war broke out all my feelings towards Ireland assumed one shape and character. I thought of nothing else but this one thing. How can I, for the first time in our long Irish connexion secure that Ireland should be on our side, and provide willingly and under democratic conditions, hundreds of thousands of fighting Irishmen living in England, Scotland and the Dominions to man our requirements and supply our regiments to sustain the reputation of Great Britain, Ireland and the Empire.'[33] The only 'savage satisfaction' he had was that his wife was dead before the Rebellion happened. 'She would have felt the *boule-versement* of our hopes even more keenly than I did, and might have been more angry than I ever could be about some of the incidents connected with it, for she was not only a devoted wife but a high-spirited woman.'[34]

Despite the sudden and overwhelming disaster he managed to keep his balance and even his sense of humour. He had critics on all sides, but his family and friends rallied to him and this was a consolation. 'It was a nasty knock which had to be endured some-how,' he told Ivy Tennyson.[35] 'I am inundated with letters, which I read grimly, but not without emotion. Considering how little I have done for anybody, the number of my friends amaze me. Real friends too.' And to Maida Mirrielees he wrote, 'As I have always found it comparatively easy to put up with the downfall of others, it would be scandalous if I could not bear my own burden of sorrow, unpopularity and blame. As the Spaniards say in the hour of discomfiture, "I have tumbled off my donkey". That I most certainly have in the eyes of all men.'[36] He went to Spain for a holiday, and told T. P. O'Connor that while there was no brightness on his horizon he was trying to find some in Don Quixote which he hoped to be able to read in the original before he died.[37]

He was on this holiday and feeling as far away from the guns almost as if he were in Achill Island when he was horrified to learn by telegram from London that Lord Kitchener and his suite had been lost when the H.M.S. *Hampshire* on which they were travel-ling to Russia was mined off Orkney. 'It seemed incredible but 'tis confirmed,' he told Magill. 'It made me very sad and wretched tho' I had no sentiment for the man, and don't suppose it will affect the vital issue.' Magill had been called back to the Irish Land Commission and Birrell hoped he would first have a holiday 'to chew the cud of sweet and bitter remembrance and mark the entrance upon a new epoch in your own and Irish history. It has been a melancholy ending of a once cheerful song and though personally now I am out of the bog on to the dull high road, I wonder how I endured the quagmire and insincerity of the whole position. I still am sorry for my *entourage* that they should have fallen with me and retired without letters after their names.' He relied upon Magill to let him have an early copy of the report of the Commission of Enquiry into the causes of the Rebellion. 'It will fall flat', he said. 'The mess of the Cabinet without me is almost as bad as if I were still a member of it.' He was agitated and tried to conceal it but Ireland, as he said, was an *un*lucky bag. Whatever you pulled out was sure to be disagreeable.'[38]

In the circumstances it comes as no surprise to read of a simple entry in his diary: 'Heart failure. Dec. 31, 1916 to March, 1917.'

Some months later, however, he was claiming that Ireland had passed completely out of his life, though not from his memory. 'From what I hear casually', he told T. P. Le Fanu, a former private secretary, 'the Irish Question is not yet settled, though the Prime Minister is thinking about it a great deal. God save Ireland.'[39] The prayer may have been directed to saving Ireland from Lloyd George who, by the end of 1916, had 'dished' Asquith and taken over the direction of the Coalition Government. For Asquith, as always, Birrell's sympathy was unbounded. 'You may be sure that it did hurt me when I fell off my donkey,' he said, 'it must have hurt Asquith more when he fell off his elephant.'[40]

Nathan resigned with Birrell. Since they had been thrown together Birrell had taken greatly to his Under Secretary, and in the hour of their common distress he told him that 'it was better to sink with some people than to go to the House of Lords with others'. So they sank together, though Nathan, unlike Birrell, rose again. But there was no question at that time of either of them being offered a peerage.

Wimborne was also recalled, but he was allowed to return to Dublin in the following August. It was pointed out to Asquith that a Chief Secretary was nominally appointed by the hand of the Lord Lieutenant; difficulty might, therefore, arise if Wimborne disappeared from office without making an appointment.[41] But this was a mere incidental. Asquith had wanted to clear out the whole Irish Government, and it was only gradually that he recognized that Wimborne's case was different from that of Birrell and Nathan.

Easter Week had been an exciting time in the Viceregal Lodge. On the Monday morning Wimborne, his wife and entourage had been about to leave for Belfast when they were told of the Rising. The motors were actually at the door to take them to the special train which was to stop at Drogheda for an Address, with National Volunteers providing a Guard of Honour. The Lodge was practically unguarded, and a defence, based on a sunken fence that curved round the building, had to be improvised. There was no real danger from the insurgents, however, but some excited soldiers who did not know where they were or what the Lodge was, created a general scare by firing intermittently and landed a shrapnel shell in the garden. In this embattled situation, and with food getting scarce, the Aides put on plain clothes and went into Dublin where they looted a barrow and wheeled it along gathering up potatoes, cauliflowers and 'all sorts of tinned things'.[42]

Wimborne's case for being retained in office was that if the actions he had recommended had been promptly taken there would have been no rebellion at all and that, when it was allowed to break out, he had taken the essential steps to see that it was quickly suppressed. His principal Aide, the influential Lord Basil Blackwood, whom he sent over to lay the case before the Prime Minister, was in a position to confirm the first point, but judging by what he told Lady Cynthia Asquith, he saw Wimborne's role during the course of the rebellion in a less favourable light. 'His Ex had simply *swilled* brandy the whole time, and his dutiful wife had busied herself filling up his glass and writing a minute diary of his day: "3.45 His Ex telephoned, etc." His Ex had been superlatively theatrical and insisted on his poor secretaries using the most melodramatically grandiloquent language down the telephone—standing over them to enforce his dictation: "It is His Ex's *command*." The pathetic thing was that it never occurred to him that there would be any retrospective blame. He was delighted to think he was at last really in the limelight and acquitting himself so well—flushed with importance and triumph. The first intimation of a floater was the telegram saying martial law was proclaimed and Maxwell coming over to take complete command. He was flabbergasted and miserable. Hitherto having magnified the trouble to add to his glory in coping with it, he now was anxious to belittle it, insinuating that Maxwell was not needed. Finding his arrival inevitable, he then wanted to get everything over before he arrived by negotiating with the rebels and coming to terms. What a ghastly floater if they had surrendered otherwise than *unconditionally*. Altogether he seems to have behaved like the Emperor of Asses. I hope Basil's advocacy was better when speaking to the P.M.! He said His Ex had "done well", then gave these amazing illustrations of his conduct. He had stridden up and down the room exclaiming, "I shall hang MacNeill!—I shall let the others off, but I shall hang MacNeill"—as though he were a plenipotentiary. Basil said Maxwell's coming had been a great blow and surprise to Birrell, too.'[43] But, strange as it may seem, it would have surprised Birrell less, we believe, had he known that Sir Henry Wilson, the Director of Military Operations on the Imperial General Staff, was urging Maxwell to have Birrell himself arrested, tried and shot.[43a] Wilson was always a bitter and active opponent of Liberal policies in Ireland, and in time he lost his life at the hands of Irish ex-servicemen who had joined the I.R.A.

4

The ignominy of Birrell did not end with his resignation, although it was obvious that his public career was at an end. He had to endure a great political funeral which took the form of a three-member Royal Commission headed by Lord Hardinge of Penshurst which enquired into the circumstances in which the rebellion had occurred, and which found that the main cause of the outbreak was the unchecked growth of lawlessness and the failure of the Irish Government to heed the warnings they had received from the police chief and the military authorities. Birrell, as administrative head of the Government in Ireland, was held primarily responsible for the situation that was allowed to arise and for the actual outbreak, and Nathan was also criticized for not having sufficiently impressed on Birrell the necessity for more active measures.

At the Commission, Birrell made it clear that the general policy on the carrying of arms was at the root of the trouble. They had made up their minds that they could not advisedly or properly or safely use the military to disarm the Ulster Volunteers, and a different policy could not be applied to the rest of the country. He was not conscious of any warnings having been received until towards the end, when General Stafford told General Friend about the German ship. He had, of course, heard at different times—who had not?—that the Castle was going to be taken, but these reports never came to anything. And he admitted that their intelligence system had failed them, particularly that of the Dublin Metropolitan Police. He was nevertheless 'a little bit at a loss to know what precisely there was to know', because the rebels had kept their secrets to themselves. For as far back as they could go the Government always had 'friends' in the rebel camp, but not this time.

But though vague and imprecise about the immediate cause of the rising, he was extremely good in explaining the remote long-term cause. It was caused, he said, by the spirit of Sinn Feinism, which we today would more accurately call the spirit of Separatism. This spirit, in his view, was mainly composed of the old hatred and distrust of the British connection, which had never died, and which was the background of Irish politics and character. The Sinn Feiners' cry was 'Leave Us Alone. We are sick of parliamentary parties. We are tired of all the talk. We shall never be happy unless we are allowed to develop ourselves in our own way.' This dislike, hatred, disloyalty so unintelligible to Englishmen was hard to define but easy to discern. It was always dangerous. Reasons were often given for its persistency. Had Catholic Emancipation accompanied the Act of Union, had Land Tenure been antedated half a century, had the Protestant Church of Ireland been disestablished a little more to please the Irish people, and not so much to gratify the British Non-conformists, had the

General Sir John Maxwell

University Question been settled earlier, it is possible that this Spirit of Sinn Feinism might have been exorcised.

The twenty years before 1916 had seen a great social and economic change. Yet, despite all that had been done, the Sinn Fein spirit had continued to live on in the Gaelic League and other kindred and influential societies. The literary Irish revival which was characterized by originality and independence of thought and expression, tended towards and fed latent desires for some kind of separate Irish national existence. It was a curious situation to watch, he said, but there was nothing in it suggestive of a revolt or rebellion, except in the realm of thought. Indeed there was evidence of a new critical tone and temper which was the deadly foe of that wild, sentimental passion which had once more led too many brave young fellows to a certain doom in the belief that any revolution in Ireland was better than none. A little more time and, but for the outbreak of the war, the new critical temper would, in his belief, have finally prevailed. There were a number of contributory causes which he detailed at length, but the basic cause of the transformation was the survival of the spirit of separatism.[44]

5

Once the rising began the military, who had been held in check by Birrell for so long, came into their own. They lost no time in quelling the disorder, although in the process the centre of Dublin was razed to the ground. Their mistakes were few; a detachment of the Sherwood Foresters was led into an avoidable situation in which heavy casualties were suffered at the hands of a handful of insurgents; an officer went mad and murdered some men, including Sheehy-Skeffington who had been doing his utmost to prevent looting; in a crowded tenement area some unoffending citizens were shot in dubious circumstances. Tragedies like these are inescapable in war and their impact in 1916 was negligible. What did profoundly worry people was the manner in which punishment was meted out to the leaders of the rising.

These were tried by court martial which is inevitably a slow process, and day by day the public read of the execution of men, most of whom were comparatively little known, like Tom Clarke, 'the tobacconist', who was the first signatory of the proclamation of the Irish Republic. Before that, reactions had been as might have been expected. The prisoners on their way to British gaols and internment camps were hooted in the streets; the Irish Party publicly condemned them, as did churchmen and the press. The *Irish Times* declared that 'the rapine and bloodshed of the past week must be punished with a severity which will make any repetition of them impossible for many generations to come', and the *Irish Independent*, with the 1913 strike possibly in mind, pointed out that 'certain of the leaders'– these included Connolly, the labour man–'remain undealt with and the part they played was worse than those who have paid the extreme penalty'. Connolly, though wounded, was taken out and shot. That further exacerbated public opinion.

Dillon gave voice to what the people were thinking in a violent protest in the House of Commons. The horrible rumours that were current were maddening the population, he said, and spreading disaffection and bitterness from one end of the country to the other. The people as a whole a week before had been the friends and loyal allies of the Government; in many cases the National Volunteers had come forward to assist the police in maintaining order. It was the first rebellion that ever took place in Ireland where the Government had a majority on its side. In return the Government had acted insanely, imposing martial law on the whole country, making wholesale arrests, disturbing the local peace and turning friends into enemies. It had let loose a river of blood; and the men they had put to death were not murderers, but men who had fought a clean fight, a brave fight, however misguided. Redmond did not go as far as that but he called for a cessation of reprisals and made it known that the resignation of Birrell had deprived him of his 'one really dependable ally in the government'. On the other hand King George told the Prime Minister that he hoped that martial law would be continued until the Sinn Feiners, all of whom he understood were known to the police, were accounted for. From what he had heard from Lord French and from a letter the Protestant Archbishop of Dublin had written to *The Times* things had by no means returned to their normal condition. In these circumstances and with the Government of Ireland remaining practically in the hands of the military[45] he concluded that the question of appointing a successor to Birrell was not pressing.

However, the overall situation was such that Asquith felt compelled to exercise a measure of personal control over it. He brought Maxwell to a Cabinet meeting on the 6th May and there the General, who had already commuted a sentence of death on the Countess Markievicz–a decision gratefully credited by the Countess's sister to the Prime Minister personally[46]–was instructed not to allow a capital sentence to be carried out in the case of any woman. It was left to his discretion to deal with particular cases involving men, but death should not be inflicted except upon ringleaders and proved murderers. It was desirable, he was also told, to bring the executions to a close as soon as possible.[47] And three days later, the Cabinet decided that the proposal to include Ireland in the Military Service Bill was impracticable.[48]

Asquith went over to Dublin on the 11th May to explore the ground for himself and to see to the machinery of government which had clearly proved itself defective. After the resignations of Birrell and Nathan, he had put Sir Robert Chalmers, the Permanent Secretary to the Treasury, into Dublin Castle to take charge of the civil administration–Birrell was sorry that the job was not given to an Irishman–and Chalmers had asked for a new political head for the Irish Office as quickly as possible. This put Asquith in a quandary. Who was to fill the job? And as he could not think of anybody he took it over himself for a while, spending days in the Castle going over the files and the problems with Chalmers and the other officials. He had a fixed idea that no successor should be appointed to the Lord Lieutenancy, which had been reduced to a cipher, to the role of a *vice-roi fainéant*, clothed with appropriate power and responsibility, but obliged in practice to content itself day by day with the crumbs that fell from the Under Secretary's table. It was not an office that any self-respecting man of parts and ability could be asked to undertake. The King, whom he consulted, wholeheartedly agreed to accept the necessity of a change and was anxious to arrange for an annual residence of himself, the Queen and the Court in Ireland. With the disappearing of the vice-royalty, Asquith saw that the fiction of a Chief Secretary would also disappear. There would instead have to be a single Minister controlling and responsible for Irish administration[49] and he thought that this was perhaps a role Lloyd George might fill.

He first invited Lloyd George to explore individually with Redmond and Carson the possibility of a political settlement which would enable the Irish Parliamentary Party to regain the power it was obviously losing. The general idea was that the Home Rule Bill would become operative immediately, subject to a decision about the exclusion of Ulster. A major triumph appeared at first to have been secured by Lloyd George as a result of his talks with the Irish leaders, but once more it was a case of the Welshman's duplicity triumphing over his ingenuity.

There was no doubt about what 'Ulster' meant; it was the six north-eastern counties. Redmond was assured that the exclusion of this area was to be limited to the war emergency period only, and that after the war, an Imperial Conference would consider the long-term future of Irish government. Carson, on the other hand, had an assurance in writing from Lloyd George that at the end of the provisional period Ulster, whether she willed it or not, would not merge in the rest of Ireland.[50] Both parties got the agreement of their close supporters to the terms to which they appeared to have agreed, the Ulster Unionists to the probable permanent surrender of three counties, in none of which of course they had an electoral majority, the Irish nationalists to the surrender, on a temporary basis, of six counties, including two in which they held the majority of votes. To secure the acceptance of these terms, Redmond had to threaten resignation of the party leadership.

At this point, Austen Chamberlain, who was Secretary of State for India, protested to the Prime Minister that the Cabinet had never authorized anybody to go as far as these talks had gone, and he had been put into the position of having to leave a deputation of South of Ireland Unionists under the impression that, much as he disliked Home Rule in any and every form, he approved of what had been done and saw no alternative to it.[51] His worries were shared by other Conservative members of the Cabinet, and produced threats of resignation from some of them, while in the subsequent public discussion of the White Paper containing the alleged headings of settlement, bitter recriminations were aroused as the divergent interpretations emerged. These led to the point at which it had to be revealed that Carson's claim for the definitive exclusion of 'Ulster' could not be resisted.[52] The repudiation of the alleged settlement followed. Asquith who, when in Ireland, had expressed the opinion that the conditions then existed for a compromise solution of the Irish Question, now told the Cabinet regretfully that owing to the complete revulsion of opinion he was no longer sanguine as to the success of his suggestion. The reasons he gave for the change of opinion in Ireland were Dillon's 'deplorable' speech, the Sheehy-Skeffington case, a letter of Bishop O'Dwyer of Limerick, the reprieve of a man who was leader of the party who murdered nine R.I.C. men at Athlone [?Ashbourne], and the unconditional release of hundreds of persons who had been arrested. One thing more than anything else that caused trouble was the ventilation of the scheme of settlement attributed to Lloyd George. It was universally regarded in Ireland as the triumph and justification of the rebellion.[53] It was in this frame of mind that the Government sent Wimborne back to Ireland – he had been exonerated by the Hardinge Commission from any blame for the Easter Rising – and appointed H. E. Duke, a Unionist lawyer, as Chief Secretary. He was, in Birrell's opinion, the best of men. The long abused anomalous system of governing Ireland was to be given another few years of life. Commenting on the whole of this extraordinary transaction Sir Horace Plunkett told Nathan that the fact that Asquith had finally come back to the Humpty Dumpty solution of the Irish trouble marked a record of English floundering in Ireland. He would have been less angry if Nathan had been invited to succeed his successor. He said nothing about Birrell in that particular letter but, for reasons going back to the early days of Birrell's appointment, he was not sorry that Birrell was being left out in the wilderness.[54]

6

That was at the end of July. By that time, as Maxwell reported, there had been a great recrudescence of Sinn Feinism. Mourning badges, Sinn Fein flags, demonstrations and Requiem Masses, and the resolutions of public bodies were all signs of a profound shift of opinion. The Sinn Fein organization was being regarded by many people as the one to follow, 'because it has in their opinion done more for Ireland than Mr. Redmond and the constitutional party; in other words, rebellion pays'. He could see no controlling influence at work. Priests, young and old, were fomenting the republican idea behind the backs of the hierarchy,[55] and a high dignitary of the Church had told him that a little spell of ecclesiastical martial law was badly needed. It was the only thing that would put an end to the foolish demonstrations of hot-headed clerics. 'At present we are in a state bordering on anarchy', he said. Maxwell did not go so far as this, but he reminded the Prime Minister that his own position required to be strengthened and regularized. He was prepared to resign if his recent actions stood in the way of an amicable political settlement, but if he was to stay on he should be given full powers to insist on the law being observed. His reports about the rise of Sinn Fein were confirmed by the police. Their information was much more alarmist, however. Assassination clubs had been formed by the Sinn Feiners and a number of prominent people singled out for attention, including General Maxwell and General Friend. Maxwell's photo had been circulated to the would-be assassins so that they would know their man. The Inspector-General of the R.I.C. attached importance to this information which had reached him, he said, from a usually well-informed source.[56]

Maxwell had friends as well as enemies and critics. 763 of them, persons of influence in Dublin and Cork, sent a memorandum to the Prime Minister to protest against any interference with the General's direction of affairs during the operation of martial law.[57] An officer on his staff, Brigadier-General Hutchinson, also wrote on his behalf to Bonham-Carter, Asquith's Secretary: 'Wish you'd speak to the P.M. re Sir John's case. He was sent over to carry out operations at very short notice and has done well. The War Office seems to be sticky about making him G.O.C.-in-Chief in Ireland (Paget's title) and naturally he wishes to keep his temporary title of general which he got in Egypt. He won't stay otherwise and it would be a misfortune if he had to leave suddenly and for such a small reason, and Kitchener and Lord French are in favour. Get this done now and so save irritation.

'As for myself I'm rather sad, for according to the C.I.G.S., here I must stay – however what must be will be. Shall look to you to keep me posted on Irish matters. Give Sir John as free a hand as you can. He can be trusted. The whole business is disagreeable and hated by the soldiers. We have had this job to do and we did it, but of the mud being thrown at us some must stick – such is the luck of a soldier.'[58]

7

Birrell's interest in Casement had revived when the ex-diplomat went to Germany in 1914. He told Nathan that 'Sir Roger C (not Roger de Coverley) seems to have gone the whole hog in Berlin. I send *very private* wire about him and his works. I don't suppose for a moment he will set foot in Ireland where his name is not worth twopence and without a name no rebel in Ireland is worth considering. Fifty thousand Germans would be a different matter.'[59] A little later he heard that Casement was said to be promising a German raid and a rising in Ireland at about Christmas time. This seemed to Birrell 'a task of incredible folly' but in dealing 'with this strain of madness and vanity nothing was impossible', he said. If the Germans came the December weather would upset their stomachs if not their plans.

To be on the safe side, however, the possibility of a German attack was taken very seriously. The military and police were given the *qui vive*. Nathan cancelled his acceptance of an invitation to spend the Christmas holidays in England, and was consoled by Birrell with the Irish maxim: 'Be aisy–and if you can't be aisy– be as aisy as you can.'[60] People living on the west coast were told what to do if the Germans came; and a yacht, the *Sayonara*, with the naval officers on board impersonating Americans, was sent cruising along the coast followed by a coastguard vessel. Now and again it entered a harbour in the hope of discovering the arrangements that were being made by the Sinn Feiners to welcome their German friends. The newspapers, of course, soon began to receive emboidered accounts of what was happening and the Castle had difficulty in dealing with them. All Galway was reported to be agog about the mystery ship and its strange occupants who used diving suits to reach the shore undetected! Ridiculous ideas were being circulated by the police in Westport, and Birrell got letters which were as illegible as his own, he said, asking was it a fact that cattle would have to be driven as far away from the coast as Athlone which was in the very centre of Ireland. The Westport people were far more interested in their beasts and in who would guarantee them their land and cattle than in the fate of the British Empire. 'Can we trust the police not to talk nonsense'? he asked. 'Some even of the County Inspectors are great asses when we meet them on their own dunghills. . . .'[61] The police seem to have become thoroughly worked up over the possibility of an invasion and their telegrams poured into the Castle when sounds of firing off the coast were heard. Birrell, again in sarcastic mood, remarked that the navy's target practice had fluttered the heart and distressed the ear of the R.I.C., but it was something to know that they were awake![62]

After this canard, for that is what it was, Casement dropped out of the picture, but he was known to be recruiting a brigade among Irish prisoners of war in Germany for service against Britain and so long as Germany backed him there was a men-

ace that had to be faced. When British Naval Intelligence discovered, by the interception of wireless messages, the date of a
projected rising in 1916, and later that a submarine was under
orders to take Casement to Ireland, they facilely assumed that he
was coming to start the rebellion. Birrell and his advisers thought
the same thing, and Nathan said so expressly to the Hardinge
Commission. He also implied that the I.R.B., and the executive of
the Irish Volunteers of which MacNeill was the head, had combined to organize the rising. On both scores he and Birrell were
wrong. Neither the Volunteer Executive as such nor MacNeill
had anything whatever to do with the rising. A group within
the I.R.B., who held half the seats on the Volunteer Executive,
planned the whole affair in response to stimulation from their
American counterparts, Clan-na-Gael, and did so without the
knowledge of MacNeill and the remaining members of the
Volunteer Executive.

The negotiations with the Germans were conducted mainly by
Devoy, the Clan-na-Gael leader in New York, and in the process
Casement was not merely cold-shouldered, but an attempt was
made to prevent him from leaving Germany by offering him
nominal ambassadorial status. The conspirators, Irish and German
alike, had found him difficult, but it was thought he would be
less of a nuisance in Germany than if he came home. At no stage
was he told who in Ireland was actually planning the rising; he
knew nothing of a division in the Volunteer Executive; he was
left to assume that there was none, and that if a rising took place it
would be led by MacNeill. When the Germans told him that their
contribution was to be limited to a shipload of arms, he insisted
on being brought home. If there was to be fighting he wanted to
be in it, he told them. In fact what he really wanted was to ensure
that there would be no fighting at all. He had lost all respect for
the Germans and wanted desperately to warn MacNeill that a rising
that was contingent on their help was doomed to failure. The
Germans pressed him to take his Irish Brigade with him to Ireland
but Casement said, 'No, that would be murder.' When he came
ashore on the coast of Kerry and lay wet, weak and unwelcomed

on the sands, he was more convinced than ever of the futility of a rising, but his arrest frustrated his personal efforts to call it off. However, Monteith, who had travelled with him from Germany, and who shared his misgivings, succeeded in sending a message to Dublin, but this, though addressed to MacNeill, was delivered into the hands of the conspirators.

The Germans in April 1918, in a communication to the I.R.B. which was handled by Michael Collins, expressed regret that they had not taken the insurrection of 1916 seriously. They proposed to deal very differently with another insurrection which they hoped was being prepared for. Full military aid would be supplied. This message in code was safely delivered through a Joseph Dowling who had been a member of Casement's Brigade, but Dowling was picked up on an island off the Galway coast by the police, and served six years of a prison sentence in the Tower of London.[63]

Casement fared far worse. After his arrest he was brought to London and lodged in the Tower with a view to bringing him to trial in the Civil Courts. The King had expressed the hope on the 6th May that this would be arranged as soon as possible, for already he noted that Cardinal Gibbons in New York was talking of leniency.[64] On the 29th June he was found guilty of high treason and sentenced to death, and on the 18th July the Court of Criminal Appeal confirmed the sentence. Already the question had been raised of exercising the prerogative of mercy in his regard, and Spring Rice, the British Ambassador in the United States, had warned that the Irish executions were establishing a firm and durable alliance between almost the entire body of Irishmen in America and the German-American organization, and this in the middle of the war with Germany was deplorable. 'As to Casement,' he wrote, 'the Irish might regard his execution as a small matter in comparison with the others. But the great bulk of American public opinion, while it might excuse executions in hot blood would very greatly regret an execution some time after the event. . . . It is far better to make Casement ridiculous than a martyr.' And later Spring Rice reported that there was great unanimity among the friends of England that from the point of view of pure expediency Casement's execution would be a very great mistake.[65]

When the matter first came before the Cabinet on the 5th July mention was made of a diary of Casement's that had been found in his lodgings and which appeared to establish that for years he had been addicted to the grossest sodomitical practices. Taking their stand on this, presumably, Spring Rice's minister, Sir Edward Grey, and Lord Lansdowne were strongly of opinion that it would be better, if possible, that Casement should be kept in confinement as a criminal lunatic than that he should be executed without any smirch on his character, and then canonized as a martyr both in Ireland and America. Others taking the contrary view it was decided that the diary should be sent to an alienist for a report. On the 12th July this report by Doctors Percy Smith and Maurice Craig was submitted. It found that Casement was abnormal but not 'certifiably insane'. As the appeal was still pending no decision was taken. On the 19th July, however, the day following the decision of the Appeal Court, the Cabinet reviewed the whole subject in the light of Home Office memoranda prepared by Sir Ernley Blackwell and tendered with supporting comments by the Permanent Secretary, C. E. Troup.[66] These dealt with the question of abnormality, and Blackwell made some preliminary points. If Casement had succeeded in reaching Dublin and had been taken with Pearse, Connolly and the rest he would have been tried by court martial and shot. (This presupposed that Casement would have joined Pearse and company in the rising.) Casement had failed to give evidence on oath; there was really no defence on the facts, nor was any defence possible. It was difficult to imagine a worse case of treason. If a decision was taken in accordance with the rules which ordinarily governed Home Office practice, there were no possible grounds for interfering with the sentence.

On the subject of abnormality, Blackwell claimed that Casement's diaries and his ledger entries, covering many pages of closely typed matter, showed that he had completed the full circle of sexual degeneracy, but no one who read Casement's report to the Foreign Office on the Putamayo atrocities (at a time when his sexual offences were of daily occurrence), his speech from the dock, etc. etc., could doubt for a moment that intellectually at any rate he was very far removed from anything that could properly be described as insanity. His excesses might have warped his judgment, but he was able to take a detached and sane view of these excessess now. He described them as his 'follies' in writing to a priest, and asked him 'to pray for him most of all in that regard, and that any evil that may have come from his folly and imprudence may not live long'.

Blackwell also addressed himself to the issue of expediency. The Foreign Office from the start appeared to have taken the view that, in order not to alienate Irish-American sentiment, they could not safely hang Casement unless they first published the fact of his private character as disclosed in his diaries. There was obviously grave objection to any sort of official or even inspired publication of such facts while the man was waiting trial or appeal, or even waiting execution, but he saw not the slightest objection to hanging Casement and *afterwards* giving as much publicity to the contents of his diary as decency permitted, so that at any rate the public in America and elsewhere might know what sort of man they were inclined to make a martyr of. 'I understand', Blackwell continued, 'that several members of the Cabinet are inclined to the opinion that it may be inexpedient to execute Casement. I suppose it is feared that in addition to the American question, the hanging of Casement may interfere with the Irish settlement. If Casement had been taken to Dublin he would have been shot and would have been a fifteenth martyr. The shooting of the fourteen leaders is said to have given a great impetus to the Sinn Fein movement. I am inclined to think that the rebellion itself and its results have given the impetus and that the situation today would have been much the same whether Pearse, Connolly and the rest had been shot or merely sent to Portland with a confident expectation of amnesty and early release. Casement's value as a martyr is already a good deal discounted. His private character is by this time pretty generally known in London.'

Raising the question as to whether if the diary was to be published, in what form? Blackwell said that it would of course be called a forgery, and the original would somehow or other have to be proved. And he ended his comments as follows: 'It seems to me that British public opinion has been entirely left out of account. Are the government prepared to face the storm of indignation with which a reprieve will be greeted in this country? .... So far as I can judge it would be far wiser from every point of view to allow the law to take its course, and by judicious means to use these diaries to prevent Casement from attaining martyrdom.'

The Cabinet may have accepted the whole of this advice but Asquith's note to the King was confined to stating that it had been unanimously resolved that Casement should be hanged. The execution took place a fortnight later. Asquith personally would have preferred a reprieve based on medical evidence, but in the absence of this he did not feel it right to treat Casement more leniently than his *supposed followers* had been treated by Maxwell.[67]

Birrell, being no longer a member of the Government, had nothing to do with the decision to execute Casement, but he was one of the first to give effect to the complementary idea of preventing Casement from becoming a martyr. Before he left for Dublin in the middle of Easter Week he showed Redmond the photographic evidence of the diaries, what he called 'this loathsome material', and by so doing prevented any effort the leader of the Irish party might have made in Casement's defence.[67a] In this regard it must be pointed out that many people, some of them still living, who knew Casement intimately, have always disputed the authenticity of the diaries.

8

The Government's understanding of what led to the rising was not enlightened by a report of Maxwell's on the state of Ireland that Asquith circulated to the Cabinet on the 24th June.[68] 'For one reason or another, things have been allowed to drift, and what is now known as Sinn Feinism came into being,' Maxwell wrote. 'They appear to have been led by a Mr. John MacNeill and an inner circle. A "split" from the constitutional–1914–party occurred some months before the actual rebellion took place. They then merged with the extremist labour party originated by Larkin, and latterly directed by J. Connolly. Those started the Citizen Army which (though not identical with the Irish Volunteers–MacNeill's army) armed and prepared for war (or rebellion) as did the Irish Volunteers. . . . MacNeill and his party, Connolly and the Citizen Army, seem to have been financed by the German-American Clan-na-Gael organization from America. This led to the Casement enterprise and the rebellion. . . . As things turned out it missed fire, and MacNeill realized too late that he was in an impossible situation, and though he tried he could not altogether stop what had been engineered for Easter. . . .'

It was presumably on some such misunderstanding of the position–we have already seen Wimborne's confusion of mind–that MacNeill was arrrested as the rising ended and condemned to death, the sentence being commuted to one of penal servitude for life. This was done despite the fact that MacNeill had taken every step open to him to avert the rising short of sending a warning to the Castle. There was indeed, as we said earlier, 'an inner circle', a military council of the I.R.B., which prepared the rising and recruited Volunteer Officers into the I.R.B. so as to ensure the participation of their units in it, but MacNeill was as unaware of its existence as the Government was. He knew individual members of this inner circle, some of them intimately, and had debated with them as Irish Volunteers the moral justification for a rising in the circumstances of the time. Some of these men believed in the idea of a blood sacrifice to redeem what they believed to be a degenerate people, and had put their names to the Proclamation of the Republic and been executed. In killing them, the Government, as Nathan perceptively remarked, had deprived itself of the means of discovering what had really happened and how.[69] Birrell, confronted with the Hardinge Commission, declared that the Three Good Men who constituted it were 'engaged in the pursuit of the unknowable' and hence would find his and Nathan's behaviour inexplicable and blameworthy. Something, however, was known, though not properly understood. Almost a full month before Maxwell wrote about the rising having been led by John MacNeill and an inner circle, he told Asquith he had read MacNeill's very interesting court-martial papers and thought some of them at least should be made public as well as being shown to the Hardinge Commission. They showed pretty plainly, he said, that if Casement's adventure had not misfired, the Government would have been up against a much more serious affair, but there was little doubt that it was that failure which caused MacNeill to countermand the Easter parades. 'I am doing all I can', he went on, 'to correct the impression in America that we caused the rebellion to start by repressive measures and making it clear that it started by the cold-blooded murder of Dublin police constables in the exercise of their ordinary duty.'[70]

This fits in with what we now know—that MacNeill, when he was told that a large consignment of arms was about to be landed, realized that this was likely to bring about the suppression of the Volunteers. This was something he was constrained to prevent, if he possibly could; so he agreed, very reluctantly, to act with the men who had planned the importation of German arms without his knowledge and in defiance of his authority. When, however, he learned that the German arms ship had been captured, he recovered the initiative and energetically set about undoing the work of the inner circle.

Maxwell, an Englishman whose soldiering had been mainly in foreign parts, could not have been expected to know much about the ins and outs of Irish affairs, but Major Price, General Friend's Military Intelligence Officer, should have been able to guide him. Price, however, suffered from blind spots. He actually tried to terrorise MacNeill into connecting Dillon and Devlin with the plans for the rising, with which, of course, they had absolutely nothing whatever to do. This was a classical example of the military stupidity of which Birrell was always complaining. And when Price's efforts were made public Wimborne was right to say, as he did, that Ireland would believe MacNeill but not, as he added, 'whatever the facts really were' but because no sane person could believe what Price was striving to prove. MacNeill put on record how he was first visited in Arbour Hill detention barracks by Maxwell who suggested that he should make a statement. Mac Neill replied that he had no statement to make. The following day he was allowed out for exercise, and was set to walk up and down in front of men who were being exercised a few yards from him. Rifles were pointed in his direction. On being returned to his cell he was followed in by Major Price who told him that he had been given a death sentence but that his life would be spared if he made a statement implicating persons higher up than himself. He said twice that it would be enough to make the statement; supporting evidence was unnecessary. MacNeill asked what persons higher up than himself were meant. Price said Mr. Dillon who was 'bitterly anti-British' and also Mr. Devlin. MacNeill said he could not connect these men with the matter in any way. Price also told MacNeill of Birrell's resignation, and spoke of it with great satisfaction.[71]

The military also appear to have known nothing of Bulmer Hobson's role in the affair. He, with others, had informed Mac-Neill on Holy Thursday night of the information that had reached them of companies of volunteers receiving orders to embark on an insurrection on the following Sunday. Hobson was busy carrying out MacNeill's direction to countermand these orders, when he was arrested by the junta and kept in confinement until the insurrection had begun. He managed, however, to get a message to MacNeill. Of all this Maxwell in his reports made no mention.

9

Wimborne, who, as we said, had been made miserable by Maxwell's appointment, reminded Asquith in September that the General's time was up. He had had an invidious job and had performed it creditably, but he would be better gone 'on promotion' for all concerned. Price, he said, was a still greater stumbling block but he made no recommendation in his regard. Birrell's successor, Duke, was very pleasant to work with; any differences between them, should they arise, would have to be kept between themselves; otherwise the temptation to play one off against the other would be too strong for 'this nation of intriguers'. The Unionists were saying that Duke would be no better than Birrell, and the Nationalists proclaimed his ascendancy proclivities, but Wimborne thought he would do well. He was perhaps a little unconscious of his difficulties, but both parties would combine to undeceive him on that point. This opinion of Duke was shared by the Treasury men. Birrell at least had the advantage of being a cynic; he assessed Irish complaints at their true value, whereas Duke seemed to swallow them all.[72]

Chalmers, Wimborne said, was about to leave and return to the Treasury, and the question of a successor as Under Secretary had to be faced. Sir Henry Robinson was an attractive candidate but, being a Kildare Street man, his appointment would emphasize the 'Unionist rule' of which the Irish Party were making a grievance. 'They avoid me now', said Wimborne, 'and say there can be no common ground between us. This is a pose of course.' He enjoyed the position of independence in which he now found himself. He told the Prime Minister that he had taken on the task of 'insidiously co-ordinating the administration' which was 'deplorably loose-jointed'. Nearly all the old public officers had a propensity to act off their own bat which was fatal. Martial law would probably be best withdrawn gradually by districts on good behaviour. The Army was essential. There was only one division left in the country beside odds and ends. The limit of prudence had, therefore, been reached. Further withdrawals would bring them all home in protest.

Nobody claimed to be able to forecast the public temper after the recent deceptions. His best advice was to go slow. Ireland needed a sedative for a time. All heroics such as compulsory service should be eschewed. Most Unionists and not a few

Nationalists regarded this as a panacea for the country, but they were not responsible for catching the hare, and he was convinced that that course would be disproportionately risky and embarrassing.

Partition was universally detested. Why incur fresh disappointments? Dillon, whom somebody had said was the most powerful man in Ireland, was frequenting extreme company, possibly with the object of recapturing it, but in saying that, Wimborne recognized that he might be sliding from facts into the realm of surmise.[73]

By this time Redmond's political fortunes had seriously declined. He was much criticized for having committed Ireland unhesitatingly to the war effort and for having compelled the assent of the Ulster Nationalists to Lloyd George's dubious 'settlement' by threatening to resign the party leadership if his advice was not taken. The state of the war did not improve his prospects. It had gone from bad to worse, and tens of thousands of Irishmen who had gone to Flanders or Gallipoli or some other theatre never returned or returned on the crowded hospital ships. A mere handful of men, 1,500 at most, had taken part in the Easter rising compared with the 150,000 who were at that time wearing the King's uniform in the British Army. There were many people now saying, in the words of a popular ballad, 'that 'twas better to die 'neath an Irish sky than at Suvla or Sed el Bar'.

The criticism of Redmond arose inside as well as outside the Parliamentary party. John Dillon had proved a loyal lieutenant since the warring elements of the old Parnellite party had reunited in 1900, but he had never shared Redmond's view of the war as a crusade on behalf of international justice and the rights of small nations. After the rising particularly, he was convinced that the party's policy should be reversed. Enough sacrifices had been made; it was now time, he believed, to look for concessions, which meant returning to the old policy of making things difficult for the Government. A majority of the Party sided with him, and they all showed a growing distrust of Lloyd George as a negotiator. For his part, Lloyd George, who displaced Asquith from the Premiership before the end of 1916, blamed his failure hitherto to settle the Irish question on the Irish themselves; their suspicion of each other, their real envy of each other. Ireland was a quagmire of distrust that made progress impossible. The truth, however, was Lloyd George's capacity for double-dealing. He could produce temporary agreements by persuading both sides to accept a solution which they interpreted in a different sense.[74]

With an eye, however, on the Americans who were being encouraged to come into the war, and for other reasons, the Government before Christmas 1916, released the majority of the Irish prisoners who had remained untried in their hands since Easter. The others were released later. By-election results pointed the way to the final success of Sinn Fein in the 1918 General Election and to the utter overthrow of the Irish party. By that time Redmond was dead, and Dillon, his successor, had been defeated by the new President of Sinn Fein, Eamon de Valera, a man who had played a significant part in the Easter rising. And the Irish soldiers as they returned from the battlefields found that their deeds of valour counted for little in their native land. In their absence Ireland had acquired other causes and other heroes.

10

On the day of Redmond's funeral (9.3.1918) 'an appreciation' of him over Birrell's initials appeared in *The Times*. It is well worth reproducing, both for what it says and how it is said. 'The impression he left on me', Birrell began, 'was of a truthful, straightforward man, who hated jobbery and corruption in all their manifold forms and branches; and when he could not always prevent them, held himself ostentatiously and scornfully aloof from them.

'Although it was not always easy to do business with him, being very justly suspicious of English politicians, he could be trusted more implicitly than almost every other politician I have ever come in contact with. He was slow to pass his word, but when he had done so you knew he would keep it to the very letter and, what was almost as important, his silence and discretion could be relied upon with certainty. He was constitutionally incapable of giving anybody away who had trusted him.

'He was, perhaps from lack of nature, out of sympathy with intellectual and aesthetic movements. His taste, outside Parliamentary oratory and platform deliverances (and these are great exceptions in the case of a political leader), was not so much defective as non-existent. In fact, he was, as so many of us are, a Philistine and in the pleasant realms of Fancy there was no place assigned for his hat and coat. He was not, however, indifferent to Irish history, as was the case with his predecessor, Mr. Parnell. He was a devout, steady Catholic, of unspeculative mind but from a purely political point of view he was, I should say, anti-clerical, after the same fashion as many an English squire. He was a faithful and affectionate friend, and from head to heel a good fellow.

'As a matter of Irish policy his famous speech in the House of Commons on the outbreak of the war was a mistake, though a noble one. He took the curve too sharply and did not carry the train with him.

'He felt to the very end, bitterly and intensely, the stupidity of the War Office. Had he been allowed to deflect the routine indifference and suspicion of the War Office from its old ruts into the deep-cut channels of Irish feelings and sentiment he might have carried his countrymen with him, but he jumped first, and tried to bargain afterwards, and failed accordingly. English people as their wont is, gushed over him as an English patriot and flouted him as an Irish statesman. Had he and his brother been put in charge of the Irish Nationalist contingents and an Ulster man, or men, been put in a corresponding position over the Irish Protestant contingents all might have gone well. Lord Kitchener, who was under the delusion that he was an Irishman no less than Redmond, was the main, though not the only obstacle in the path of good sense and good feeling.'

CHAPTER VI

In Retirement
1916–1933

BIRRELL lived at 70 Elm Park Road in Chelsea, but he also had a seaside cottage called 'The Pightle' at Sheringham in Norfolk. After his resignation he went there for a while. The continuing war and the strikes of later days left him occasionally with the sense of being marooned, but the small-boat fishermen who were his neighbours amused him with their chatter; and honey, lobsters, crabs and flat fish were plentiful. The war seemed remote except when a high wind one night carried the noise of the German bombardment of Yarmouth across the excited countryside. Norfolk was lovely in the summer months, but when the winter drew in and he tired of 'staring the North Pole out of countenance'[1] he was glad to return to his quarters in Chelsea where he was widely known and respected. Like Carlyle before him, he became the 'sage of Chelsea' and was an honoured visitor at the Arts Club. He declined, however, an invitation to unveil a statue of the Greek mythological princess Atalanta on the Embankment near Albert Bridge. He was too old, he said, to be stripping women in public.

He read widely and deeply and was understandably intrigued by the biography, published in 1917, of Sir Charles Dilke, whose ministerial career had ended tragically like his own though in very different circumstances. He also, but more leisurely, resumed his writing, without either raising or lowering his literary reputation,[2] in the opinion of R. C. K. Ensor and Lord Crewe, the authors of the generally inadequate entry in the *Dictionary of National Biography*. Birrell's repute rested particularly on his *Obiter Dicta* which were much admired. His epigrammatic 'Birrellisms' added to his fame. Some of these have achieved permanency in Dictionaries of Quotations: 'That great dust-heap called history', for instance, or his 'Happy is the land whose annals are dull'. He had a light, unbuttoned style all of his own, sometimes known as Birrelling, which a magazine editor, looking for an article from him, described as being 'all about nothing and then off at a tangent'. Beatrice Webb in 1910 had observed 'the same jovial litterateur pleasantly speaking about nothing with a group of admiring women.'[2a]

A book on his father-in-law Frederick Locker-Lampson, for whom he entertained the warmest affection, took up a good deal of his time. He was working on this in 1919 when the weather was trying and the industrial outlook depressing. 'No one would think we have just emerged from a triumphant war,' he said.[3] Locker-Lampson's work had been criticized by the American James Brander Matthew, a writer who had had the curious experience of being trained from boyhood to be a millionaire and then never to become one. This misadventure he had borne with dignity and almost indifference, but his criticisms left Birrell a little uncomfortable and uneasy. He thought, however, that Matthew had been driven into this attitude by 'our British insular and ignorant insolence to everybody and everything save our sweet selves and our productions. But what does it matter?' he added. 'We men are a little breed wherever born.'[4]

The cynical and agnostic streak in his sensitive make-up hardened with adversity and old age. He supposed it was the choice of the profession of teaching that had enabled a friend of his to preserve the freshness of Truth and the disposition to 'argle-bargle'. 'This passion has died down with me', he said, 'for I couldn't bring myself to cross the road either to assert or to deny the existence of a Supreme Being. And as for history, be damned to it. What's history done for me? To this melancholy plight am I reduced.'[5] He wrote these words in October 1919, less than a year since the war had ended, and a General Election had resulted in a triumph for the Lloyd George-Bonar Law coalition and in disaster for such of the Liberals as had remained independent. Asquith had been defeated and with him many of Birrell's former colleagues who, unlike himself, had sought re-election. He tried to console his old leader, and made suggestions as to how he could recover his lost prestige by calling a new world into existence to redress the deficiencies of the old. 'I have been smoking my pipe over the fire,' he told him, 'turning over the misfortunes of my friends, one by one, and tho' the tears may have trickled down my cheeks, I find myself able to say with my national poet – not yours (R. Burns) – "Strength to bear it has been given, my spouse Nancy –" and you surely are better out of it, for the time, than "to lead apes to Hell", or to speak less profanely, to march through Coventry at the head of such a ragged retinue as seems left. . . .'[6]

Birrell found himself thrown more and more into the company of people of his own age, and even this circle narrowed so quickly that already in 1918 he was complaining that his friends were mostly 'old men, tormented with rheums and catarrhs, and either living alone in melancholy plight in chambers or inhabiting tall houses in South Kensington, nagged at by an elderly crone, who once in the early '70s was the slim goddess of their idolatry and the inspiration of their long since silenced Muse'.[7] The Tennysons, Medleys and Locker-Lampsons kept in touch, and as Sir James Dougherty lived nearby the air of Dublin Castle, as he said, was around him; but happily not yet the habits and customs of that false symbol of Empire. He was glad that Magill, for whom he had a deep regard, was out of its precincts. Dublin could hardly be a desirable place to live in, he thought, but he understood that Sir Henry Robinson was optimistic about the future, although how he managed to do it he could not even guess. The Abbey Theatre's *Whiteheaded Boy* had proved a great favourite when given a London production. 'So we laugh and groan at the same time, but history will revile us for our cowardice and crime.'[7a]

But for regular company he had to rely on his two sons. With Tony, the younger of these, conversation was limited, for Tony was 'languid to the verge of immobility'.[8] At his birth, Birrell had sanguinely prophesied that he would be a prop for himself in his old age, but this was not to be the case. He never grew up and was unable to cope with anything but the surface of a well-ordered

THE CHIEF SECRETARY

life.'⁹ Frankie amply made up for his brother's deficiencies, however. He was 'restlessly active',¹⁰ and the reincarnation of his father inasmuch as he could write when he set his mind to it, and being gay and 'garrulous, was always ready to debate the problems of the age into the early hours. Inside the Bloomsbury circle to which he belonged, Frankie, though something of a snob, was regarded as 'a rare and beautiful spirit'. But D. H. Lawrence couldn't stand him, finding him 'horrible, unclean, and nasty, like a black beetle'.¹¹ Jealousy underlay this judgment. Lawrence's wife, Frieda, had fallen for Frankie on first meeting him, and when they met again they got on much too well for Lawrence's taste, and their noisy snobbish conversation about titled Germans whom they both knew only made things worse.

Through Frankie, Birrell met some of the Bloomsbury set, but it is unlikely that he relished their company. Years before, when he read H. G. Wells's 'tremendous book'¹² *Ann Veronica* and heard of the tangles in which authors like Wells and 'our poor sentimental Tommy J. M. Barrie' were involving themselves in the pursuit of freer love, he was glad he belonged to the older generation. 'The world never was and never will be a nice place', he told Maida Mirrielees, 'until men and women have ceased to generate upon it. *Then* the Fauna and the Flora and all the Crustaceans and Molluscs . . . will behave as they do now, quite nicely, but there will be no one with a microscope to watch their silly goings on.'¹³ What he would have made of 'the silly goings on' described in the recent biography of Lytton Strachey,¹⁴ we can only imagine.

We know from that book, however, what Strachey made of 'old man Birrell' when he met him in May 1917 for the first time. 'He was decidedly a Victorian product. Large and tall and oddly like Thackeray to look at–with spectacles and sharp big nose and a long upper lip that moves about and curls very expressively– white hair, of course, and also rather unexpectedly sensitive and even sometimes almost agitated fingers. Altogether, a most imposing façade! And there he sits, square and solid, talking in a loud deep voice–can you imagine it?–and being very entertaining for hour after hour–telling stories and interjecting reflections and all the rest of it–and all with the greatest gentility–taking up one's remarks most good-humouredly, and proceeding and embroidering with an impression of easy strength. Underneath–there really seems to be almost nothing. The ordinary respectabilities and virtues, no doubt, and a certain bookishness, gleaned from some rather narrow reading, and then–blank.'[15] Birrell was perhaps just Birrelling, talking all about nothing and then off at a tangent. But this was only one side of the man: in his family he was regarded as the 'practical' person to whom different problems were brought for solution, and civil servants found him very satisfactory to work with, being adroit and quick to come to conclusions, a minister who never sat on papers. That was Sir Henry Robinson's considered judgment. Birrell's real interest, however, was in literature. 'If left to himself,' Magill said, 'he would be found buried in a book in his library at Elm Park Road, a curious half-underground room where the electric light was required even on summer afternoons. I can see him still sitting at the fire dressed in an extraordinary yellow tweed which he had got on some of his trips to the west of Ireland, with a large black cat stretched luxuriously on his knee, and with the ashes of his cigar descending gracefully on his waistcoat, immersed in some book from which I felt ashamed to distract his attention to deal with some problem. . . .'[15a]

Frankie's close friend, David Garnett, first encountered Birrell when he was 'a Liberal Minister who was holding an impossibly difficult job' in Ireland.[16] He found him charming, witty and humane but 'a character based in part on Dr. Johnson' for whom, it was true, Birrell had an unusual feeling.[17] He might have added that Birrell was indiscreet in talking so much to a son who was apt to pass on what he had heard to his friends. Much of this talk was concerned with the difficulties Birrell had experienced in keeping his political associates straight on the Home Rule issue. Kitchener had tried to wreck the Bill. Asquith was loath to estrange the Conservatives. Sir Edward Grey was opposed, and Birrell had

threatened to resign unless the Bill were passed. In this emergency
he had found an unsuspected ally in Winston Churchill, who saw
that the alternative was to immobilize two Army Corps in Ireland.
Lloyd George cared for nobody except himself and Wales, but he
feared that he would himself suffer if Birrell led a secession group
and forced Asquith to form a coalition and depend upon the Conservative vote. At the last minute, Grey realized that American
opinion depended upon the influence of Redmond and might
easily be lost if Home Rule was dropped. He therefore came out in
support of Birrell, but it was a very near thing. Frankie also told
Garnett that his father was not on speaking terms with Kitchener,
who refused the suggestion that a large proportion of the new
army should be trained in Ireland. The money they would have
spent there, Birrell believed, would have made them very welcome
and would have constituted a powerful influence against Sinn
Fein.[18]

But all the striving of the past in which he had been so intimately involved took on a ridiculous aspect at the end of 1921
when, as he said in his autobiography, 'after months of horrors,
all of a sudden the "Government"–and he put the word like that
in inverted commas–'capitulates, and signs a Treaty with "Sinn
Fein", and declares Ireland (minus an undefined Ulster) to be a
Free State, with full control over both Customs and Excise, with
her own police and her own army. Nor is it thought necessary
to take the opinion of the country upon a question that has
severed it into two rival camps for forty years. In pursuance of the
terms of this Treaty, and without waiting for Parliamentary
approval, Dublin Castle is "surrendered" to the rebels, and our
soldiers evacuate the land.'[19] Shortly afterwards there was a Mr.
Cosgrave in power in Ireland who by a stroke of the pen abolished
the Dublin Corporation, one of Birrell's *bêtes noires*. Now if he
had attempted to do the same piece of good work, Unionists and
Nationalists would have combined to hound him out of office.[20]
Times had changed with a vengeance. The prolonged Irish controversy had been dismissed from the English political arena but
'do not, do not ask me how', he said.[21]

2

The time came, however, when Frankie sensed that his father was growing reluctant to speak about the past; his own sad experience in Ireland and the decline of the Liberal Party grieved and humiliated him too much. He was never more humiliated perhaps than when he put up fifty-six volumes of the *Liberal Magazine* for auction to make more room in his still growing library. They realized one shilling! In his letters to Maida Mirrielees he did sometimes look back, but not without a twinge of remorse. Of the death of an old domestic who often opened the door when he went courting Maida's sister he wrote: 'What a sweet Innocent I was in those far off days! Would you believe it, that I don't believe that during all those years I ever gave her as much as five shillings. What a stingy, ill-bred cur she must have taken me for... R.I.P.'[22]

To Magill, who had gone to work for the Government of Northern Ireland, Birrell revealed his mind in a Christmas letter in 1925. 'All my old friends seem to have retired on pensions, insufficient I dare say but better than a blow in the eye with a blunt stick, which is all that has come my way. What a medley of recollections my ten years in Ireland have provided me with. To think of all our futile wranglings over Gladstonian Home Rule, with its "safeguards" for the Union and the Empire, when all the time Providence had up its sleeve the Repeal of the Union and the hauling down of the Union Jack, to be accomplished at midnight by the leaders of the so-called Unionist Party, who would never hear of the least tampering with the Act of Union. Well, now three-fourth's of Ireland has a Republic (for the Oath of Allegiance will soon disappear) and Craig and Moore govern Ulster! Let us take off our hats to the Course of Events which control the world. I saw Dillon the other day at dinner with Tay Pay [T.P. O'Connor]; the first time I have exchanged a word or letter with him since 1916. He was little altered in appearance, but his point of view was wholly different....'[22a]

Times got harder with the trade depression of the 1920s. He found it difficult to keep up 'The Pightle' and was obliged to let it for the summer months. He had long known that 'to live by your pen is all Betty Martin, unless you can write some school book and bribe the Teaching Professor to insist on all the pupils to buy it'.[23] Nevertheless he managed to have an occasional holiday on the Lake of Geneva, staying at the *Trois Couronnes* in Vevey where he had often gone with his wife, and where in his political days he could rest and cogitate better than by the banks of the Thames or the Liffey.[24] But now he sorely missed Eleanor. He had become forgetful. He could not recognize people he knew intimately if he met them unexpectedly. He went about in a wide-brimmed black felt hat, and otherwise dressed more eccentrically than usual. He had always odd sartorial inclinations; for instance, he wore his tie above his collar instead of below it until a newspaper cartoon drew Eleanor's attention to what he was doing. When she was no longer there to check him his idiosyncrasies became more pronounced.[24a] On preparing to dress for a dinner-party one night at a country house where he was a visitor he found that his only dress shirt was badly stained. Not at all perturbed he put on an old yellow flannel cricket shirt with his white waistcoat and tail coat and strolled quite unconcernedly into his host's drawing-room. For a time he wore on his tie an enormous imitation pearl, until a gang of thieves on a cross-Channel steamer stole it from him believing that it was worth hundreds of pounds.[25] And the eccentric streak further revealed itself when in the *Trois Couronnes* he began to apostrophize the guests in French so vilely pronounced as to be completely unintelligible.[26]

There were two memorable days in 1929; one in January when old friends, including Sir Matthew Nathan, entertained him to lunch for his seventy-ninth birthday, and the other in November, when the Senate of the National University of Ireland told him of their desire to make their founder a Doctor of Literature. He replied immediately to say how greatly honoured he felt, and we can imagine his excitement at the prospect of seeing Ireland again after so many years and in circumstances which showed that one at least of the things he had done for that country was still appreciated. There were difficulties, of course–the Irish sea and his shaky limbs, and these he mentioned in his letter. 'I most certainly hope to be able to attend the ceremony on the fifth of next month (my first visit to Ireland since 1916) but must put in a *caveat* about the weather, for my recollection of the little bit of water that separates us still lives in my memory. If I come, as I hope to do, my son will accompany me to lend me an arm.'[27]

His old enemy, 'that little bit of water that separates us', had the final victory. For days in early December what, in the newspaper cliché, was the worst storm in living memory swept Britain and Ireland, wrecking ships and taking toll of human life. Travel was impossible. So Birrell had to receive his degree *in absentia*, as did Hilaire Belloc, G. K. Chesterton and other good papists. Birrell probably knew these men already; he could have met Chesterton and Belloc many times on English soil; but one man he had never met and was looking forward to meeting, we may assume, was the Irish President, W. T. Cosgrave, who headed the list of proposed honorary graduates. To have talked with Cosgrave would have added greatly to the interest of coming for the last time to the island that had played so fatal a part in his affairs. 'I often in my dreams visit Connemara and the mountains of Kerry,' he told Magill, 'but never either the Castle or the Lodge. I should like to see Achill Sound again, but I do not suppose I ever shall. I should find it dull without my wife, and Sir Henry Robinson to drive the motor. To recapture former experiences is impossible. . . .'[27a] Magill, he noted, was still sticking to the Northern State and Indexing the Statutes which was not an occupation exciting enough to make a gloomy city like Belfast endurable.

About a year later he was confessing that he had no news from Ireland–'It might no longer exist for us'–but he was soon saying that could he visit Dublin as a disembodied spirit he would certainly go there again and tread the once familiar streets. And he followed with close attention the political changes that occurred in the spring of 1932. 'I see as I expected De Valera has not been beaten,' he told Magill. 'We English will never understand the Irish R.C. race and the sooner we part company the better. It is a thousand pities that the two islands were so near one another. I like them both!'[27][b]

In the summer of 1930 Lytton Strachey found him extraordinarily vigorous and younger than anyone in a group that contained men as young as his son, Frankie, but a decline set in soon afterwards. In the autumn of that year he told J. L. Hammond, the social historian, that for more than two months he had been a prisoner in the house. 'There is nothing whatever the matter with me except lack of vitality, chiefly in my legs, supposed to be due to my heart having gone on the dole and refusing to pump, and after 80 years' pumping, who can blame it?' Hammond was a lucky dog, he said, to be able to write books; he was reduced to reading them.[28]

He was a bad patient. When an accident sent him to bed for a stretch in 1928 his *bonhomie* deserted him. 'The nurses and other nuisances' got on his nerves. He grew moroser every day, but he knew he had to learn to put up with his fellow creatures even as they had to put up with him.[29] He had always been a great walker and now that he was confined to an invalid chair with only the top half of him, as he said, all right, he realized the end could not be far off. Yet he refused as he had always done to look at death and what lay beyond it. 'I ought never to engage in even the semblance of argument about the subject', he had told Maida Mirrielees, 'for not only am I ignorant, but I am constitutionally averse to all allegory and mystery and am content to wait and see whether anything happens after death about which we know and can know nothing. We are creatures imprisoned in Time and Space and I cannot even fancy "unconditioned" life. So I must be left to perish in my pride. Happily there are hundreds of other things to talk about.'[30]

He died in November 1933, a few months after he had closed down 'The Pightle' and removed the furniture. He was eighty-four. Within thirteen months Frankie was dead too, of a brain tumour like his mother. He had endured great strain during his father's illness and after his death. The delicate Tony lived on a good while longer in the care of the devoted Miss Tattersall.

3

Asquith was frequently called upon to make a funeral oration and his practice was, when bored at a Cabinet meeting, to distract himself by composing tributes to his colleagues. 'He looked around the table,' Birrell said, 'selected a victim, and we knew upon what exercise his mind was engaged. It was highly uncomfortable when, after circling around the table, the Prime Minister's obituary eye rested suddenly upon oneself.'[31] But Asquith predeceased Birrell, so that the comprehending words he could have spoken about his minister for Ireland were never uttered. The writer of the notice of Birrell's death in *The Times* appeared to be touching the heart of the matter, however, when he said that 'the responsibility for the affairs of Ireland then [1914] and afterwards was his but certainly not his alone....' Redmond, as we saw earlier, was prepared to share responsibility with Birrell for what went wrong, and Asquith should possibly have done the same. Birrell never suggested, however, that he had become a scapegoat for his political associates, but he did say that the policy which laid him low 'was then the Government policy'. It was a policy of minimum repression of the Sinn Feiners, a policy that obliged him to walk warily and run risks for fear of endangering the over-all Liberal commitment to conciliation and friendship towards Ireland. From a practical British point of view this was sound policy and might have succeeded had the war not dragged on as it did. Because the alternative meant putting a large army of occupation into Ireland instead of taking out of Ireland the Irish recruits that were sorely needed to sustain the campaign against the Central European powers.

Birrell was prepared to admit, however, that he had badly mistaken the rebel mentality; but so had his military and civilian advisers, except the few who clamoured for provocative and expensive action and these were all members of the Old Gang who advised action from inbred hatred of the National Sentiment, and not from any fear of a rebellion.[32] The discovery that the Sinn Feiners were hand in glove with the German enemy made further deferment of major action against them impossible; action that, incidentally, would have forestalled the rising had it been taken as promptly as Wimborne wanted. As it was, the insurgents moved at noon on Easter Monday, whereas the steps that Birrell authorized at the same hour were probably intended to be taken less than twenty-four hours later. Birrell's career and reputation hung on as little as that.

The figure he, therefore, presents is one for pity, and this indeed *The Times*' obituary suggested, though for reasons that Birrell would have dismissed as sheer nonsense, namely, that he had been wrongly appointed to a position for which he was unsuited; that his fault had been the fault of a too sanguine temperament; that he was a too great lover of ease, and of those quiet pursuits in which the best of him appears, to be well fitted for the hard and suspicious battles of politics; that in spite of the skill in debate which he often exhibited, he seemed always to walk in the political field with the air of a stranger, as if a misunderstanding of his qualities and of his deepest affections had somehow drawn him thither against his own instincts. Birrell would have said that it had taken a long time to discover his deficiences. He had been Chief Secretary for nine years, three or four times longer than any of his predecessors, and at no time had there been any question of dismissing him; on the contrary, every move in the direction of retirement had come from himself. He had been kept on in Ireland because his tenure of office there had been highly successful, and because he had gained and retained the esteem and affection of Liberals and Nationalists alike.

Other writers disposed of Birrell the politician as *The Times* and, later, the *Dictionary of National Biography* did, but more briefly and sometimes more offensively. He was indolent, incompetent, a 'light-weight', 'an innocent essayist', 'an intellectual coon', or, if he was none of these, he was 'the queerest Minister ever', a man who treated every subject with a humour almost amounting to levity.[33] This was how Viscount Snowden described him, remembering no doubt Birrell's quip about Snowden's colleague, George Lansbury, apropos of his championing of the Suffragettes, that the trouble with him was that he would let his bleeding heart run away with his bloody head.[34] In the search for tags to pin on Birrell, Moran of the *Leader* produced 'the Bristol Buffoon' and 'London's Leading Liberal Light Comedian',[34a] and thus helped to spread the idea, even in the Civil Service, that the Chief Secretary was a bit of a playboy.[34b] From this it was an easy progression to see in him the 'Playboy of the Western World',[35] for how could anyone who persistently sees the funny side of public affairs and of human behaviour be seriously regarded as an efficient Minister or administrator? A sense of humour is out of place in dull company. Birrell discovered this once when some remarks he made after a Johnson supper at the *Old Cock* restaurant gave offence. He was amazed. 'What is the world coming to?' he asked. 'Is there no place left where a man may enjoy himself and poke his fun? I have no recollection of what I said except that it *was* all in fun and entirely impromptu. . . .' He thought that his critic must have eaten something that disagreed with him.[36]

It is interesting and somewhat ironical to find Irishmen, and Irishmen from within the I.R.B. camp at that, giving a more complimentary account of Birrell, not of himself personally for, of course, they did not know him, but of his policy and strategy. Two examples come to mind. The first is by the friend, confidant and biographer of Michael Collins, Piaras Beaslai, who worked tooth and nail to bring about the rising and took part in it. 'There exists a curious idea in England to this day', he wrote in 1926, 'that Mr. Asquith and Mr. Birrell were in some mysterious way responsible, by their "tolerance" of the Irish Volunteers, for the insurrection of Easter Week. I can testify that the biggest obstacle that we had to contend against was the cleverness of Mr. Birrell's policy. The one thing that would have rallied support to our side was drastic coercion on the part of the English Government, but Mr. Birrell cleverly contrived to appear as not interfering with us while taking care that we were effectively silenced . . .'.[37] Birrell's second Irish apologist was P. S. O'Hegarty, the author of *The Victory of Sinn Fein* and of *A History of Ireland Under the Union*, and an outstanding authority on Irish separatism. In his *Victory of Sinn Fein* O'Hegarty recorded his belief that as late as 1918 a policy of Birrellism, as he called it, might have held Ireland still for England, but instead the Irish were given the mailed fist: the German Plot, Partition, Conscription–everything combined to throw more and more elements in the country over to Sinn Fein.[38] Reviewing the position in 1952 he said that 'Birrell's mild, apologetic, non-aggressive administration entirely bamboozled Irish public opinion and the Irish Parliamentary Party, and brought Irish nationality into the greatest danger in which it ever stood. Birrell was an Englishman 'playing Ireland as a skilled angler plays a fish'.[39]

Birrell would not have liked the suggestion that he bamboozled anybody; that was a role he would have left to Lloyd George. And he could have denied emphatically ever endangering Irish nationality, for, taking his cue from his predecessor, Bryce, he had done his best, as he conceived it, for the Irish language and had otherwise shown his interest in Irish cultural manifestations.[40] But he would not have objected, we think, to have been likened to a skilled angler playing a fish. He might, however, have thought that O'Hegarty should have made it clear what the fish was. It was a loyal Ireland inside the United Kingdom, and he himself might have added that, while he did not quite succeed in landing the fish, he very nearly did.

NOTES

CHAPTER I

1. Campbell-Bannerman Papers, Add. Mss. 41,208, 30.10.1907.
2. *Things Past Redress*, 198. 3. Margot Asquith, *More Memories*, 72.
4. J. G. Swift MacNeill, *What I have Seen and Heard*, 276. 5. Birrell,
Collected Essays, vol. 2, p. 346, 'What Happened at the Reformation'.
6. Liverpool Univ. Mss. 8.3(3), To T. P. Le Fanu, Easter Sunday, 1913.
7. Fyfe, *T. P. O'Connor*, 286. 8. Asquith, *Memories and Reflections*,
vol. 1, p. 105. 9. Ibid. 10. Taylor Bequest, Autog. d. 23, 8.2.1888.
11. Campbell-Bannerman Papers, Add. Mss. 41,235, 6.1.1900. 12.
Beatrice Webb, *Our Partnership*, 380. 13. Parliamentary Debates,
CLXIX, col. 198, 13.2.1907. 14. *Things Past Redress*, chapter 10.
15. Campbell-Bannerman Papers, Add. Mss. 41,239. 16. Ms.
Asquith 19, f. 136. 17. Campbell-Bannerman Papers, Add. Mss.
41,239, f. 192. 23.12.1906. 18. Amery, *My Political Life*, vol. 1, p. 59.
18a. Royal Archives, R.28/2. 19. Digby, *Horace Plunkett*, 114.
20. *Irish Times*, 24.1.1907. 21. *Things Past Redress*, 125. 22. Birrell,
Collected Essays, vol. 2, Essay on Nationality. 22a. Speech at the
Eighty Club, 25.7.1910. 23. Birrell, *Collected Essays*, vol. 1, p. 405.
24. MacLeod, *Neville Chamberlain*, 50. 25. Parliamentary Debates,
CLXIX, col. 203, 13.2.1907. 26. Ibid. cols. 198–199. 27. Ms. Asquith
11, f. 69, Birrell to Asquith, 11.4.1908. 28. O'Brien, *An Olive Branch
in Ireland*, 304. 29. A. S. Green Papers, 15073 (8), 24.10.1901. 30.
Ibid. 15073 (5), 14.3.1905 and 3.5.1905. 31. O'Brien, *An Olive
Branch in Ireland*, 304. 32. Quoted by R. B. McDowell, *Alice Stopford
Green*, 91. 33. *The Leader*, 18.5.1907. 34. Campbell-Bannerman
Papers, Add. Mss. 41239, f. 250. 35. A. S. Green Papers, Ms. 15097
(3). Joseph O'Neill to Mrs. Green, n.d. 36. MacDonnell Papers,
Eng. Hist. c. 354. September 1907. 37. A. S. Green Papers, 15089
(11), 10.5.1901. 38. Campbell-Bannerman Papers, Add. Mss. 41240,
30.10.1907. 39. MacDonnell Papers, Eng. Hist. c. 250, 29.8.1907.
40. Ibid. 41. Campbell-Bannerman Papers, Add. Mss. 41240, f. 127,
30.10.1907. 42. Liverpool Univ. Mss. 10.3. 43. Birrell to Walsh,
31.12.1907. 44. Amery, *My Political Life*, vol. 1, 59. 45. *Things
Past Redress*, 202. 46. Ms. Nathan 449, To Nathan, 27.3.1915.

47. 31.12.1907. 48. *Things Past Redress*, 203. 49. Birrell to Walsh, 8.7.1908. 50. N.L.I. Bryce Papers, 11016, 30.1.1908. 51. Randolph S. Churchill, *Winston S. Churchill*, II, 363. 52. Jenkins, *Asquith*, 184. 53. C. P. Curran, *Struggle with Fortune*, 228–229. 54. Lee, *King Edward VII*, 474. 54a. Magill Memoirs. 55. *Irish School Weekly*, 13.4.1907. 56. Ms. Nathan 454–455, f. 145, 4.10.1915. 56a. Ibid. 57. Ibid. 460–461, 6.10.1915. 57a. Ibid. 57b. Ibid. 58. *Things Past Redress*, 206. 59. Ibid. 198. 60. Ibid. 212. 61. Ibid. 209. 62. A. S. Green Papers, 15093 (8) 25.10.19. 63. Robinson, *Further Memories of Irish Life*, 103. 64. Beatrice Webb, *Our Partnership*, 408. 65. Robinson, *Memories: Wise and Otherwise*, 195–196. 66. *Things Past Redress*, 214. 66a. Lady Cynthia Asquith, *Diaries*, 307. 67. *Royal Commission on the Rebellion in Ireland* (Cd. 8311), Minutes of Evidence, p. 21. 68. *Things Past Redress*, 210–211. 69. Ibid. 211. 70. Cathal O' Shannon to author. 71. Parliamentary Debates, CLXIX, col. 663, 18.2.1907. 72. Ms. Nathan 449, Nathan to Birrell, 23.1.1916. 73. Ms. Asquith 36, f. 4, Birrell to Asquith, 1.2.1910. 74. Public Record Office, London, C.O.904/161/2.

CHAPTER II

1. *Ulster Guardian*, 23.9.1911. 2. Ibid. 30.9.1911. 3. Ibid. 14.10.1911. 4. Public Record Office, London, C.O.906/18, Robinson to Birrell, n.d. 5. *Ulster Crisis*, 51. 6. Public Record Office, London, C.O.906/18, 28.1.1912. 7. Ibid. 26.1.1912. 7a. Churchill to Cabinet, 24.2.1911 and 1.3.1911. 8. Bodleian, J. C. Medley Dep., 8.2.1912. 9. Parliamentary Debates, XXXVI, col. 1444, 11.4.1914. 10. Parliamentary Debates, XXXVII, col. 1705, 30.4.1912. 10a. Public Record Office, London, C.O.904/13. 11. *Freeman's Journal*, 20.7.1912. 12. Ms. Asquith 22, C. E. Troup to Gladstone, Home Secretary, 27.9.1909. 13. Irish State Paper Office, G.F.41. 13a. Headlam, *Irish Reminiscences*, 124. 14. *Freeman's Journal*, 20.7.1912. 15. Liverpool Univ. Ms.8.3(3) 12.8.1912. 16. *Freeman's Journal*, 21.9.1912. 17. Nicholson, *King George V*, 297. 18. Ms. Asquith 38, f. 109, To Asquith, 24.7.1913. 19. Nicholson, *King George V*, 296. 20. Ms. Asquith 38, f. 122. 30.8.1913. 21. Jenkins, *Asquith*, 285–286. 22. Ms. Asquith 38, f. 220, 3.10.1913. 23. Ibid. f. 196, 20.9.1913. 24. Ibid. f. 220, 3.10.1913. 25. Ibid. f. 128, 8.9.1913. 26. Ibid. f. 196, To Asquith,

20.9.1913.   27. Cabinet Papers, vol. 107, 8.9.1911.   28. Ibid. 62,
April 1912.   29. Ibid. 66, 14.4.1912.   30. Garnett, *Golden Echo*, 205.
31. Ms. Asquith 38, f. 128, 8.9.1913.   32. Ibid. f. 210, 26.9.1913.
33. *Annual Register*, 1913 (231),   34. Ms. Asquith 38, f. 243, 28.10.1913.
34a. Public Record Office, London, Cab. 41/34, 12.11.1913.   35.
14.11.1913.   36. *Report of Dublin Disturbances Commission* (Cd. 7269),
1914.

CHAPTER III

1. Jenkins, *Asquith*, 289–291.   2. Ms. Asquith 38, f. 235.   3. Ibid.
f. 243, 28.10.1913.   4. Ibid. 39, f. 20.   5. Gwynn, *Life of John
Redmond*, 237–238.   6. Ibid. 239.   7. Jenkins, *Asquith*, 301.   8. Horgan, *Parnell to Pearse*, 228.   9. Cabinet Papers, vol. 120, 2.4.1914.
10. Public Record Office, London, C.O.904/14, 17.7.1908.   11. Ibid.
July 1908.   12. Le Roux, *Tom Clarke and the Irish Freedom Movement*,
98.   13. Gwynn, *Life of John Redmond*, 245.   14. Fergusson, *The
Curragh Incident*, 88.   15. Stewart, A.T.Q., *Ulster Crisis*, 143.   16. Ms.
Asquith 41, 26.4.1914.   17. Ibid. 41, f. 71.   18. Jenkins, *Asquith*, 318.
19. Add. Redmond Papers, Redmond to M. J. Ryan, 17.9.1914.
20. Cabinet Papers, vol. 120, 15.6.1914.   21. Ms. Asquith 41, ff. 125–
129.   22. Jenkins, *Asquith*, 322.   23. *Ulster Guardian*, 3.10.1914.
24. Add. Redmond Papers, Redmond to T. B. Fitzpatrick, 16.12.1914.
25. Ibid. Redmond to M. J. Ryan, 17.9.1914.   26. J. C. Medley
Deposit, Aberdeen to Birrell, 18.8.1914.   27. Ibid. Robinson to
Birrell, 18.8.1914.   28. Gwynn, *Life of John Redmond*, 382.   29. F. X.
Martin, *Irish Historical Studies*, March 1961, 240–241.   30. *The
Observer*, 14.2.1915; and Ms. Nathan 449, 14.2.1915.   31. A. S. Green
Papers, 15121.   32. Ibid. 15114(23).   33. Ibid. 15073(8), 30.11.1914.
34. Ms. Nathan 449, 6.12.1914.   35. *The Irish Volunteer*, 5.12.1914.
36. Cabinet Papers, vol. 123, 19.1.1915.   36a. Magill Memoirs.

CHAPTER IV

1. Ms. Nathan 454–455, 14.4.1914.   2. *The Leader*, 1.8.1914.   3. Ms.
Nathan, 449, 6.11.1914.   4. Ibid. 460–461, f. 156, 4.11.1914.   5. Ibid.
221–232, 24.3.1916.   6. Ibid. ff. 188–189, 5.4.1915.   7. Ibid. 449,

27.3.1915. 8. Ibid. 4.11.1914. 9. Ibid. 27.3.1915. 10. Add. Redmond Papers, Birrell to Redmond, 27.12.1914. 11. Ms. Asquith 26,
f. 82, 29.10.1914. 12. Cabinet Papers, vol. 123, 19.1.1915. 13. Ms.
Nathan 449, 10.11.1914. 14. Ibid. 29.11.1914. 15. Ibid. 16. J. C.
Medley Deposit, Cabinet Papers, Nov. 1914. 17. Ibid. Nathan
to Birrell, 10.11.1914. 18. Ibid. 3.12.1914. 19. Ms. Nathan 449,
28.2.1915. 20. Ibid. 21.2.1915. 21. Ibid. 21.1.1915. 22. J. C.
Medley Deposit, Nathan to Birrell, 3.3.1915. 23. Ms. Nathan 449,
28.12.1914. 24. B.M. Add. Mss. 41210, 28.12.1906. 25. Malcolm
Thomson, *David Lloyd George*, 102. 26. B.M. Add. Mss. 41,239,
f. 196, 12.1.1907. 27. *The Leader*, 17.3.1914. 28. Sir Charles
Tennyson to author. 29. Brian O'Higgins, *The Voice of Banba*, 44.
30. Ms. Nathan, 460–461, f. 178, 3.3.1915. 31. Ms. Asquith 38, f. 235,
16.10.1913. 32. G. C. Duggan to author. 33. Pentland, *A Bonnie
Fechter*. 34. Ibid. also Salter, *Mirror of a Public Servant*, 70. 35. Haddo
House Papers, 7.10.1914. 36. *Sinn Fein*, 17.10.1914. 37. *Irish Times*,
31.10.1914. 38. Haddo House Papers, 8.11.1914. 39. Ms. Asquith
46, f. 97, 8.10.1914. 40. Pentland, *A Bonnie Fechter*, pp. 178–179.
41. *The Leader*, 26.12.1914. 42. Haddo House Papers, 8.11.1914.
43. Ms. Asquith 4, f. 60. 44. Ibid. f. 70. 45. Ibid. 46, f. 99.
46. Ms. Nathan 449, 22.12.1914. 47. Ibid. 456–457, f. 190. 48. A. S.
Green Papers, Mrs. Green to R. Best, 6.2.1915. 49. Ms. Nathan 449,
21.1.1915. 50. Haddo House Papers, 31.12.1914. 51. Ms. Nathan
449, 11.2.1915. 52. Ibid. 15.2.1915. 53. *The Leader*, 11.4.1908.
54. Lennox Robinson, *Curtain Up*, 83. 55. Sir Henry Robinson,
Memories: Wise and Otherwise, 228. 56. Ms. Nathan 449, 4.11.1914.
57. Ibid. 14.12.1914. 58. Ibid. 59. Ms. Nathan 454–455, 'Old
Harrovian' to Wimborne. 60. Ibid. 449, 21.1.1915. 61. Ibid.
7.1.1915. 62. Ibid. 21.2.1915. 63. Ibid. 460–461, f. 176. 64. Add.
Redmond Papers, 27.12.1914. 65. Liverpool Univ. Mss. 8.3(3).
65a. Lady Cynthia Asquith, *Diaries*, 126–128. 66. Ms. Nathan 449.
15.1.1916. 67. Sir Charles Tennyson, *Alfred Tennyson*, 497. 68.
Sir Charles Tennyson to author. 69. *Stars and Markets*, 56. 70. Ibid.
71. Ms. Nathan 449, 21.12.1914. 72. *Stars and Markets*, 121. 73. Ms.
Nathan 449, 14.2.1915. 74. B.M. Add. Mss. 49372, 20(?).3.1915.
75. Redmond Papers, 13.3.1915. 76. Sir Sidney Lee Corres., 26.3.1915
77. Ms. Nathan 449, 13.1.1915. 78. Ibid. 22.3.1915. 79. Liverpool
Ms. 8.2(3). 80. Ibid. 80a. Lady Cynthia Asquith, *Diaries*, 128.
81. Ms. Nathan 449, 21.4.1915. 82. Jenkins, *Asquith*, 356. 83. Ibid.

359.   84. Ms. Nathan 449, 11.5.1915.   85. Ibid. 15.5.1915.   86. Ibid. n.d.   87. Ibid. 1.6.1915.   88. Gwynn, *Life of John Redmond*, 427. 89. Ibid.   90. Ibid. 430.   91. Ibid. 432.   92. Ms. Nathan 449, 10.6.1915.   93. Ibid. 12.6.1915.   94. Ibid.   94a. Ms. Nathan, Nathan to Redmond, 2.6.1915.   95. Ms. Nathan 449, 7.7.1915. 96. Ibid. 9.7.1915.   97. Ibid. 12.7.1915.   98. Ibid. 3.8.1915.   99. Ibid.   100. Ibid. 9.7.1915.   101. Ibid. 6.9.1915.   102. Ibid. 2.9.1915. 103. Ibid. 15.9.1915.   103a. Ibid. 24.9.1915.   104. Ibid. 20.10.1915. 105. Ibid. 3.11.1915.   106. Ibid. n.d.   107. Ibid. 16.11.1915.   108. *Letters of W. B. Yeats*, ed. Allan Wade, 535.   109. Ms. Nathan 449, 25 (?28).12.1915.   110. Ibid. 14.11.1915.   111. Ibid. n.d.   112. Ibid. 13.12.1915.   113. Robinson, *Memories: Wise and Otherwise*, 190. 114. A. S. Green Papers, 15073(8).   115. Liverpool Univ. Ms. 8.3(3), To Le Fanu 21.2.1915.   116. A. S. Green Papers, 12.12.1911.   117. Ms. Nathan 449, 8.12.1914.   118. Ibid. 30.9.1915.   119. Ibid. n.d. 120. Ibid. 14.2.1915.   121. Ibid. 21.1.1915   122. Ibid. 24.4.1915. 123. Ibid. 11.5.1915.   124. Liverpool Univ. Mss. 8.3(3), 24.1.1916. 125. A. S. Green Papers, 15073(8), 2.2.1913.   126. Trinity College Dublin, Mahaffy Autographs, 33.   127. J. G. Swift MacNeill, *What I have Seen and Heard*, 277.   128. Parliamentary Debates, LXXII, col. 539, 15.6.1915.   129. G. C. Duggan to author.   130. Haddo House Papers, 9.7.1915.   131. Liverpool Univ. Ms. 8(3), 9.8.1910.   132. Hone, *W. B. Yeats*, 249.   133. *Stars and Markets*, 54.   134. Bodleian Ms. Eng. lett. e.94, To R. F. Charles, 17.5.1906(?).

CHAPTER V

1. Ms. Nathan 449, 9.1.1916.   2. Ibid. 13.12.1915.   3. Ms. Nathan 456–457, f. 32.   4. Lady Cynthia Asquith, *Diaries*, 126–128.   5. Ms. Nathan 449, Birrell to Nathan, 1.2.1916.   6. Ibid.   7. Ibid.   8. Quoted *Dublin Castle and the 1916 Rising*, 51–52.   9. Gwynn, *Life of John Redmond*, 400.   10. Irish State Paper Office, C.B.S. 11174. 11. Ms. Nathan 449, 'Sunday night'.   12. Ibid.   13. Ibid.   14. Ibid. 19.3.1916.   15. Ibid.   16. Ibid.   17. Ibid.   18. B.M. Add. Mss. 49372, 13.12.1915.   19. Ms. Nathan 449, 19.3.1916.   19a. Ibid.   20. Ibid. 9(?).4.1916.   21. Ibid. 5.4.1916.   22. Ibid. 20.3.1916.   23. Ibid. 12.4.1916.   24. Ibid. 22.4.1916.   25. Ibid.   26. *Dublin Castle and the*

1916 Rising, 144 et seq.   27. Hankey, *The Supreme Command*, 1914–1918, vol. 2, p. 475.   28. Lady Cynthia Asquith, *Diaries*, 161.   29. MacDonagh, *Life of William O'Brien*, 222.   30. Parliamentary Debates, LXXXII, cols. 31–39, 3.5.1916.   31. Ibid.   32. Letter to Magill, n.d.   32a. B.M. Add. Mss. 49372, 23.5.1916.   33. B.M. Add. Mss. 49382B, To Henry Jackson, O.M., 23.11.1916.   34. *Things Past Redress*, 221.   35. Liverpool Univ. Mss. 8.2(3).   36. B.M. Add. Mss. 49372, 23.5.1916.   37. Fyfe, *T. P. O'Connor*, 249.   38. Letter to Magill, n.d.   39. Liverpool Univ. Mss. 8.3(3), To T. P. Le Fanu, 7.4.1917.   40. *Stars and Markets*.   41. MS. Asquith, f. 181.   42. N.L.I. Ms. 11016, 'From a letter written by an Irishwoman in Dublin immediately after the Rebellion in April, 1916.'   43. Lady Cynthia Asquith, *Diaries*, 163.   43a. Bernard Ash, *The Lost Dictator*, p. 204.   44. *Royal Commission on the Rebellion in Ireland* (Cd. 8311), Minutes of Evidence, 19.5.1916.   45. Ms. Asquith 4, f. 192.   46. Ibid. 31, f. 28.   47. Ibid. 41, f. 151.   48. Ibid. f. 132.   49. Cabinet Papers, vol. 148, 21.5.1916.   50. Colvin, *Life of Carson*, vol. 3, p. 166.   51. Ms. Asquith 37, f. 68.   52. Cabinet Papers, vol. 152, 19.7.1916.   53. Ibid. 23.6.1916.   54. Ms. Nathan 460–461, f. 45.   55. Cabinet Papers, vol. 150, 24.6.1916.   56. Ms. Asquith 44, f. 26.   57. Ibid. 41, f. 90.   58. Ibid. 37, f. 2.   59. Ms. Nathan 449, 26.11.1914.   60. Ibid. 26.12.1914.   61. Ibid. 8.2.1915.   62. Ibid. 4.11.1914.   63. O'Hegarty, *A History of Ireland under the Union*, 721.   64. Ms. Asquith 4, f. 192.   65. Cabinet Papers, vol. 150. 28.6.1916.   66. Ibid. vol. 151, 15/16.7.1916.   67. Jenkins, *Asquith*, 404.   67a. Gwynn, *The Life and Death of Roger Casement*, 18.   68. Cabinet Papers, vol. 150, 24.6.1916.   69. Ms. Nathan 466, Nathan to Birrell, 11.5.1916.   70. Ms. Asquith 37, f. 23.   71. N.L.I. Ms. 8798 (3) and *Freeman's Journal*, 6.9.1917.   72. Headlam, *Irish Reminiscences*, 193.   73. Ms. Asquith 37, f. 119.   74. Gwynn, *The History of Partition*, 148.

CHAPTER VI

1. Bodleian Ms. Eng. lett. e.94, To R. F. Charles, 21.10.1919.   2. *D.N.B.*, 1931–1940, p. 83.   2a. Webb, *Our Partnership*, 447.   3. University of London Mss., To Dobson, 3.2.1919.   4. Ibid. 16.5.1919.   5. Bodleian Ms. Eng. lett. e.94, To R. F. Charles, 21.10.1919.   6. Ms. Asquith 33, f. 25.   7. *Stars and Markets*, 126.   7a. Letter to Magill,

21.2.1921.   8. *Stars and Markets*, 128.   9. David Garnett to author.
10. *Stars and Markets*, 128.   11. Garnett, *The Flowers of the Forest*, 53.
12. B.M. Add. Mss. 49372, To Maida Mirrielees, 11.10.1909.   13. Ibid.
14. Michael Holroyd, *Lytton Strachey*.   15. Ibid. vol. 2, 230.   15a.
Magill Memoirs.   16. Garnett, *The Flowers of the Forest*, 10.   17. Ibid.
82.   18. Ibid. 11/12.   19. *Things Past Redress*, 220.   20. Ibid. 219.
21. Ibid. 253.   22. B.M. Add. Mss. 49372, 10.1.1927.   22a. Letter to
Magill, 27.12.1925.   23. Ibid. 10.3.1908.   24. Liverpool Univ. Mss.
8.3.(3).   24a. Leslie Ward, *Forty Years a Spy*, 215.   25. *Stars and
Markets*, 55.   26. Ibid. 132.   27. National University of Ireland
Papers.   27a. Letter to Magill, 27.12.1912.   27b. Letters to Magill
5.12.1929, 29.12.1931 and 28.1.1933.   28. Hammond Papers, 16,
f. 147.   29. B.M. Add. Mss. 49372, 15.9.1928.   30. Ibid. 5.8.1927.
31. Salter, *Mirror of a Public Servant*, 70.   32. B.M. Add. Mss. 49382B,
23.11.1916.   33. Viscount Snowden, *Autobiography*, vol. 3, 145.   34.
Ibid. 258.   34a. *The Leader*, 23.5. 1914.   34b. Joseph Brennan to
author.   35. Dangerfield, *The Strange Death of Liberal England*, 1910–
1914.   36. Sir Sidney Lee Corres, 15.12.1911.   37. *Michael Collins
and the Making of a New Ireland*, vol. 1, 58–59.   38. *Victory of Sinn Fein*,
29.   39. *A History of Ireland under the Union*, 695.   40. *Things Past
Redress*, 214–215.

BIBLIOGRAPHY

PRINCIPAL MANUSCRIPT SOURCES

Bodleian Library, Oxford: Nathan Papers, Asquith Papers, Bryce Papers, MacDonnell Papers, Taylor Bequest, Sir Sidney Lee Correspondence, J. Christopher Medley Deposit (Birrell Papers), C. P. Magill Deposit (Birrell Letters and Memoirs of A. P. Magill).

British Museum: Campbell-Bannerman Papers and Birrell Papers.

Public Record Office, London: Cabinet Papers and Colonial Office Papers.

Haddo House, Aberdeen: Aberdeen Papers.

Liverpool University Library: Birrell Papers.

National Library of Ireland: Redmond Papers, Additional Redmond Papers, Alice Stopford Green Papers, Bryce Papers and MacNeill Papers.

OTHER MANUSCRIPT SOURCES

London University Library, Newcastle upon Tyne University Library, Trinity College Library, Dublin, State Paper Office, Dublin, and *National University Registrar's Office, Dublin.*

PRINCIPAL PRINTED SOURCES

Books: Augustine Birrell (1937): *Things Past Redress*; Sir Charles Tennyson (1957) *Stars and Markets*, and Leon O Broin (1966) *Dublin Castle and the 1916 Rising.*

Newspapers and Periodicals: Freeman's Journal, The Irish Times, The Times, The Observer, The Leader, The Spark, Sinn Fein, The Irish Worker, Workers' Republic, Irish School Weekly, Annual Register.

Reports of Royal Commissions: Disturbances in Dublin (1913), Landing of Arms at Howth (1914) and the Rebellion in Ireland (1916).

BIBLIOGRAPHY

AMONG OTHER BOOKS CONSULTED

Aberdeen, Marquis and Marchioness (1925) *We 'Twa.'*

Arthur, Sir George (1932) *General Sir John Maxwell.*

Asquith, Lady Cynthia (1968) *Diaries.*

Asquith, Margot (1933) *More Memories.*

Beaslai, Piaras (1926) *Michael Collins and the Making of a New Ireland.*

Beckett, J. C. (1966) *The Making of Modern Ireland.*

Birrell, Augustine (1922) *Collected Essays.*

Bonham Carter, Violet (Baroness Asquith of Yarnbury) (1965) *Winston Churchill as I knew him.*

Churchill, Randolph S. (1966) *Winston S. Churchill.*

Digby, Margaret (1949) *Horace Plunkett.*

Dudley Edwards, O., and Pyle, F. (1968) *1916– The Easter Rising.*

Fergusson, Sir James (1964) *The Curragh Incident.*

Figgis, Darrell (1927) *Recollections of the Irish War.*

Fingal, Countess of (1937) *Seventy Years Young.*

Fisher, H. A. L. (1927) *Life of Viscount Bryce.*

Fox, R. M. (1943) *The History of the Irish Citizen Army.*

French, Gerald (1931) *Life of Field-Marshal Sir John French.*

Fyfe, Hamilton (1934) *T. P. O'Connor.*

Garnett, David (1953) *Golden Echo* and *The Flowers of the Forest.*

Gwynn, Denis (1931) *The Life of John Redmond,* and *The Life and Death of Roger Casement.*

Gwynn, Stephen (1919) *John Redmond's Last Years.*

Hankey, Lord (1961) *The Supreme Council, 1914–1918.*

Headlam, Maurice (1947) *Irish Reminiscences.*

Healy, T. M. (1928) *Letters and Leaders of my Day.*

Horgan, J. J. (1948) *Parnell to Pearse.*

Hyde, H. M. (1953) *Carson,* (1960) *Roger Casement.*

Jenkins, Roy (1964) *Asquith.*

Larkin, Emmet (1965) *James Larkin.*

Lee, Sir Sidney (1925) *King Edward VII.*

Le Roux, L. N. (1936) *Tom Clarke and the Irish Freedom Movement.*

ed. Leslie, Shane (unpublished) *Memoirs of Gordon Shepherd.*

Lynch, D., and O'Donoghue, F. (1957) *The I.R.B. and the 1916 Insurrection*.

MacColl, Rene (1956) *Roger Casement*.

MacDonagh, M. (1928) *Life of William O'Brien*.

McDowell, R. B. (1964) *The Irish Administration, 1801–1914*. (1967) *Alice Stopford Green*.

MacLeod, Iain (1961) *Neville Chamberlain*.

MacNeill, J. G. Swift (1925) *What I have seen and heard*.

Macready, Sir C. F. Nevil (1924) *Annals of an Active Life*.

Magnus, Philip (1964) *King Edward the Seventh*.

Marjoribanks, E. and Colvin, I. D. (1932–1936) *Life of Lord Carson*.

Martin, F. X. (1961) *MacNeill on the 1916 Rising* (Irish Historical Studies). (1963) *The Irish Volunteers, 1913–1915,* (1964) *The Howth Gun-running,* (1967) *Leaders and Men of the Easter Rising*.

Moody, T. W., and Beckett, J. C. (1959) *Queen's, Belfast, 1845–1949*.

Nicholson, Harold (1952) *King George V*.

O'Brien, Conor Cruise (1960) *The Shaping of Modern Ireland*.

O'Brien, William (1910) *An Olive Branch in Ireland*.

O Broin, Leon (1966) *Dublin Castle and the 1916 Rising: the story of Sir Matthew Nathan*.

O'Hegarty, P. S. (1924) *The Victory of Sinn Fein*. (1952) *A History of Ireland Under the Union, 1801–1922*.

Oxford and Asquith, Earl of (1928) *Memories and Reflections*.

Pentland, Marjorie (1952) *A Bonnie Fechter*.

Robinson, Sir Henry (1923) *Memories: Wise and Otherwise*. (1924) *Further Memories of Irish Life*.

Ryan, A. P. (1956) *Mutiny at the Curragh*.

Salter, Lord (1960) *Memoirs of a Public Servant*.

Spender, J. A., and Asquith, Cyril (1932) *Life of Lord Oxford and Asquith*.

Stewart, A. T. Q. (1967) *The Ulster Crisis*.

Webb, Beatrice (1948) *Our Partnership*.

INDEX